Driver & Vehicle
Standards
Agency

D0183002

The **OFFICIAL DVSA GUIDE** to
DRIVING
the essential skills

London: TSO

Written and compiled by the Learning Materials Section of the Driver and Vehicle Standards Agency (DVSA).

First edition Crown copyright 1992
Second edition Crown copyright 1997
Third edition Crown copyright 1999
Fourth edition Crown copyright 2001
Fifth edition Crown copyright 2005
Sixth edition Crown copyright 2007
Seventh edition Crown copyright 2011
Eighth edition Crown copyright 2014
Seventh impression 2018

ISBN 978 0 11 553290 0

A CIP catalogue record for this book is available from the British Library

Other titles in the Driving Skills series

The Official DVSA Theory Test for Car Drivers
The Official DVSA Theory Test for Car Drivers (DVD-ROM)
The Official DVSA Guide to Learning to Drive
The Official DVSA Guide to Better Driving
The Official DVSA Guide to Hazard Perception (DVD-ROM)

The Official DVSA Theory Test Kit iPhone/Android App
The Official DVSA Highway Code iPhone App
The Official DVSA Hazard Perception Practice iOS App

The Official DVSA Guide to Riding – the essential skills
The Official DVSA Theory Test for Motorcyclists
The Official DVSA Theory Test for Motorcyclists (DVD-ROM)
The Official DVSA Guide to Learning to Ride
Better Biking – the official DVSA training aid (DVD)

The Official DVSA Guide to Driving Buses and Coaches
The Official DVSA Guide to Driving Goods Vehicles
The Official DVSA Theory Test for Drivers of Large Vehicles
The Official DVSA Theory Test for Drivers of Large Vehicles (DVD-ROM)
Driver CPC – the official DVSA guide for professional bus and coach drivers
Driver CPC – the official DVSA guide for professional goods vehicle drivers

The Official DVSA Guide to Tractor and Specialist Vehicle Driving Tests
The Official DVSA Theory Test for Approved Driving Instructors (DVD-ROM)

Every effort has been made to ensure that the information contained in this publication is accurate at the time of going to press. The Stationery Office cannot be held responsible for any inaccuracies. Information in this book is for guidance only.

All metric and imperial conversions in this book are approximate.

We're turning over a new leaf.

100% recycled
This book is printed
on 100% recycled paper

RECYCLED
Paper made from
recycled material
FSC
www.fsc.org
FSC® C002151

Find us online

❯ GOV.UK – Simpler, clearer, faster

GOV.UK is the best place to find government services and information for

- car drivers
- motorcyclists
- driving licences
- driving and riding tests
- towing a caravan or trailer
- medical rules
- driving and riding for a living
- online services.

Visit **www.gov.uk** and try it out.

You can also find contact details for DVSA and other motoring agencies like DVLA at **www.gov.uk**

You'll notice that links to **GOV.UK**, the UK's new central government site, don't always take you to a specific page. This is because this new kind of site constantly adapts to what people really search for and so such static links would quickly go out of date. Try it out. Simply search what you need from your preferred search site or from **www.gov.uk** and you should find what you're looking for. You can give feedback to the Government Digital Service from the website.

Driver & Vehicle Standards Agency

The Driver and Vehicle Standards Agency (DVSA) is an executive agency of the Department for Transport.

We improve road safety in Great Britain by setting standards for driving and motorcycling, and making sure drivers, vehicle operators and MOT garages understand and follow roadworthiness standards. We also provide a range of licensing, testing, education and enforcement services.

www.gov.uk/dvsa

The Driver and Vehicle Agency (DVA) is an executive agency within the Department of the Environment for Northern Ireland.

Its primary aim is to promote and improve road safety through the advancement of driving standards and implementation of the government's policies for improving the mechanical standards of vehicles.

nidirect.gov.uk/motoring

⊕ Contents

⊛ A message from the Chief Driving Examiner

The UK has some of the safest roads in the world and we have a reputation for being well-mannered and considerate drivers. However, while things have steadily been getting better, too many people are still being killed and seriously injured on our roads every year. So, there's still work to do.

Safe and responsible driving is all about recognising that we'll generally get where we want to go more quickly, and in one piece, if we cooperate with other road users. It's about understanding that others may not be as able or as experienced as we are – and that however skilled we think we are, or however long we've been driving, we can all make mistakes.

This book is designed to guide you through everything you need to know to drive safely. If you follow this guidance – ideally with the help of an approved driving instructor – you'll be well prepared to drive for yourself and enjoy the experience. You'll also be prepared for the responsibility that comes with carrying passengers, such as friends and family, and driving for work. You'll be much more likely to avoid incidents, and as an added benefit you'll keep your insurance premiums down.

Driving is both an enjoyable activity and a very valuable contribution to our social and working lives. I want all drivers to gain the maximum benefit from their driving and to avoid the heartbreak that comes when things go wrong. I strongly encourage you to read this book carefully and to take on board the lessons it provides.

Lesley Young
Chief Driving Examiner

Section one
➡ The driver

This section covers

- Attitude
- Good practice
- Health
- Learner drivers
- New drivers
- Older drivers
- Disabled drivers
- Reviewing your driving

⊕ Attitude

No matter how fast, expensive or efficient your vehicle is, it's you, the driver, who determines whether it's a safe means of transport.

Being a good driver doesn't mean being a perfect driver – in fact, it's very doubtful whether a perfect driver exists. A good driver is somebody who knows that they can always get better and is willing to make the effort.

With experience your practical skill will improve, but that alone won't make you a good driver. To achieve that goal, you'll also need to take responsibility for the way you approach driving. You need to develop your ability to

- concentrate and not allow yourself to be distracted
- scan the road ahead of you and learn to anticipate risky situations
- be patient with other road users
- understand your own state of mind and health, and how they may affect your driving
- have confidence in your abilities.

Together, these qualities make up what's generally known as the driver's attitude. It's your attitude, together with personal characteristics such as mood, emotional state, and levels of fatigue and stress, that will affect how you behave on the road.

There's a lot of enjoyment and satisfaction to be gained from showing not only your skill and ability but also courtesy and consideration to those around you.

REMEMBER, nearly all road traffic incidents are caused, to some degree, by the driver. Doing all you can to prevent incidents is the responsibility of every driver.

Developing a safe and responsible attitude and adopting 'good' behaviour will come more easily to some drivers than to others. But these qualities are so important to safe driving that it's vital for every driver to make the effort to keep working on them. The best drivers are always trying to improve their skills. Even when they've been driving for years, they know that there's always something new to learn.

Responsibility

As a responsible driver, you must always be concerned for the safety of

- yourself
- your passengers
- all other road users.

Yourself

See the information on health later in this section for more about your own safety.

Your passengers

Be aware of your passengers' needs. For example, they may have mobility problems or be suffering from an illness that might need additional attention. Also, make sure you understand your responsibilities regarding your passengers' use of seat belts.

Other road users

Be tolerant; remember that everyone is entitled to use the road. This may mean making allowances for other road users, particularly the most vulnerable, such as

- children and older people
- people with disabilities
- cyclists and motorcyclists
- people in charge of animals.

Look around you and plan your actions well ahead to avoid causing danger or inconvenience. That way, you can avoid the need to act hastily.

Recognise your own limitations and those of other people.

> **REMEMBER,** the responsibility for safe driving rests with you.

Concentration

To be able to drive safely in today's traffic conditions, you must concentrate fully at all times.

3

If you let your mind wander, even for a moment, the risk of making a mistake increases – and mistakes can lead to incidents.

Avoid driving if you're

- feeling tired or unwell
- distracted in any way
- upset or annoyed
- under a lot of mental or emotional pressure.

FACTS A contributing factor in around 42% of collisions attended by a police officer between 2009 and 2012 was that the driver/rider failed to look properly.

Concentration is the key to anticipation and is helped by having

- good vision
- good hearing
- good health
- self-awareness.

If you have any in-vehicle technology such as a satellite navigation (sat-nav) system, don't let it distract you from driving. Keep any visual or manual interaction with the system to an absolute minimum. You should find an appropriate, safe and legal place to stop before making any adjustments.

Before you set out
- turn your phone off, put it in silent mode or put it out of reach. That way, you won't be tempted to make or answer phone calls, read or reply to texts, play games or use social media
- if you're using a sat-nav, set your destination and make sure the device doesn't block your view.

While on the move don't
- use your phone for calls, texting or social media
- look at road maps, and only look at your sat-nav very briefly
- get distracted by tuning the radio, changing CDs or using MP3 players

- let conversation take your attention away from the road (an argument with your passengers can be particularly distracting)
- listen to loud music or use headphones of any kind, as these can mask other sounds
- be distracted by eating, drinking, smoking or vaping.

In addition, don't
- stick non-essential stickers on the windows of your vehicle, as they can restrict your view
- hang objects (eg dolls, dice) where they might distract you and restrict your view.

Passengers
Passengers can be a major source of distraction if they're

- talking to you
- using a mobile phone
- behaving irresponsibly.

Those who drive with young children in the vehicle may face increased distractions while driving. Preparation and planning are especially important. It's sensible to come up with ways to cope with situations that may occur. For example, make sure that small children have enough to occupy them during a journey, so they're less likely to get bored and cry.

Mobile phones

Driving requires all of your attention, all of the time.

You **MUST NOT** use a hand-held mobile phone or similar device when driving, except to call 999 or 112 in a genuine emergency when it's unsafe or impractical to stop.

Using any phone or microphone, even if it's hands-free, can take your attention off the road. It's far safer not to use any phone while driving.

Let your incoming calls go to voicemail and stop before checking your messages. Likewise, if you need to make a call, find a safe place to stop first.

These rules apply even if you're not driving, but are supervising a learner driver.

> **FACTS** You're four times as likely to crash if you use a mobile phone while driving.

Anticipation

Anticipation in driving means planning well ahead and being prepared to take early action. With experience it should become an instinctive part of your driving.

You need to continually question the actions of other road users.

If you plan ahead and try to anticipate the actions of others, you can

- avoid the need for a sudden reaction
- maintain a comfortable safety margin
- prevent some hazards from developing
- save fuel by anticipating situations early. Braking late and heavily, then accelerating as the situation improves, increases fuel consumption.

Take early action in response to those hazards that do develop.

Anticipation and good planning are essential to developing defensive driving techniques (see section 10).

Patience

If you're upset by the bad behaviour of another driver, try not to react. If necessary, slow down to calm yourself, even if you feel like making a more aggressive response. Consider stopping to take a break. While your brain is processing strong emotions, such as anger, your attention can be taken away from driving tasks. As a result, your powers of concentration, anticipation and observation are likely to be much reduced. This will make a road traffic incident much more likely.

We all make mistakes from time to time, so be prepared to make allowances for someone else's mistakes.

REMEMBER, your actions can affect the behaviour of other drivers. Setting a good example can have a positive effect on their driving.

Do

- keep calm
- show restraint
- use sound judgement.

Don't

- drive in an aggressive or competitive way
- use aggressive language or gestures
- try to teach another road user a lesson, even if they've caused you inconvenience.

Learner drivers

Be patient if the vehicle ahead of you is being driven by a learner. They may not be as skilful at anticipating and responding to events as a more experienced driver.

REMEMBER, not every vehicle showing L plates (D plates in Wales) is fitted with dual controls, and the person accompanying the driver might not be a professional instructor.

Don't

- drive up close behind a learner, as this is intimidating and could cause them to panic
- show your impatience, for example by revving your engine, if the learner is slow to move off
- cut in sharply after overtaking.

Expect a learner to make mistakes. Allow for their mistakes and don't give them a hard time. Learners may not take the action you expect. Remember that it may take them longer to do things. Don't forget we were all learners once.

Drivers who have recently passed their test may be displaying a green P plate or other warning sign to alert others that they're new drivers. Be patient and make allowances for their lack of experience.

Read more about learner drivers later in this section.

Older drivers

Although they have more driving experience, older drivers may have slower reactions than younger drivers. Make allowances for this.

Confidence

Confidence is part of a driver's attitude and is closely related to

- skill
- judgement
- experience.

Confidence levels are likely to change throughout a driver's life. Many drivers begin with a relatively high level of confidence in their ability, but after six months their confidence is often much lower. Experiences such as being involved in an incident can have a negative impact on a driver's confidence.

Overconfidence can occur when a driver overestimates their abilities and can lead to

- unsafe driving behaviour
- risk taking
- traffic and speed violations.

It's important to assess your driving ability regularly. Many people think they're better drivers than they really are, so it's important to be honest with yourself and work on any areas you think could be improved. Many driving instructors offer refresher lessons for nervous drivers who would like to build their confidence.

The National Standard for Driving sets out the skills, knowledge and understanding that are required to be a safe and responsible driver. If you meet the standard, then you'll be in a great position to pass your test and well on your way to becoming a safe driver for life.

You can view the National Standard for Driving at **www.gov.uk**

⊕ Good practice

Planning your journey

- Make sure your vehicle is roadworthy. For example, tyre pressures may need adjusting if your route includes motorway travel, if you're carrying a load or if you're towing a trailer.
- Plan refuelling stops.
- Check the weather to see how it may affect your route or journey.
- If it's a long journey, plan enough time for breaks and refreshment.
- If you have a sat-nav, program it before you start your journey. Select the route you prefer and think about traffic congestion and times of day, as this can help you to avoid delays and save fuel.
- Don't rely on your sat-nav alone, as it may have out-of-date or incomplete information at any given time. Use road and street maps as well, or check your route on the internet.

- Give yourself plenty of time for your journey. Hurrying leads to mistakes, and mistakes can lead to incidents.

Before you set out, plan your journey by visiting **www.gov.uk** or check the smartphone apps from Highways England (formerly the Highways Agency) for live traffic updates. You could also listen to local and national radio for news of roadworks and traffic congestion (see section 18).

> **FACTS** Figures from the Highways Agency (now Highways England) show that more than 11 000 people ran out of fuel on the English motorway network between April 2010 and September 2011.

> Always make sure that you have enough fuel for your journey and don't leave it until the tank is running low before you fill up.

Clothing and shoes

Make sure you're comfortable. Wear appropriate clothing, especially on a long journey.

High heels and slippery soles can be dangerous as they can cause your feet to slip off the pedals. Shoes that are too wide, or that easily fall off, can be just as dangerous.

It's a good idea to keep a suitable pair of shoes in your vehicle, just to wear while you're driving.

The weather

The weather is another factor to consider when you're planning a journey. If it's really bad, it might be best to postpone your trip or use public transport. Always try to avoid driving in thick fog or icy conditions, as the risk of a road traffic incident is far higher.

Many drivers run into difficulties in very bad weather. Follow the weather forecasts and general advice to drivers through local and national media.

Animals

If you're taking animals with you on a journey

- keep them under control
- don't allow them to be loose in the vehicle
- don't leave them in the vehicle for any length of time, especially in hot weather
- never let animals loose on the public road – they can cause incidents.

Driving close to home

Many incidents happen close to home on regular daily or routine journeys. If you drive to work every day, don't leave yourself the bare minimum of time to get there.

Don't let familiarity with your surroundings lead you to start taking risks simply because you feel you know every detail.

Remember that other road users won't necessarily have the benefit of local knowledge, so they might drive more cautiously than you feel they should.

 Health

Your eyesight

All drivers must be able to read, in good daylight, a current-style number plate (on vehicles registered since 2001) from 20 metres. Glasses or corrective lenses may be worn if necessary. If you do need to wear glasses or corrective lenses to read the number plate, then you must also use them while driving.

For more information on drivers' eyesight requirements, see **www.gov.uk**

Fitness to drive

You must

- be medically fit to drive

- understand that some medicines shouldn't be taken if you intend to drive. Check with your doctor that it's safe to drive on prescription medicine

- notify the Driver and Vehicle Licensing Agency (DVLA) in Swansea (Driver and Vehicle Agency (DVA) in Northern Ireland) if your health is likely to affect your ability to drive either now or, because of a worsening condition, in the future.

Don't drive if you're feeling tired or unwell. Even a cold can make it unsafe for you to drive. If you find you're losing concentration or not feeling well, keep your speed to a safe minimum and give yourself more time to react. Take a break when possible and consider handing over the driving to someone else.

It's also important to be physically fit to drive. You must have full control of your vehicle at all times.

Remember that, for example

- a twisted ankle can reduce pedal control
- a stiff neck can make it difficult to look behind when reversing or checking blind spots.

Alcohol

Alcohol will seriously reduce your judgement and ability to drive safely. You must be aware that

- driving with alcohol in your blood is potentially very dangerous. There are severe penalties if you drive or attempt to drive while over the legal limit
- if you drink in the evening, you might still be over the legal limit and unfit to drive the following morning.

Alcohol is removed from the blood at the rate of about one unit an hour, but this varies from person to person. If you know how many units you've had, you can work out roughly how many hours it will take for your body to be alcohol-free. To be on the safe side you should start counting from when you had your last drink.

To be absolutely sure there's no alcohol left in your body the morning after drinking, you can check yourself with a home breath-testing kit. The only safe limit, ever, is a zero limit.

You **MUST NOT** drive if your breath alcohol level is higher than the legally permitted level – see **www.gov.uk**

REMEMBER, if you drink, don't drive – and if you drive, don't drink.

Drugs

Driving when you're under the influence of drugs is an offence. This includes some prescription medications that can affect your ability to drive safely.

The effects of drugs can be unpredictable and you may not be aware of them. The direct effects of some drugs can last up to 72 hours.

A new offence of driving with certain illegal drugs in your body came into force in March 2015. The new rules mean that it's an offence to be over the specified limits for certain drugs, such as cannabis, cocaine and ecstasy. Even using a small amount of illegal drugs could result in a positive test and a conviction.

The penalties are a 12-month driving ban, a criminal record and a possible prison sentence.

Visit **www.gov.uk** for more information.

> **FACTS** During 2012, 55 300 people in England and Wales were convicted of driving after consuming alcohol or taking drugs.

Fatigue

Fatigue can mean feeling tired, sleepy or lacking energy. Symptoms can include

- slower reflexes
- poor decision making
- headaches
- lack of concentration
- muscle weakness
- irritability.

Driving while you're tired increases your risk of being involved in a collision.

Don't begin a journey if you feel tired – make sure you get a good night's sleep before starting a long journey.

Try to avoid driving between 2.00 am and 7.00 am, because this is when the 'body clock' is in a daily dip.

If you begin to feel sleepy, stop in a safe place before you get to the stage of 'fighting sleep'. Sleep can come upon you more quickly than you would imagine. Also, when you're very tired, you can experience micro-sleeps, which means that you could lose consciousness for up to 30 seconds.

If it's not possible to stop immediately, open a window for fresh air. Stop as soon as it's safe and legal to do so. On a motorway, pull in at the nearest service area or leave the motorway. The only time you may stop on the hard shoulder of the motorway is in an emergency, so you **MUST NOT** stop there to rest.

The most effective ways to counter sleepiness are caffeine and a short nap. The combination of a caffeinated drink (for example, caffeinated coffee), followed by a short nap of up to 15 minutes, is particularly effective. Caffeine takes 20–30 minutes to be absorbed and act on the brain, which will give you the opportunity for a nap. However, this shouldn't be used as a long-term solution to your sleepiness.

Don't drive for too long without taking a break. Your concentration will be much better if you plan regular stops for rest and refreshments. It's recommended that you take a break of at least 15 minutes after every two hours of driving. This is especially important at night.

⊕ Learner drivers

Attitude

Your attitude to driving and to other road users can affect the way you drive and how enjoyable you find driving. It's easy to become anxious or frustrated, especially if there's a lot of traffic or you're on unfamiliar roads. When you're learning to drive it can feel like the whole world is in a rush and you might be holding them up.

If you're a learner, try to remember that experienced drivers were once learners too. Although you're bound to see some poor behaviour on the road, most people want to get to their destination with the minimum of fuss. Most drivers are courteous to other drivers and road users, and forgive their mistakes. And everyone makes mistakes – even experienced drivers.

Learner drivers have the opportunity to begin their driving careers with a safe and responsible attitude. It's important at this very early stage to start developing the behaviours that will keep everyone safe on the road and make driving an enjoyable experience.

If you're a novice, you need to be responsible and show patience and courtesy to become a good driver. And, hopefully, more experienced drivers will show you the same respect.

Planned lessons

A planned approach to learning is advisable, particularly in the early stages. Everyone learns differently, so it's important that, together with whoever teaches you to drive, you develop a learning plan that suits your needs.

Who should teach you?
The best way to learn is by having

- regular planned lessons with a professional instructor
- each lesson matched to your needs and abilities
- as much practice as possible.

Once you understand the basics, it's a good idea to combine professional instruction with as much practice as you can get with relatives or friends. This helps you to gain experience by driving in a wide variety of situations.

If you pay someone for driving lessons, they must be an approved driving instructor (ADI) or a potential driving instructor (PDI) with a trainee licence.

Approved driving instructor (car)

An ADI must

- pass a three-part examination to qualify
- have their name entered on the register held by the Driver and Vehicle Standards Agency (DVSA)
- display a green ADI identification certificate on the windscreen of the vehicle being used for a driving lesson
- reach and maintain the standards required by DVSA.

Some trainee instructors who haven't yet completed the qualifying examination may hold a trainee licence to help them gain instructional experience.

Trainee instructors must display a pink identification certificate on the windscreen of the vehicle being used for a driving lesson.

How to choose an ADI

You should choose an instructor who can provide exactly what you need as a learner. Some ADIs will also be able to help you develop your skills after passing the test – for example, by teaching you how to drive at different times of day, in different weather conditions and on types of road you may not have experienced while you were learning to drive.

Choose an instructor

- who has a good reputation
- who's reliable and punctual
- whose vehicle suits you (eg engine size, has dual controls, etc)
- who you think you'll get on well with.

You should ask if the instructor is an ADI or a trainee. ADIs are graded on their performance and you can ask what grade they are. Visit **www.gov.uk** for more information on ADI grading.

You can find your nearest ADIs by using the 'Find driving schools and lessons' tool on **www.gov.uk**. Put in your postcode and it'll come up with a list of ADIs in your area. You can also find out which ADIs are voluntarily developing their own skills (continuing professional development – CPD) or observing the voluntary ADI code of practice.

Trainee instructors aren't listed on this website.

You could also ask friends and relatives to recommend an ADI.

Take advice from your ADI on

- all aspects of driving
- what learning materials are available; for example, books, DVD-ROMs, downloads, eBooks and apps
- how to practise
- when you'll be ready for the driving test.

The official syllabus

If you learn with an ADI, make sure they cover the official syllabus fully. See **The Official DVSA Guide to Learning to Drive** for more details. The syllabus is also shown in the Driver's Record. The Driver's Record will help you to monitor your progress and is available from your ADI or can be downloaded from **www.gov.uk**

All practical driving tests include a period of independent driving. This assesses your ability to drive on your own while making decisions for yourself without instruction. The examiner will be looking for evidence that you have the required skills, knowledge and attitude to be a safe driver.

This is important because you'll be able to drive unaccompanied as soon as you've passed your driving test. During the independent drive you'll be asked to

- drive following traffic signs to a destination, or
- drive following a series of verbal directions

or a combination of both.

Accompanying a learner

If you're accompanying a learner, you should try to encourage confidence. It's also important not to put them in a situation that requires more skill than they can be expected to show.

Don't let them try to run before they can walk. Overestimating a learner's skill can set back their progress and could lead to incidents for both the learner and other road users.

Anyone supervising a learner must

- be at least 21 years old
- have held for at least three years (and still hold) a full EC/EEA licence for the category of vehicle being driven.

The Official DVSA Guide to Learning to Drive includes a section that will help you to understand what a learner driver needs to practise. It also points out the hazards you may encounter when accompanying a learner driver.

Learning by example

People often learn by example. You, as the accompanying driver, should therefore

- show a learner how to drive with quiet confidence
- point out when other drivers make a mistake and discuss with the learner how they could approach the situation better
- discourage them from developing bad habits and using excuses such as 'Everyone else does it, so why shouldn't I?'

Taking on too much

The enthusiastic learner should be careful not to take on too much. Overconfidence can lead to carelessness, risk-taking and incidents. Also, as the accompanying driver, you should understand the learner's level of experience and skill as a driver. You can take advice from the learner's ADI about the level they've reached and the skills they should be practising.

The training vehicle

A vehicle being driven by a learner must display L plates (or D plates in Wales), which should be removed or covered at all other times.

If you own a car or intend to buy one, it might be best to find a driving school that uses a similar model.

At a later stage, it might also be possible to have lessons in your own car.

Avoid fixing L plates (D plates) to the windscreen or back window, as they can restrict your view.

⊕ New drivers

New drivers are vulnerable because they lack experience on the roads. They can be involved in incidents early in their driving careers. Young drivers may be especially vulnerable.

Incidents involving new drivers are usually caused by

- lack of experience and judgement, especially when driving 'high-performance' cars
- competitive behaviour, racing and lack of consideration for others
- being overconfident in their own ability.
- the natural spirit of youth and tendency to push boundaries
- showing off to friends; being 'egged on' by passengers looking for excitement.

Profiles of incidents involving new drivers tell us that these incidents are most likely to occur

- at night
- at weekends
- on rural roads
- when driving with friends
- when alcohol and drugs are involved.

If you're a new driver, avoid

- driving too fast; speed reduces the time you have to react, and increases the force of the impact if you're involved in a collision
- reckless driving; drive with consideration and care
- showing off; if you want to impress your friends, show them how smooth and safe a driver you are
- being 'wound up'; keep calm
- an aggressive attitude and behaviour; stay calm and safe
- loud music; this could interfere with your concentration or with your hearing at a critical moment
- driving beyond your capabilities; always leave yourself a safety margin
- being distracted by passengers.

Above all, be responsible and show courtesy and consideration to other road users.

False perceptions

Many younger drivers wrongly believe that fast reactions and the ability to handle their vehicle will make them a good and safe driver. They fail to recognise that vehicle handling skills alone won't prevent road traffic incidents.

Having the right attitude and a sound knowledge of defensive driving techniques is essential.

Pass Plus

New drivers can take further training after they've passed their test. Pass Plus was created by DVSA for new drivers who would like to improve their basic skills and safely widen their driving experience. If you take the Pass Plus course, you may also receive reduced insurance premiums.

Ask your ADI for details of the scheme or visit **www.gov.uk** for more information.

⊙ Older drivers

Although they're experienced, older drivers can also be vulnerable, but for different reasons. The natural and gradual deterioration in physical fitness and ability that comes with age can affect judgement and concentration. Physical frailty can mean that those involved in incidents are more likely to be injured.

Generally, older drivers are as safe as any other driver. They're involved in far fewer drink-drive or single-vehicle incidents than younger people.

However, older drivers have slower reaction times than young drivers. This means it can take them longer to react to hazards and other situations that require quick decisions – for example, high-speed junctions and slip roads.

If you're an older driver, be responsible and

- have your eyesight checked regularly, including your night vision. It's common for eyesight to deteriorate with age. If you find you need glasses for driving, you **MUST** wear them whenever you drive
- avoid driving at night if you find the glare from headlights dazzles you
- be aware that you may find driving more tiring as you get older
- be honest with yourself about your driving. If you believe that you're no longer safe on the road, it may be time to stop driving.

You might choose to restrict your time behind the wheel by avoiding driving

- long distances
- at rush hour
- in bad weather.

REMEMBER, recognise your own limitations and don't take risks.

⊕ Disabled drivers

Advances in technology offer many more disabled people the chance to drive. All standard vehicles can now be modified for a physically disabled driver.

Modifications

These can include

- hand controls for braking and acceleration
- steering and secondary control aids
- left-foot accelerator conversions
- clutch conversions
- parking-brake devices
- additional car mirrors
- seat-belt modifications
- harnesses
- special seating
- wheelchair stowage equipment
- joystick and foot steering; a four-way joystick can now be used to steer, accelerate and brake

- infra-red remote control systems that enable a wheelchair user to get into or out of a vehicle with complete independence.

Assessment

Mobility centres for disabled people are available to

- test driving ability
- give advice on the sort of controls and adaptations needed to drive safely and in comfort.

For a complete list of mobility centres, visit

drivingmobility.org.uk

For information about paying for modifications and adaptations, visit

motability.co.uk

The major motoring organisations and some motor manufacturers offer special services for disabled drivers.

⊙ Reviewing your driving

To be a safe and responsible driver it's essential to review and adjust your behaviour over your lifetime. Keeping up to date with changes in the law and driving technology, as well as regularly and honestly reviewing your performance as a driver, will make all the difference to your own safety and other people's safety. As you progress through a lifetime of driving, there'll be changes in circumstances. The context in which you drive will change and you'll also probably change as an individual.

For example, there are likely to be changes

- to the law and to the rules of the road
- to vehicle and related technologies
- in your personal circumstances

- in the reasons why you drive
- in your health and physical condition
- in your attitudes and behaviours.

Safe and responsible drivers make sure they maintain their skills by reviewing their driving and continuously seeking to improve.

As a continuously improving driver you should

- learn from experience
- avoid becoming self-satisfied and thinking you know everything
- watch out for the development of bad habits. Try to keep your driving up to the standard you were taught and, if you think it's slipping, do something about it
- develop and maintain considerate and responsible driver behaviours.

The competent driver needs

- a sense of responsibility
- to concentrate on the task of driving
- good anticipation
- patience
- confidence
- courtesy and consideration.

There's a wide range of opportunities for drivers who want to review and assess their driving, develop their competence and respond to changing circumstances. For example

- read **The Official DVSA Guide to Better Driving**, which explores how emotions, attitude and behaviour can affect your driving. It will also teach you – through real-life scenarios and test-yourself questionnaires – how to manage stress and anxiety behind the wheel
- newly qualified drivers can take a Pass Plus course
- you can practise your driving with an experienced accompanying driver, who can give you feedback on how you've driven
- if you already have a licence, but feel that you could do with improving your skills or you've lost your confidence, you can book some lessons with an ADI
- advanced driving courses are available if you want to improve your driving further.

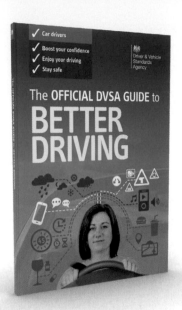

If you find the context of your driving has changed, it's important to review and assess your skills and knowledge in the new environment. For example, you may have to drive for work or as a new parent, or you may move from the city to the countryside. As the context changes you may find that you need additional training, knowledge or support.

Driving for work

Driving for work is one of the most high-risk contexts in driving, because of the amount of time you'll spend behind the wheel and the pressure you may be under. If you drive for work – perhaps a van or a company car – you'll probably face lots of different driving conditions and you may be expected to reach your destination quickly. In this situation, you and your employer should think about how to balance your work commitments with driving within the law. Your stress and fatigue levels should also be taken into account.

All drivers

All drivers need to be alert to changes in their physical or mental condition. Ill-health or relevant age-related changes can have a significant impact on driving and should be considered and addressed.

Constantly and honestly reviewing how well you're driving should help you have a long and safe driving career.

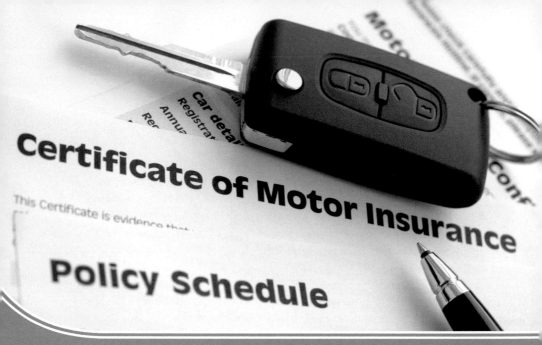

Section two

⊙ The driver and the law

This section covers

- Licence requirements
- Insurance
- Vehicle registration certificate (V5C)
- Vehicle tax
- The MOT test
- Roadworthiness
- The Highway Code
- Seat belts
- Loading your vehicle

⊕ Licence requirements

The law in Northern Ireland

The laws relating to driving and the processes you need to follow to get the right paperwork aren't always the same in Great Britain and Northern Ireland. For example, in Great Britain your vehicle is required to pass an MOT test three years after the date of first registration, but in Northern Ireland an MOT isn't required until four years after registration.

> If you drive in Northern Ireland, you should check the NI Direct website for the most up-to-date advice on the driver and the law.
>
> **nidirect.gov.uk**

Your driving licence

Driving any vehicle carries with it legal requirements, and you must satisfy some of these before you begin to drive on the public road. Others apply after you start to drive.

For the category of vehicle you intend to drive, you **MUST** have one of the following

- a valid provisional driving licence
- a valid full driving licence

or, in certain circumstances

- a signed, valid International Driving Permit (IDP)
- a full driving licence issued outside the UK.

Your age

You **MUST** be at least 17 years old to drive a car. As an exception, you can drive a car when you're 16 if you get, or have applied for, the enhanced rate of the mobility component of Personal Independence Payment (PIP).

Changes to your driving licence

If you change your name and/or address, you must complete the details on your licence and send it to: DVLA, Swansea, SA99 1BN (DVA in NI) or you can do this online at **www.gov.uk**

Provisional licence

You can apply for a provisional driving licence online at **www.gov.uk**

Alternatively, you can apply by post by completing a D1 application form, which you can get from the Driver and Vehicle Licensing Agency (DVLA) form-ordering service or from a post office. You'll also need to include

- original documentation confirming your identity
- a colour passport-style photograph
- the current fee.

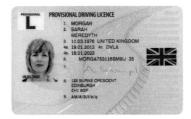

When you receive your provisional licence, check that all the details are correct.

L plates (D plates in Wales)
You **MUST** display L plates (D plates) which conform to legal specifications, and which are clearly visible from both in front of the vehicle and from behind the vehicle.

If the vehicle is NOT being driven by a learner driver, the L plates (D plates) should be removed or covered.

Your accompanying driver
You **MUST** be accompanied by a driver who's at least 21 years old and who holds a full EC/EEA licence for that type of car (manual or automatic) and has held one for three years.

Motorways
Holders of provisional car licences weren't allowed to drive on a motorway at the time this book was published. However, in 2018 it's proposed that learner car drivers will be allowed to have driving lessons on a motorway, provided that they're accompanied by an approved driving instructor (ADI) and are in a vehicle fitted with dual controls. Please check **www.gov.uk** for the latest information.

Full licence

To obtain your full licence you **MUST** pass a theory test, followed by a practical test for the category of vehicle you wish to drive. You'll then be able to drive unaccompanied and on a motorway. Your car licence also allows you to drive a light van of up to 3.5 tonnes maximum laden weight, but different speed limits apply to vans over 2 tonnes maximum laden weight.

Electronic driver record

On 8 June 2015, the paper counterpart to the photocard driving licence was discontinued. Details of the vehicles you can drive and any penalty points or bans you've received are now stored electronically. You can view this information at **www.gov.uk/view-driving-licence**

You can also share this information with anyone who needs to see your details (for example, an employer or car-hire company) by generating a 'check code'. Visit the link above for more information.

Note: if you have a paper driving licence that was issued before the photocard licence was introduced in 1998, it remains valid.

Visitors and new residents

Visitors and new residents with a full, valid EC/EEA driving licence may use that licence to drive/ride a car or motorcycle in Great Britain until they're 70 years old, or for three years after becoming resident in Great Britain, whichever is longer. If your EC/EEA licence was obtained by exchanging a non-EC/EEA licence, you may drive/ride on your licence in Great Britain for no more than 12 months.

Those with licences from outside the EC/EEA may drive/ride a car or motorcycle in Great Britain for up to 12 months from the date they last entered or became resident in this country. After this period, they must obtain a full British licence.

If you come from certain designated countries (see **www.gov.uk** for more details), you may exchange your full driving licence for a British one within five years of becoming a resident. If you come from any other country, you can obtain a full British licence by applying for a British provisional licence and passing a British driving test.

Different rules apply if you wish to drive a lorry, minibus and/or bus. See **www.gov.uk** for full details.

Renewing your driving licence

You must renew a photocard licence every 10 years. You'll receive a reminder in the post before your current licence ends. There are three ways to renew

1. online at **www.gov.uk**
2. at a participating post office (find your nearest suitable post office at **postoffice.co.uk/uk-driving-licence-photocard-renewal**)
3. by post with DVLA (visit **www.gov.uk** for more details).

Your driving licence should arrive within one week if you apply online.

Renewing your driving licence if you're 70 or over

All drivers must renew their licence at the age of 70, and every three years thereafter.

You can renew online at **www.gov.uk** for free if you're 70 or over (or soon will be). Alternatively, you can apply by post using the D46P application form. DVLA will automatically send you this form 90 days before your 70th birthday. If you haven't got the D46P form, you can use a D1 Application for a driving licence form, which you can get from your local post office.

⊕ Insurance

The registered keeper of a vehicle **MUST** make sure the vehicle has motor insurance unless it's kept off the road and a Statutory Off-Road Notification (SORN) has been made (see later in this section). As part of Continuous Insurance Enforcement (CIE), the registered keeper will be notified when their vehicle appears to be uninsured. If they don't act on the letter and insure the vehicle, they'll risk

- a fixed-penalty fine of £100
- a court prosecution and a fine of up to £1000
- having the vehicle clamped, seized and destroyed.

It's the driver's responsibility to make sure that they're insured to drive the vehicle they're using. Uninsured drivers can now be detected by the police and roadside automatic number-plate recognition (ANPR) cameras, which are linked to the motor insurance database. The penalties for uninsured drivers include

- an unlimited fine
- 6–8 penalty points on their licence
- having the vehicle seized by the police, taken away and destroyed.

Motor insurance can be arranged online or in person with an insurance company, broker or other insurance provider.

Types of insurance

Third-party

This is the legal minimum and generally the cheapest insurance cover. 'Third party' means anyone you might injure or whose property you might damage. You're not covered for damage to the vehicle you're driving or injury to yourself.

Third-party, fire and theft

This is the same as third-party, except that it also covers you against your vehicle being stolen or damaged by fire.

Comprehensive
This is the best type of insurance, but the most expensive. Apart from covering other persons and property for injury and damage, it also covers damage to your vehicle. Additional benefits, such as cover for the contents of the vehicle, may be offered.

The cost of insurance

This depends on a number of factors, including

- your age; the younger you are, the more it will cost, especially if you're under 25
- whether you've completed the Pass Plus scheme
- how long you've been driving
- the make and power of your vehicle
- where you live and keep your car overnight
- how you intend to use your vehicle
- when and how you drive (with telematics insurance)
- any court convictions and fixed-penalty offences
- any no-claims discount you've earned.

It can also vary from one insurer to another, so it pays to shop around.

You must answer all questions on the insurance application honestly as, in the event of a claim, your policy could be worthless if the insurance company discovers that you haven't told the truth. They then have the right to void the policy, which would leave you open to prosecution for being uninsured. For example, a young person is committing fraud if they state that an older, more experienced driver is the main user of their vehicle to reduce the cost of their cover. This is known as 'fronting' and insurance companies look out for it.

Telematics insurance

These policies (also known as black box insurance) offer a personalised price for car insurance based on when and how you drive. A 'black box' is fitted into your car and uses GPS technology to measure your driving performance.

Your insurer uses this information to calculate your premiums. The idea is that by driving safely you can save money but poor driving could result in your premiums increasing.

What's insured

This also varies from company to company. Read your insurance policy carefully and ask your insurer or broker if you're in any doubt. Otherwise you might have difficulties when you claim.

If you do make a claim, you'll often have to pay part of the cost yourself – this is called the 'excess', and it's usually higher for young and inexperienced drivers.

> Before driving someone else's vehicle, check your insurance cover. You're probably only covered for third-party risks. You might not be covered at all!

Insurance documents

Certificate of insurance

This short and simple document shows

- who's insured to drive the vehicle
- the vehicle covered
- the period of cover
- what type of use the vehicle is insured for
- whether there's cover to drive other vehicles.

Sometimes a broker will give you a temporary certificate or 'cover note' while you're waiting for the certificate.

Certificate of Motor Insurance

Registration mark of vehicle	**ANY 1234**	Certificate number	**000123456**
Name of Policyholder	**Mr A N Other**		
Effective date of the commencement of insurance for the purposes of the relevant law	**01/07/12** (Noon)	Date of expiry of insurance	**01/07/13** (Noon)

Persons or classes of persons entitled to drive	• The Policyholder • The Policyholder may also drive with the owner's permission a motor car not owned by the Policyholder and not hired or leased to the Policyholder under a hire purchase or annual leasing agreement. • Any person named below who is driving on the Policyholder's order or with the Policyholder's permission: **Mrs A N Other** (Spouse)	provided that the person driving holds a licence to drive such motor car or has held and is not disqualified for holding or obtaining such a licence and is not breaking the conditions of their driving licence.
Limitations as to use The Policy covers: The Policy does not cover:	• use for social, domestic and pleasure purposes • use by the Policyholder or by the Policyholder's spouse each in person in connection with the businesses of the Policyholder or spouse • use for racing, competitions, rallies, trials, track days or 4x4 off road events. • use for hire and reward • use for any purpose in connection with the motor trade. • use to secure the release of a motor car, other than the vehicle identified above by its registration mark, which has been seized by, or on behalf of, any government or public authority	
Certification	I hereby certify that the Policy to which this Certificate relates satisfies the requirements of the relevant law applicable in Great Britain and Northern Ireland, the Republic of Ireland, the Isle of Man, the Island of Guernsey, the Island of Jersey and the Island of Alderney. UK Insurance Limited Authorised Insurers Chief Executive Advice to third parties: Nothing in this Certificate affects your right as a third party to make a claim.	

A cover note normally lasts for one month.

Showing your certificate

Keep the certificate safe and produce it

- if the police ask you to
- if you're involved in an incident.

The policy document

This contains the full details of the contract between you and the insurance company and how to claim. Insurance companies also supply a summary of cover showing the main cover, terms and conditions. If there's anything you don't understand, ask your broker or the insurance company to explain.

⊕ Vehicle registration certificate (V5C)

A vehicle registration certificate (V5C), also known as a logbook, contains information about the vehicle. It shows

- the name and address of the vehicle's registered keeper
- information about the vehicle, including the make, model and engine size
- the date the vehicle was first registered.

The registered keeper is the person who's responsible for taxing the vehicle, even if they aren't the legal owner. If you're the registered keeper of a vehicle, it's your responsibility to keep the details of your V5C up to date. You must tell DVLA when

- you change your address
- you change your name
- you change any of the details of your vehicle (eg colour)
- you no longer have the vehicle.

You can update your V5C by filling in the relevant section and sending the whole form to DVLA, which will issue a new V5C. Informing DVLA ensures your V11 (tax reminder) is sent to the correct address, enabling you to tax your vehicle.

When a vehicle is sold, both the seller and the buyer must complete and sign the V5C and the seller must send the relevant part of the V5C to DVLA.

You can get more information about the V5C on the form itself, or from **www.gov.uk**

If you lose your V5C, you can request a replacement from DVLA, although a fee may be charged.

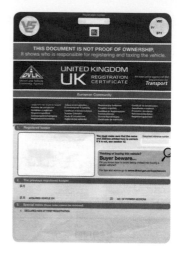

REMEMBER

- the registered keeper is responsible for informing DVLA in the event of any changes to their name, address or details of the vehicle
- the registered keeper must notify DVLA when they no longer have the vehicle
- the V5C isn't proof of ownership.

⊕ Vehicle tax

You can pay your vehicle tax online at **www.gov.uk**. Alternatively, you can use DVLA's automated phone service on **0300 123 4321** or visit certain post office branches.

The paper tax disc is now a thing of the past. You still have to pay your vehicle tax, but you no longer receive a paper disc to display in your windscreen.

When you buy a vehicle, the tax is no longer transferred with it; you need to pay the tax yourself before you can use the vehicle. You can do this online, by telephone or at the post office, using the New Keeper Supplement (V5C/2) part of the vehicle registration certificate (V5C).

DVLA will send you a renewal reminder through the post when your existing vehicle tax is about to run out.

When you sell a vehicle, you should tell DVLA. They'll automatically send you a refund for any full calendar months left on your vehicle tax.

The registered keeper of a vehicle also needs to tell DVLA when the vehicle is off the road, or has been sold, transferred, scrapped or exported; otherwise they remain liable for taxing it. Once DVLA has been notified about a sale or transfer, or that the vehicle is off-road, it will issue an acknowledgement, which should be kept as proof that the vehicle record has been changed.

If you don't relicense your vehicle

Keepers who fail to relicense their vehicle (or make a SORN) incur an automatic penalty. DVLA carries out a computer check each month to identify untaxed vehicles. It's no longer necessary for the vehicle to be seen on a public road before a penalty is issued, but on-road enforcement will continue.

Statutory Off-Road Notification (SORN)

If you don't intend to use or keep the vehicle on a public road, you can make a SORN and then you won't have to pay vehicle tax. Once you've made a SORN, it will remain valid until the vehicle is taxed, sold or scrapped.

You can make a SORN by

- applying online at **www.gov.uk**
- contacting DVLA on **0300 123 4321** or minicom **0300 790 6201**
- filling in a SORN declaration form V890 and sending it to DVLA. These forms are available from licence-issuing post office branches or can be downloaded from **www.gov.uk**
- filling in the relevant section of your renewal reminder form V11 and taking it to a licence-issuing post office branch
- using form V14 Application for a refund of vehicle tax, if you're also applying for a refund and the vehicle is to remain in your possession.

Remember, to keep a vehicle untaxed and off the road, the registered keeper **MUST** make a SORN. If you don't and you ignore any subsequent reminders sent to you as the registered keeper, then you risk

- a fixed-penalty fine of £100
- court prosecution and a fine of up to £1000
- having the vehicle clamped, seized and destroyed.

⊕ The MOT test

The MOT test applies to most motor vehicles three years old and over. If your vehicle is more than three years old and isn't exempt from the MOT test, you must have a current MOT test certificate. You won't be able to tax your vehicle without it.

Motor vehicles manufactured before 1 January 1960 are exempt from the requirement to have an MOT – although they can be submitted for a test voluntarily. Owners are still legally required to ensure that these vehicles are safe and in a proper condition to be on the road.

Certain vehicles, including the following, **MUST** be tested one year after registration and annually thereafter

- large goods vehicles (LGVs) over 3.5 tonnes gross weight
- passenger-carrying vehicles (PCVs) with more than eight seats
- ambulances
- taxis.

The purpose of the MOT test is to ensure that your vehicle's safety and environmental systems and components meet the required minimum legal standards.

The test must be carried out every year by a vehicle testing station appointed by the Driver and Vehicle Standards Agency (DVSA).

For details of DVSA's MOT text reminder service, see **www.gov.uk**

> You can have your vehicle tested as much as one month before the current certificate runs out. The expiry date of the new certificate will be one year after the expiry date of the old one.

Your certificate

An MOT test certificate isn't a guarantee that the vehicle will remain roadworthy and comply with the minimum standards of the certificate. Neither does it imply that the engine and transmission systems are in good condition – these items aren't critical to safety and aren't covered by the MOT test.

Fees

Ask any vehicle testing station about their current test and retest fees.

The maximum fee that may be charged is set by the government and depends on the type of vehicle. See **www.gov.uk/getting-an-mot/mot-test-fees** for the latest figures.

Failure

If your vehicle fails its MOT and you want to continue to use it, you must make arrangements to have the necessary repairs carried out without delay. The vehicle must pass a retest before it's used on the road, except when

* driving it away from the testing station after failing the test
* driving to and from a garage carrying out the repairs
* driving to an MOT test appointment booked in advance.

Even in these circumstances you can still be prosecuted if your car isn't roadworthy under the various regulations governing its construction and use. In addition, check that your insurance cover remains valid.

You can go online at **www.gov.uk** to check your vehicle's MOT status and history.

Appeals

If you consider the vehicle has been incorrectly failed, you have the right to appeal. Information on how to appeal may be obtained at **www.gov.uk**

Exhaust emission limits

Remember, the test includes a strict exhaust emission test. This means your engine must be correctly tuned and adjusted.

There are prescribed emission limits for the engines of vehicles registered after 1975 and the MOT test will check that these limits aren't exceeded.

⊕ Roadworthiness

You must ensure that the vehicle you intend to drive

* is legally roadworthy
* is insured for you to drive
* has a current MOT test certificate if required
* has up-to-date vehicle tax.

Components that need checking include the following.

The braking system

The vehicle's brakes, including the parking brake (also known as the handbrake), must be in good working order and correctly adjusted.

Tyres

All tyres on the vehicle **MUST** meet current requirements for condition and depth of tread (see section 14).

Lights/indicators

All lights, including lenses and reflectors, must be in working order, even during daylight hours.

Exhaust

A silencer must be fitted which reduces noise to an acceptable level.

For cars and light goods vehicles, exhaust emissions mustn't exceed the prescribed limits. Any MOT testing station will be able to tell you the limits for your vehicle.

For best fuel economy, have the engine tuned according to the manufacturer's recommendations.

Instruments and equipment

Appropriate mirrors must be fitted.

All instruments and equipment must be in good working order, including

- speedometer
- horn
- windscreen wipers and washers.

Vehicle modifications

Some vehicle modifications, such as heavily tinted windows, may restrict vision. Others may potentially endanger pedestrians, as in the case of bull bars.

Disability modifications

If your vehicle has been adapted for your disability, make sure that the modifications don't affect the safe control of the vehicle.

⊕ The Highway Code

The Highway Code contains essential advice for all road users.

A set of rules

Its purpose is to prevent road traffic incidents by ensuring that we all adopt the same rules when we use the road.

Road traffic law has developed over the years into a comprehensive set of rules, many with underpinning legislation. Use of **MUST** or **MUST NOT** in red within a rule indicates that direct legislation applies, and a reference to that legislation also appears beneath the rule.

If you disobey these rules you're committing a criminal offence. The Highway Code explains these rules as simply as possible, to make them easy to understand.

Road traffic law changes from time to time, and so do the penalties for breaking it. Make sure you keep up to date. The Highway Code is updated frequently, and you should study and apply the contents of the current edition.

Road signs and signals

You **MUST** know and comply with

- all traffic signs and road markings
- signals given by police officers, traffic wardens, school crossing wardens, traffic officers, DVSA officials and any other authorised person (for example, road workers operating 'stop/go' boards)
- traffic signals at
  - junctions and crossroads
  - roadworks
  - narrow bridges
  - pedestrian crossings
  - fire and ambulance stations*

- level crossings*
- tramway (light rail transit) crossings.

*usually red flashing lights

Road safety

In everyday driving, you need to follow the rules set down in The Highway Code for your own safety and that of all road users.

Even if you're an experienced driver, you need to know The Highway Code thoroughly and apply it in your everyday driving.

You **MUST NOT** drive

- dangerously
- without due care and attention
- without reasonable consideration for other road users.

Although not all the rules in The Highway Code are legal requirements, they can be used in court proceedings to establish liability and support prosecutions under the Traffic Acts.

Look on The Highway Code as an aid to safe driving. **Don't** look on it as a restriction.

The Highway Code is available as a book, an eBook and an iPhone app.

 Seat belts

Seat belts save lives and reduce the risk of injury. Unless you're exempt, you must wear a seat belt if one is available.

The following table summarises the legal requirements for the wearing of seat belts. It's important that seat belts are always correctly adjusted and are comfortable, with both the lap belt and the diagonal belt, where available, protecting the body.

The driver is responsible for ensuring that all children under 14 years old wear seat belts or use an approved child restraint.

You may temporarily release your seat belt while carrying out any manoeuvre involving reversing. However, you **MUST** refasten it once the manoeuvre has been completed.

If an inertia reel seat belt has temporarily locked because the vehicle is parked on a gradient, you may move the vehicle to release the mechanism. As soon as the mechanism has released, you should stop and put on the belt.

	Front seat – all vehicles	Rear seat – cars and small minibuses*
Driver	Seat belt **MUST** be worn if fitted	–
Child under 3 years old	Correct child restraint **MUST** be used	Correct child restraint **MUST** be used*
Child from 3rd birthday up to 1.35m in height (or 12th birthday, whichever they reach first)	Correct child restraint **MUST** be used	Correct child restraint **MUST** be used where seat belts fitted**
Child over 1.35m (approx 4ft 5ins) **in height, or 12 or 13 years**	Adult seat belt **MUST** be worn if available	Adult seat belt **MUST** be worn if available
Adult passengers aged 14 years and over	Seat belt **MUST** be worn if available	Seat belt **MUST** be worn if available

* If the correct child restraint isn't available in a licensed taxi or private hire vehicle, the child may travel unrestrained.

** If the correct child restraint isn't available in a licensed taxi or private hire vehicle, or for reasons of unexpected necessity over a short distance, or where two occupied child restraints prevent fitment of a third, then an adult seat belt **MUST** be worn.

Carrying children

A child restraint appropriate to the child's weight and size **MUST** be used when carrying children under 1.35 metres tall. Types of restraint include

- baby seat
- child seat
- booster seat
- booster cushion.

Child seat restraints **MUST** be correctly fitted in accordance with the manufacturer's instructions. If in doubt, seek specialist advice.

Adults **MUST NOT** put one seat belt around both themselves and an infant on their lap. This doesn't comply with the law and could result in severe internal, and/or fatal, crush injuries to the child in the event of a crash.

When carrying children in a vehicle, you should also ensure that

- they're kept under control
- child safety door locks are used, where fitted
- they don't sit behind the rear seats in an estate car or hatchback, unless a special child seat has been fitted.

Learn more about carrying children safely and car seats at this website.

childcarseats.org.uk

Airbags

Rear-facing child seats **MUST NOT** be used in a seat protected by an airbag. In a collision, the airbag would hit the child seat with such force that the child would almost certainly receive serious or fatal injuries.

Smoking in your vehicle

It's illegal to smoke in a private enclosed vehicle if one or more of the occupants is under 18.

This means that it's an offence

- for a person of any age to smoke in a private vehicle that's carrying someone under 18
- for a driver (including a provisional driver) not to stop someone smoking if one of the occupants is under 18.

The rules don't apply to e-cigarettes.

⊕ Loading your vehicle

It's your responsibility as a driver to ensure that your vehicle isn't overloaded.

Never exceed the weight limits for your vehicle as this can be dangerous. It will also mean that your vehicle uses more fuel as the engine has to work harder.

You **MUST** also ensure that any load

- is fastened securely
- doesn't obscure your view
- doesn't stick out dangerously.

Make sure that any objects or animals you carry are secured safely.

- Dogs should be strapped in with a special car harness or travel behind a grille. Other animals should be carried in cages or special carry-boxes, which should be secured with the seat belt.

- Make sure packages are securely stored, preferably in the boot of the vehicle, where they should be strapped down or wedged in to stop them moving around.

If you do need to carry packages inside the car, make sure that they won't move if you have to brake or turn suddenly. In particular

- strap down any large or heavy object with the seat belt
- don't put anything where it would obstruct your vision
- don't carry any items in the driver's footwell. If you put something elsewhere on the floor, make sure that it can't roll around the vehicle.

Carrying a heavy load may have an effect on the handling of your car, so

- allow a greater stopping distance
- adjust your headlights and increase your tyre pressure to take account of the load
- distribute the weight evenly, as any change to the vehicle's centre of gravity will affect the braking and steering.

Consider fitting

- a specially designed roof box to carry bulky items. This is streamlined to save fuel and will also hold the load more securely
- special cycle racks on top of or behind the car to carry cycles more securely. If they're fitted behind the car, make sure that the number plates and lights aren't obscured.

Section three

⊙ **The controls**

This section covers

- Your vehicle handbook
- Driving position
- The hand controls
- The foot controls
- Switches
- Other controls

⊕ Your vehicle handbook

In-car controls and technologies – when used correctly – help you drive and manage your vehicle. New technologies appear all the time and they vary between different models of vehicle. Make sure you're familiar with the particular vehicle you're in charge of and follow the manufacturer's guidelines.

⊕ Driving position

You must adopt a suitable driving position before you can use the controls on the car safely.

You must be able to

- reach and use each control easily and comfortably; for example, you should be able to operate the clutch pedal without stretching your left leg

- control the vehicle by keeping a suitable grip on the steering wheel; your arms should be relaxed and not restricted at the elbows

- see the road ahead clearly.

Driving seat adjustment

You should make sure that the seat is adjusted to suit you. Most driving seats can be adjusted for

- 'rake' – the angle of the seat back

- position – the seat will move forwards or backwards.

Sometimes, the driving seat will also adjust for height.

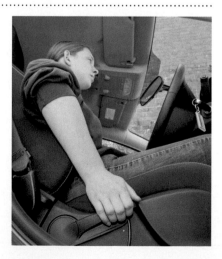

The driver and front passenger should avoid sitting too close to the steering wheel or dashboard.

If someone else has been driving the vehicle, make any necessary adjustments before you start to drive.

Never adjust your seat while the vehicle is moving.

Remember, after adjusting your seat, make sure it's firmly locked in position. Listen for, or feel for, the locking mechanism engaging. An insecure driving seat is dangerous.

As soon as you're seated, check that the parking brake is applied.

Steering column adjustment

On some vehicles, you can adjust the steering column to suit you. You can move it towards or away from you, and adjust the angle of tilt.

When making an adjustment, take care not to allow the steering wheel to interfere with your view of the instrument panel. Also, make sure you secure the locking mechanism after any adjustment.

Never attempt to adjust your steering column while the vehicle is moving.

Head restraint adjustment

Head restraints are provided to protect against neck and spine injuries, commonly called whiplash.

> See why it's important to adjust the head restraint correctly, and how to do it, in this video.
>
> youtube.com/watch?v=wIYIPuRvwtM

For maximum protection, the head restraint should be correctly adjusted – but it's easy to overlook.

The head restraints should be adjusted so that the rigid part of the head restraint is

- at least as high as the eyes or top of the ears
- as close to the back of the head as is comfortable.

An incorrectly adjusted head restraint offers little or no protection against whiplash injuries.

Don't remove the head restraints; they're fitted for your safety and can save you from more serious injuries in the event of an incident.

Remember, it's a head restraint, not a head rest.

Seat belt adjustment

Adjust the seat belt properly. Place the lap belt as low as possible over the hips. Ensure the shoulder belt lies on the chest and over the shoulder.

Many cars are now fitted with height adjusters for the diagonal strap. The diagonal strap should be adjusted to lie centrally over the shoulder and away from the neck. Adjust the strap so that it lies in contact with your shoulder and slopes up and back to the anchorage point.

⊙ The hand controls

The positions of some of the controls, such as indicators, light switches and windscreen wipers, vary from model to model.

Before you drive an unfamiliar vehicle, you should get to know the positions of all the controls. You should never have to fumble or look down for them when you're driving.

Keep your eyes on the road.

The steering wheel

The steering wheel should normally be controlled with both hands.

Function

The steering wheel controls the direction in which you want the vehicle to travel.

It controls the steering mechanism, which turns

- the front wheels in most vehicles
- all four wheels in vehicles with four-wheel steering – limited to a small number of models.

How to use the steering wheel

For best control

- keep both hands on the wheel, unless you're changing gear or working another control with one hand. Return that hand to the wheel immediately after you've finished the task
- avoid resting your arm on the door, which can restrict your movement
- grip the wheel firmly, but not too tightly; when the vehicle is moving you need very little effort to turn the wheel.

REMEMBER, never take both hands off the wheel when the vehicle is moving.

Steering lock*

This is the angle through which the front wheels turn when you turn the steering wheel; it can be either 'right lock' or 'left lock'.

Turning the steering wheel as far as it will go is called 'full lock'. The amount of lock varies from vehicle to vehicle.

Small cars will generally turn in a smaller circle than larger vehicles. Taxi cabs are an obvious exception as they have a very small turning circle.

* Not to be confused with the steering-column locking mechanism, which engages when the ignition key is removed on most modern vehicles as an anti-theft device.

Steering

You should

- place your hands on the steering wheel in a position that's comfortable and which gives you full control
- keep your movements steady and smooth
- turn the steering wheel to manoeuvre round a corner at the correct time.

Oversteer and understeer

Vehicles vary in how they behave when turning at various road speeds.

Some respond more than you would expect in relation to the amount of turn you give the wheel (oversteer). Some respond less (understeer).

You must get to know the characteristics of your vehicle before you drive in traffic, and drive extra carefully until you're familiar with its behaviour.

Power-assisted steering

Power-assisted steering (PAS) is generally standard in today's vehicles.

PAS makes steering easier by reducing driver steering effort and gives a lighter feel to the steering.

On some vehicles the amount of power assistance reduces with increased speed.

PAS is most useful at low speeds, such as when manoeuvring in a tight corner or parking.

With PAS the steering feels light and you can easily turn the wheel too much, especially if you're used to driving a vehicle not fitted with it.

Not all vehicles have PAS. For example, it's often not fitted in older vehicles. The steering can feel heavy if it's not fitted. Consult the vehicle handbook before driving a car you've not driven before.

'Dry' steering

When you're manoeuvring, try to avoid turning the steering wheel when the vehicle is stationary. This is known as 'dry' steering and may cause

• damage to the tyres

• wear in the steering mechanism.

This applies whether you have PAS or not.

Power-assisted steering helps to manoeuvre the car more easily, especially when turning a tight corner or parking.

The gear lever

The gear lever is normally to the left of the driving seat, either on the floor or on a raised console.

Some cars have the gear lever protruding from the instrument panel; others have a gear lever on the steering column.

Function

The gear lever enables you to change from one gear to another.

The gearbox

The gearbox contains the gears, which control the relationship between engine speed and road speed.

First gear provides the greatest force at the driving wheels and is normally the one you use to get the vehicle moving.

As you speed up, you change up to the higher gears, each one giving you less gear force but more road speed. Top gear provides the least force, but usually has the widest range of speeds. Using as high a gear as possible for speed and road traffic conditions saves fuel.

Most modern cars have five or six forward gears, while heavier vehicles often have many more.

As well as the five or six forward gears, there's a reverse gear.

In neutral, no gear is engaged.

The clutch links the engine to the road wheels through the gearbox and allows the gradual connection of the engine to the wheels.

Four-wheel-drive vehicles may have a double gearbox with high- and low-ratio ranges, which effectively double the number of available gears. The lower range is normally used off-road.

Gear positions

Most cars have five-speed or six-speed gearboxes. On a five-speed gear lever, the first four gears normally form an 'H', while reverse and fifth form an additional 'I'. Many cars are designed so that you can't move straight from fifth to reverse gear, and the gear lever automatically springs back into neutral when no gear is engaged. This tendency of the gear lever to line up with particular gears is known as bias. Third and fourth gears are often lined up.

Some older cars have four-speed gearboxes. These have the gears in an 'H', with reverse extended on the left or right.

Avoid looking down at the gear lever

You should have a mental picture of the gear layout. This will enable you to change gear without looking at the diagram on the top of the gear lever. Your eyes should be on the road.

With practice, changing gear becomes second-nature.

For automatic transmission systems, see section 22.

The parking brake

Sometimes the parking brake is referred to as the handbrake.

Position

The parking brake lever is normally mounted on the floor, just behind the gear lever. In some vehicles it's just under the instrument panel, while on other models the parking brake is applied by operating an additional pedal.

Function

The parking brake holds the vehicle still when it has stopped.

In most cars the parking brake operates on the rear wheels only. If it's applied while the vehicle is moving, there's a real danger of locking the braked wheels and skidding.

The parking brake shouldn't be used to stop a moving vehicle, except in an emergency such as footbrake failure – very unlikely with dual-circuit braking systems.

> **REMEMBER,** when you park your vehicle, always leave it in gear and make sure that the parking brake is fully on.

Applying

Apply the handbrake firmly according to your manufacturer's guidelines. Refer to your vehicle handbook to check the correct procedure for your vehicle.

Releasing

Pull the lever up slightly and press the button in to release the ratchet. Then, keeping the button in, move the lever to the 'off' position.

On some vehicles, instead of pressing a button, the parking brake is released by twisting the hand grip.

Electronic parking brake

Some modern vehicles are fitted with an electronic parking brake which is operated with a switch or button and releases automatically when you drive off.

⊙ The foot controls

The accelerator/gas pedal

This is operated by the right foot and is positioned on the extreme right of the group of three pedals.

Function

The accelerator controls the ratio of fuel and air that's supplied to the engine. The name 'gas pedal' is derived from 'gasoline', the American word for petrol.

Petrol engines

All modern cars have an electronic fuel-injection system, designed to give optimum engine performance.

Older cars had a carburettor that mixed the fuel with air as it was drawn into the engine.

Diesel engines

A high-pressure fuel injector delivers the fuel into the cylinders. This is known as a compression-ignition engine.

In both engine types

The more you press the accelerator, the more fuel goes to the engine, the more power is generated and the higher the engine speed.

Knowing the right amount of pressure to put on the accelerator takes practice. Accelerating fiercely wastes fuel and creates noise.

When moving off, you need just the right amount. Too little, and the engine stalls. Too much, and the vehicle can surge forward.

The footbrake

The right foot operates the footbrake as well as the accelerator. You shouldn't need to use both controls at the same time.

The footbrake is the middle of the group of three pedals, so the right foot can travel smoothly and quickly from one to the other.

Function

The footbrake is used to slow down or stop the vehicle.

Using the footbrake

The more pressure you put on the footbrake, the more the vehicle will slow down.

Slowing down under control isn't just a matter of slamming the footbrake on as hard as you can. As with the other foot controls, using the footbrake needs practice.

Press the footbrake with the ball of your foot. Use enough pressure to slow the wheels without allowing them to lock.

Progressive braking

In normal circumstances, always press lightly on the brake pedal to begin with and gradually press harder as the brakes begin to act. This is known as progressive braking, and will give maximum control as well as smoother stopping.

Dual-circuit braking

Modern cars are equipped with dual-circuit braking systems. These systems ensure that, in the rare event of a braking system failure, there remains some braking available when the brake pedal is pressed. Under these conditions it may be necessary to push the brake pedal harder than normal.

Anti-lock braking system

Many cars either have an anti-lock braking system (ABS) fitted or have it available as an option.

If ABS is fitted it activates automatically. It prevents the wheels from locking, so that you can continue to steer the vehicle while braking. You should refer to the vehicle handbook for details of the manufacturer's recommended method of use.

ABS is only a driver aid; it doesn't help the vehicle to stop more quickly. Nor does it remove the need for good driving practices such as anticipating events and assessing road conditions. You still need to plan well ahead and brake smoothly and progressively.

The clutch

The clutch pedal is operated by the left foot and is on the left of the group of three pedals.

Function

The clutch is the connection between the engine and the gearbox. It's a connection over which the driver has control, but which requires practice in its use.

How it works

In its simplest form, the clutch is made up of two plates. One is connected to the engine and rotates all the time the engine is running. The other is linked to the gearbox and rotates only when it's held against the first plate by springs.

When you press the clutch pedal, you force the plates apart, breaking the drive connection.

In neutral, even though both plates are touching, the wheels don't turn because no gear is engaged.

The 'biting point'

The point of engagement, when the two plates begin to make contact and the load on the engine increases, is known as the 'biting point'.

You'll learn with practice to judge the biting point exactly. You'll feel it, and hear it because the engine speed will drop slightly.

The feel of the clutch will vary with different vehicles. Also, as the clutch plates begin to wear, the biting point may change.

Clutch control

Being able to sense the biting point is a crucial part of clutch control.

The other important part is allowing the clutch plates to engage fully and smoothly. If the plates come together too suddenly, the engine can stall or the vehicle may lurch sharply.

Good clutch control comes only with practice, and is essential when moving off or changing gear.

 Switches

Sidelights and headlights

Position

On many vehicles, the lighting controls are on a stalk at the side of the steering column.

This stalk normally has three positions

1. off

2. sidelights (or dim–dip), rear and number-plate lights

3. headlights (main or dipped beam) and the dip control. On some vehicles the dip control is a separate switch.

Some vehicles have 'dim–dip' headlights, which come on as the sidelights are switched on. It's impossible to drive these vehicles with only the sidelights switched on.

The sidelights normally work without the ignition being switched on.

Use

This is covered in section 13.

Fog lights

Fog lights should work only when the sidelights or headlights are on. Modern vehicles must be fitted with at least one rear fog light. Front fog lights are often fitted as an option.

Position

Since they're only used in bad weather, the fog light switches are usually on the instrument panel rather than on the steering column.

Use

You must only use fog lights when visibility is seriously reduced, ie 100 metres (328 feet) or less. You mustn't use fog lights in any other circumstances, because they can dazzle and distract other drivers.

When using front fog lights, a warning light will show so that you know they're on.

A warning light will show when the rear fog lights are on.

Automatic and adaptive headlights

Automatic headlights

These work through sensors which detect the level of light outside the vehicle. When the sensors detect a certain level of darkness, the headlights switch on.

Drivers shouldn't rely on such technology and should continue to turn on their headlights manually if needed.

Adaptive headlights

These are designed to improve visibility at night around corners and over hills. The headlights adjust according to the driver's input and the driving conditions to illuminate the road without dazzling other drivers.

Direction indicator

Position

The direction indicator switch is usually on a stalk, which may be on either side of the steering column.

Function

The direction indicators enable you to show other road users which direction you intend to take. Correct use of the direction indicators is vital to safe driving.

Self-cancelling indicator switches might not cancel after a slight change of direction.

Always check that the signal has been cancelled. You can do this by checking the

- repeater warning light
- audible warning, usually a ticking noise when the indicators are flashing.

Most modern vehicles are fitted with lane change indicators. Flicking the indicator stalk in either direction gives you three flashes and removes the need to cancel the indicator. This functionality is especially useful for overtaking when driving on motorways and dual carriageways.

Use

You should be able to operate the direction indicators without taking your hand off the steering wheel.

Hazard warning lights

Position

The position of this switch varies. Some vehicles have it on the steering column, others on the instrument panel. It's usually

- within easy reach of the driver's hands
- clearly marked to prevent accidental use.

Use

Hazard warning lights should be used to warn other road users when you're temporarily obstructing traffic; for example, when

- you've broken down
- you have to slow down quickly on a motorway or unrestricted dual carriageway, because of a hazard ahead. Use them only long enough to ensure that your warning has been seen.

Don't use them to excuse stopping in a restricted area, such as on double yellow lines, regardless of how brief your stop.

Because the lights flash at the same rate as normal indicators, if another driver is unable to see both sides of your vehicle, the hazard warning lights could be mistaken for a turning or moving-out signal.

Windscreen washers and wipers

Position

The windscreen washer and wiper controls are usually on stalks mounted on the steering column. You should be able to find the controls without taking your eyes off the road.

On most vehicles, the same stalk controls both the washers and wipers. Both are essential in bad weather.

Where they're provided, rear washers and wipers have separate controls. Some vehicles may be fitted with miniature washers and wipers to keep the headlights clear.

Increasingly, vehicles are fitted with rain sensors which automatically adjust the speed of your wipers according to the amount of rain. This means you don't have to regularly adjust the speed of your wipers, or switch them on and off.

Function

The windscreen washers and wipers keep the windscreen clear of rain, spray, snow or fog.

Use washers before wipers

Use your washers first to wet the surface before you switch on your windscreen wipers. Wiping a dry windscreen can cause scratches to the screen as well as shortening the life of the wiper blades.

Avoiding excessive dirt build-up can also help to stop scratches on your windscreen. Tiny bits of grit can scratch the surface and make driving at night very difficult.

Wash your windscreen regularly with a sponge and plenty of water. Wash the wiper blades as well.

Regular checks

Check the windscreen washer bottle and keep it topped up.

You can use additives to prevent smearing, assist cleaning and, especially in the winter, to prevent icing up.

Wiper blades

Wiper blades wear and become ineffective, causing smears and streaks across the windscreen. You **MUST** replace them if this happens.

Horn

Position

On most vehicles, the horn switch is either

- on the steering wheel

- on the outer end of the stalk which controls the direction indicators.

Function

The horn is used to warn other road users of your presence.

Use

Use it to tell other road users you're there, if this is necessary.

Aggressive sounding of the horn is dangerous. It can distract and alarm other road users.

You mustn't sound your horn (unless there's a danger from another vehicle) when your vehicle is stationary or when driving in a built-up area between 11.30 pm and 7.00 am.

Heated windscreen and rear window

Most cars have heated rear windows, and some have heated front windscreens as well.

Function

The front and rear windscreen heaters keep the windscreen and rear window clear of

- internal condensation
- frost and ice on the outside.

Use

They should be used as necessary to keep your windscreen and rear window clear, especially in wet and cold conditions.

Demister

Once the engine has warmed up, you can set the controls to direct warm air to the windscreen and, on some vehicles, the front side windows.

The fan control can be set to boost the warm air flow.

Ignition switch and starter

Position

The ignition switch is usually positioned on the steering column.

Before operating the starter

Make sure that

- the parking brake is on
- the clutch is disengaged (pressed in) if required to start the car
- the gear lever is in neutral.

On most vehicles, the ignition and starter are incorporated in the same switch and operated by the ignition key. Some vehicles have a separate starter button.

On most vehicles, an anti-theft device is incorporated into the ignition switch and operated by the ignition key. The mechanism locks the steering column, so a slight movement may need to be applied to the steering wheel while turning the ignition key to release it.

The first position

This operates some of the electrical equipment, such as the radio.

The second position

This switches on the ignition, instrument panel and gauges. A red ignition warning light will usually show when the key reaches this position.

The third position

This operates the starter.

The direction indicators, and on some vehicles the headlights, will only operate when the ignition is switched on.

Use

The starter is usually operated by turning the ignition key to its maximum. As soon as the engine starts, release the key. Don't operate the starter when the engine is running. This can damage the starter motor and the engagement mechanism.

Being towed

When the vehicle is being towed, the anti-theft device locking the steering column must be released by inserting the ignition key and ensuring that the steering wheel is free to move (unless a suspended tow is being used).

REMEMBER, without the ignition switched on, the steering will be heavy and the brakes won't work properly.

⊕ Other controls

Instrument panel

For detailed information and guidance on this, see your vehicle handbook.

The main visual aids on the instrument panel are

- speedometer, to tell you how quickly the vehicle is travelling in miles and kilometres per hour. It's usually a dial, with a needle showing the speed, but it may be a digital display

The visual aids are grouped on the instrument panel in plain view of the driver.

- direction indicator repeater light(s)

- fuel gauge

- high-beam indicator light (usually blue)

- rev counter (on some vehicles), to tell you the engine speed in revolutions per minute (rpm)

- warming-up coil indicator light (on diesel engines)

- temperature gauge (may be a warning light).

Cruise control

This is a device, usually electronic, which enables the driver to select and maintain a fixed speed on the open road.

Use cruise control on your vehicle if it's fitted. The sophisticated electronics in the engine management system precisely measure the amount of fuel the engine needs to work most efficiently for a given speed. If you use this where you can, it may reduce your vehicle's fuel consumption.

Cruise control relieves the driver of the physical effort involved in keeping an even pressure on the accelerator pedal for long periods. It's only suitable where changes of speed are unlikely to be required.

Normal control can be resumed immediately should the need arise. In most cases this happens as soon as the driver uses the accelerator, clutch or footbrake.

Adaptive cruise control

This technology uses radar to detect other vehicles ahead. Unlike normal cruise control, this system can automatically adjust your vehicle's speed in order to maintain a safe following distance from the vehicle in front. This technology shouldn't be relied upon, and a driver should use their judgement in maintaining a safe separation distance.

Speed limiter

This technology operates in a similar way to cruise control and allows the driver to set a maximum speed for the vehicle.

Like cruise control, it's normally operated using simple switches mounted on the steering wheel. Whereas cruise control maintains a constant speed, a speed limiter prevents you from accelerating beyond the selected speed. You can slow down by taking your foot off the accelerator, as normal.

On some vehicles (particularly commercial vehicles), the maximum speed is fixed and the speed limiter can't be adjusted by the driver.

Warning lights

Function

These lights help you to

- drive safely

- monitor the performance of the engine

- protect your engine and other equipment against damage

- see the functions selected.

Types of light

Many different types of light may be fitted, including

- oil pressure light (often red) – this shows if the oil level is dangerously low or the oil isn't circulating as it should be. It should light up as you turn the ignition on, but go out as the engine starts

- ignition warning light (usually red) – if this comes on when the engine is running, it shows you have a problem with the electrical charging system
- ABS warning light – this should light up as you turn the ignition on and may not go out until the car is travelling at 5–10 mph
- brake condition warning light
- water temperature light (or gauge) – this tells you if the engine is overheating
- 'doors open' and/or 'boot lid unlocked' light
- 'parking brake applied' light
- airbag failure warning light – this indicates a problem with the system and is a safety risk, as the airbag may not operate in a collision
- four-way hazard warning lights
- rear fog light warning light
- rear window heater indicator light
- seat belt warning lights
- fog lights/headlights/sidelights indicator lights
- tyre pressure warning light – this tells you if the tyre pressure is below the recommended setting.

Oil pressure

Parking brake warning and brake condition

Doors open

Seat belt

Choke

All vehicles with petrol engines have some form of choke. This reduces the amount of air in the air/fuel mixture, and helps to start the engine from cold. Most cars have an automatic choke but some older cars may have a manual choke. The further you pull the control out, the richer the mixture. You must push in the control as soon as the engine warms up.

A pre-heating device is incorporated in some vehicles with diesel engines. The starter should only be operated when the indicator light goes out (where fitted).

Section four
➡ Mirrors

This section covers

- Mirrors
- Adjusting mirrors
- Using mirrors
- Blind spots
- The mirrors and hazards
- MSM routine

⊕ Mirrors

Using the mirrors has to be part of a safe, systematic routine such as Mirrors – Signal – Manoeuvre (MSM). You must always know how your driving is likely to affect traffic behind you.

The MSM routine includes interpreting what you see in the mirrors and acting appropriately. Regular and sensible use of the mirrors is an essential element of safe driving.

Modern cars are required to have an offside (driver's side) mirror fitted, as well as an interior mirror. However, most vehicles have three driving mirrors

- an interior mirror
- two exterior mirrors: one on the nearside (left-hand) door and one on the offside (right-hand) door.

Vans and other vehicles with a restricted view to the rear must have an exterior mirror on each side.

Function

Your mirrors

- give you a view of the road behind and to the sides
- enable you to keep up to date with what's happening behind and to the sides of your vehicle
- help you to make safe and sensible decisions, based on the position and speed of other traffic.

Defensive driving

Mirrors are one of the keys to defensive driving. Always use them to keep up to date with what's behind and to the sides of your vehicle.

> **REMEMBER,** don't just look into your mirrors; act safely and sensibly on what you see.

Flat mirrors

Most interior and some exterior door mirrors have flat glass.

Flat mirrors don't distort the picture of the road behind. This makes it easier to judge the speed and distance of traffic behind you.

Convex mirrors

Many exterior mirrors have convex glass, which

- is slightly curved
- gives a wider field of vision.

This makes accurate judgement of speed and position of vehicles behind you more difficult.

A vehicle behind seems smaller in a convex mirror, so it could be closer than you think.

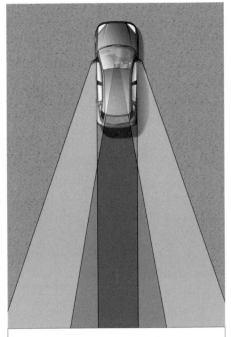

The view covered by your interior and exterior mirrors.

Some cars have 'split' mirrors, which give a wider field of view.

Extended-arm mirrors

Some caravans and trailers block your interior mirror's view of the road behind, which means you must rely on your exterior mirrors.

If you're towing a caravan or a wide trailer, fit side mirrors with extended arms to enable you to see past the caravan or trailer.

⊙ Adjusting mirrors

Before moving off, make sure all mirrors are clean and adjusted to give you the best possible view of the road behind.

While in your normal driving position, adjust your mirrors so that you require the minimum of head movement to get a good view of traffic behind.

Always check your view as part of your 'cockpit drill' (see section 5).

When adjusting mirrors, grip them at the edge to avoid getting fingermarks on the surface. Fingermarks can distort and blur the view in the mirror.

Interior mirror

Adjust your interior mirror so that you get the best possible view through the rear window, especially to the offside, with a minimum of head movement.

Exterior mirrors

Adjust your exterior mirrors

• to give the best view behind

• so that the side of the vehicle is only just visible.

Don't adjust the mirrors while you're driving. Do it before you move off, or at any time your vehicle is stationary.

Check when you get into your vehicle that they've not been knocked out of position.

Remember to check that your exterior mirrors are still positioned correctly after you've been through a car wash.

Keep your exterior mirrors clean. In bad weather, check they're clear of frost and condensation before you move off.

Electric mirrors

Many vehicles have door mirrors which can be adjusted electrically using switches inside the vehicle.

Some of them have a heating element to keep them clear of frost and condensation.

Anti-dazzle mirrors

The interior mirror usually has an anti-dazzle position. When driving at night, you can use this to prevent dazzle or distraction by the lights of traffic behind you. You'll still be able to see the lights, but the dazzle will be greatly reduced.

REMEMBER to reset the mirror for normal use.

⊕ Using mirrors

Using your driving mirrors regularly and sensibly is vital to good driving.

Learning to judge the speed and distance of vehicles behind you takes time.

Try the following exercise when your vehicle is stationary.

• Compare the different impressions you get when you view vehicles through the interior mirror and the exterior mirror. The vehicles may seem smaller in the exterior mirror. Then look over your shoulder to get the real view.

- Also while you're stationary, look for blind spots. These are the areas that your mirrors don't show you, which are explained later in this section.

Which mirror to use

Your use of the mirrors should be linked to the manoeuvre you intend to make and the type of vehicle you're driving.

Normally you should use the interior mirror first, followed by the exterior ones if necessary.

Your use of the exterior mirrors will depend on the manoeuvre and the situation. For example, before turning left in slow-moving traffic, your nearside exterior mirror will help you to look for cyclists filtering on your left.

When to use your mirrors

You should always

- use your mirrors in good time, that is, well before you
  - approach a hazard
  - slow down, change lane or begin any manoeuvre
- act sensibly on what you see
- begin the MSM routine early (see later in this section).

Always use your mirrors before

- moving off
- signalling
- changing direction or lane, turning left, turning right or overtaking
- slowing down or stopping
- opening your car door.

When you look in your mirrors, ask yourself

- How close is the traffic behind you?
- How fast is it moving?
- What's it doing?

- Is the manoeuvre safe?
- How will my signal affect following drivers?

It's also important to use the mirrors early enough to allow other road users time to react to any signal you need to give. Use your mirrors to check their reaction.

Check your internal mirrors

Check your external mirrors

Blind spots

A blind spot is an area that can't be seen either when using normal forward vision or when using the mirrors. The main blind spots are

- the area between what you see as you look forward and what you see in your exterior mirror
- the area obscured by the bodywork of the vehicle when you look in your mirrors. Vehicles of different shapes have different blind spots.

Some vehicles – such as 4x4s – have very large blind spots, which can block the driver's view of pedestrians, motorcyclists or even small cars.

Exterior mirrors and reverse-assist technology can help reduce blind spots, but remember that they won't show you everything behind you. You can buy auxiliary mirrors to mount on the surface of your exterior mirrors. These give an even wider angle of vision and go some way towards reducing blind spots, but won't entirely eliminate them.

Similarly, vehicle manufacturers are introducing systems that use radar or cameras to warn drivers – by flashing a light or making a sound – if a vehicle encroaches into a blind spot. If you have such technology installed, it's still vital to check your mirrors as normal.

Even though you've used your mirrors, always look round over your right shoulder to check the blind spot before you move off.

Don't rely on your mirrors before opening your car door; always look behind you. A cyclist or motorcyclist could easily be hidden from view.

Check your blind spot

Checking blind spots on the move

On occasion it will be necessary to check blind spots while you're on the move. These blind spots will be to either side and shouldn't require you to look round, but rather to give a quick sideways glance.

Looking right round to check blind spots on the move is unnecessary and dangerous, especially when driving at high speeds; in the time it takes, you'll lose touch with what's happening in front.

Regular and sensible use of the mirrors will keep you up to date with what's happening behind. You will, however, still need to know when a glance into the blind spots is needed.

Take a quick sideways glance

- before changing lanes
- before joining a motorway or dual carriageway from a slip road
- before manoeuvring in situations where traffic is merging from the left or right.

Recognise where other drivers' blind spots will be and avoid remaining in them longer than necessary. This is particularly important when overtaking large vehicles.

⊕ The mirrors and hazards

A hazard is any situation that involves you being in some risk or danger. Hazards may cause you to slow down or change course.

When approaching a hazard, you should use your mirrors and be prepared to change speed and/or direction.

Hazards include

- bends in the road
- junctions
- pedestrian crossings

- roadworks
- livestock on the road.

Always check your mirrors in good time, and before you change direction, to decide

- whether a signal is necessary
- whether it's safe to change speed or direction.

Keeping up to date

Keep up to date with the position and speed of traffic behind you.

Good drivers always know as much about the conditions behind as they know about the situation ahead.

Traffic positions change rapidly on some roads. Frequent glances in mirrors keep you up to date with what's behind. How frequently you do this depends on road and traffic conditions.

Driving on high-speed roads

When driving on motorways or dual carriageways, check your mirrors earlier than you would on ordinary roads.

Higher speeds are more difficult to judge and situations can develop more quickly.

⊙ MSM routine

Regardless of your driving experience, you should make the Mirrors – Signal – Manoeuvre (MSM) routine an integral part of your driving.

Remember this routine

- **MIRRORS** – check the speed and position of traffic behind you
- **SIGNAL** – consider whether a signal is necessary. If it is, signal your intention to change course or slow down clearly and in good time
- **MANOEUVRE** – a manoeuvre is any change of speed or position.

Manoeuvre

This is broken down into

P – Position

S – Speed

L – Look.

Position
Your vehicle must always be in the correct position for the manoeuvre. When a change of direction is required, move into position in good time.

Speed
Ensure that the vehicle is travelling at the appropriate speed and in a suitable gear to complete the manoeuvre safely.

Look
The 'look' phase consists of four elements (**LADA**)

- **L**ooking – What can you see?
- **A**ssessing – What are your options?
- **D**eciding – Depending on what you see.
- **A**cting – Either continue or wait.

Using MSM

Always use the MSM routine before

- moving off
- signalling
- changing direction
    - turning left or right
    - overtaking or changing lanes
- slowing down or stopping.

Never

- signal without checking mirrors first
- rely solely on mirrors when you're reversing. Keep looking around to watch for other road users
- assume that, because you've signalled, you can carry out the intended manoeuvre safely. Check to be sure, because other road users might not
  - have seen your signal
  - understand your intention.

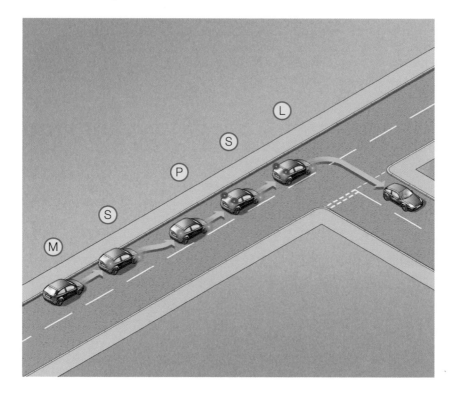

(M) Mirror   (S) Signal   (P) Position   (S) Speed   (L) Look

Section five

→ Starting to drive

This section covers

- Getting started
- Starting the engine
- Moving off
- Braking
- Stopping in an emergency
- Skidding
- The parking brake
- Steering
- Changing gear
- Signalling
- Moving off at an angle
- Moving off on hills

⊕ Getting started

Before you drive on busy roads and in traffic, you should master the basic techniques of starting, moving off and stopping. You must have full control of your vehicle at all times. This involves

- a good working knowledge of the various controls
- being able to coordinate hand and foot controls.

In addition, you need to have

- an understanding of the rules of the road
- respect for the needs of other road users
- a basic knowledge of your vehicle. That way, you can check it to make sure everything's working properly and it's safe to start your journey.

Driving isn't just a matter of starting the engine and moving off.

Cockpit drill

Make these checks for the safety of yourself, your passengers and other road users.

Every time you get into your vehicle, check that

- all doors are properly closed and the parking brake is on
- the driving seat is adjusted so that you can see clearly in all directions and reach all the controls comfortably
- the head restraint is in the correct position (see section 3)
- the mirrors are clean and correctly adjusted (see section 4)
- you and your passengers have seat belts on
- the gear lever is in neutral (if you're driving an automatic, the gear lever should be in 'P' or 'N')
- you have enough fuel for your journey. If not, plan where to refuel the vehicle.

Driving a vehicle unfamiliar to you

Before you start your journey, make sure you know and understand the vehicle's

- controls: where they are and how they work
- handling: front-, rear- or four-wheel drive
- brakes: if anti-lock (ABS) brakes are fitted, know how to check and use them.

Consult the vehicle handbook if anything is unfamiliar to you.

➡ Starting the engine

After you've made the preliminary checks and you're settled comfortably in the driving seat, begin the drill for starting the engine.

- Check the parking brake is on by trying to pull it on slightly further.
- Check that the gear lever is in neutral (or 'P' or 'N' if driving an automatic).
- Pull the choke out if your vehicle has one. Most vehicles have an automatic choke.
- Switch on the ignition by turning the key. The ignition and oil pressure light, if fitted, will come on. Other warning lights should also come on. With a diesel engine you might have to wait for a glow-plug light to go out.
- Operate the starter by turning the key further, or use the separate starter switch, if one is fitted.

- Release the starter key or switch as soon as the engine begins running; otherwise the starter could be damaged. Don't operate the starter if the engine is already running.

If the engine fails to start

If the engine fails to start first time

- release the key or switch
- wait a moment
- try again.

When the engine starts

You may need to press the accelerator slightly to keep the engine running.

The engine should now be idling ('ticking over').

The ignition and oil pressure warning lights should go out when the engine is running. If either light stays on, switch off the engine and have the fault checked. Never drive a vehicle with the oil pressure warning light showing – it could damage the engine.

If your vehicle has a manual choke, push it in as the engine warms up. Don't drive with the choke out any longer than necessary. This wastes fuel, causes wear to the engine and can be dangerous, especially with automatic transmission.

Move off as soon as possible after starting the engine. Allowing the engine to warm up while you're stationary wastes fuel and causes pollution.

⊕ Moving off

With your left foot, press the clutch pedal fully down and hold it there.

Move the gear lever into first gear. If it won't engage, move the gear lever to neutral, then let out the clutch and repeat the first two steps.

To prepare to move off

- With your right foot, press the accelerator slightly and hold it steady.
- Slowly and smoothly, let up the clutch pedal until you hear the engine noise change slightly. This change means the clutch is at the biting point (see later in this section). With experience, you'll be able to feel the biting point.
- Hold the clutch steady in this position.
- Now make your final safety checks, use your mirrors and look over your right shoulder to check the blind spot.
- Decide if a signal is necessary. The timing of any signal is crucial. Avoid waiting with the clutch at biting point.
- If it's safe to move off, be ready to release the parking brake.
- Look round again if necessary and keep an eye on your mirrors.
- When you're sure it's safe and convenient to move off, release the parking brake and at the same time, let the clutch pedal come up a little more. The vehicle will begin to move. Tight clutch control is needed, so keep the clutch pedal just above the biting point.

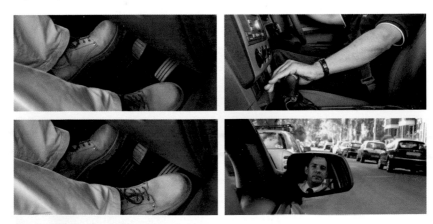

- Gradually depress the accelerator for more speed and let the clutch come up smoothly, then take your left foot off the clutch pedal. Accelerating fiercely wastes fuel.

Biting point

The 'biting point' is when the clutch plates start to engage. You must be able to find this point confidently when you bring up the clutch pedal. Although you can press the pedal down quickly, you mustn't let it come up too fast. Practise finding the biting point until you become familiar with it.

Although this process is the same for all vehicles with manual gearboxes, there can be slight variations in how different vehicles feel, and sound, when at the biting point. If you have to use a different vehicle on occasion while learning, take a few minutes to practise finding its biting point first, before driving on the roads.

This advice also applies after you've passed your test, whenever you have to drive an unfamiliar vehicle.

Practice makes perfect

Getting these steps in the right order is difficult at first. Choose a quiet, level road to practise starting, moving off, and stopping.

Don't

- signal and move out regardless
- sit with the signal showing when you can't move out safely.

Defensive driving

- Check all round before moving off.
- Signal if necessary.
- Don't move out into the path of oncoming traffic.
- Don't rush.

 Braking

Safe and controlled braking is vital to good driving. Try to slow down gradually and smoothly.

Anticipation

If you anticipate properly, you'll seldom need to brake fiercely.

Good anticipation will give you time to brake progressively over a longer distance.

Late, harsh braking is a sign of poor anticipation and of reduced safety margins.

Braking and steering

Braking shifts the weight of the vehicle forward. This can make steering more difficult.

If you have to brake hard, try to do so when you're travelling in a straight line.

Whenever you brake, you should consider

- the safety and peace of mind of everyone concerned, including your passengers
- wear and tear on brakes, tyres and suspension
- vehicles behind you whose brakes might not be as powerful as yours.

REMEMBER, the greater your speed when you brake

- the more difficult it is to control the vehicle
- the greater the distance you need to stop the vehicle.

Braking on bends

If you have to brake on a bend, remember that the weight of the vehicle is thrown outwards as well as forwards. The front tyre on the outside of the curve will have an increased load on it and this can lead to skidding.

Road surface conditions can have a big effect in these situations. Watch for uneven, loose or slippery surfaces.

Think ahead

Think well ahead to avoid the need for harsh, uncontrolled braking.

You should never drive too fast or too close to the vehicle in front. Other drivers might be affected by your actions.

Always use your mirrors before braking and give yourself plenty of space.

Consider

- your own speed of reaction
- the size and weight of your vehicle and its load
- the gradient of the road
- whether the road has a camber or bend
- the weather and visibility
- the road surface. Is it rough, smooth, loose, wet, muddy, or covered with wet leaves, ice or snow?

Five rules for good braking

1. Anticipate. Think and look well ahead.

2. Know your own limitations and those of your vehicle.

3. Take note of the state of the road and its surface.

4. Give yourself plenty of time and distance to brake progressively.

5. Avoid the risk of skidding, rather than trying to control it.

Defensive driving

If the vehicle behind is too close, slow down gradually to increase your distance from the vehicle ahead so that you can avoid having to brake suddenly.

Stopping

The drill for stopping is always the same, except in an emergency. You must learn it thoroughly from the beginning.

The amount of pressure you need to apply to the footbrake depends on

- your speed
- how quickly you need to stop.

To stop you should

- use the mirrors
- decide whether you need to signal your intention to stop
- signal if necessary
- take your foot off the accelerator. The engine will slow down
- push down the brake pedal lightly with your right foot and then more firmly (see 'Progressive braking', later in this section)
- press the clutch pedal right down with your left foot just before the vehicle stops. This disengages the engine from the driving wheels and prevents stalling. Don't do it too soon; the engine's resistance helps slow the vehicle down

- ease the pressure off the footbrake just as the vehicle stops
- apply the parking brake
- put the gear lever into neutral
- take both feet off the pedals.

Check your mirrors before braking.

Brake after you've checked your mirrors.

Changing down before you stop

When stopping normally, you can stop in the gear that you're in; you don't necessarily have to change down. However, your vehicle should always be in the right gear for the road speed and conditions.

Progressive braking

This is a safe driving technique that

- allows other drivers time to react
- prevents skidding
- saves wear and tear on brakes, tyres and suspension
- uses less fuel than harsh braking
- is more comfortable for your passengers.

To brake progressively

- put light pressure on the brake at first
- gradually increase the pressure as required to stop the vehicle

- when the vehicle has almost stopped, ease off the pressure so that the vehicle stops smoothly. There should be little or no pressure as the vehicle actually stops.

Practise

Find a quiet road and make sure you won't affect another road user. Choose a particular point at which you would like to stop. See how near to it you can get.

It's better to stop short of the mark than to overshoot it. You can always ease off the brakes and run forward a bit more.

Stopping at the kerb needs practice too. Aim to stop reasonably close to the kerb without hitting it.

Keep full control of the steering so that you can accurately position the car as you stop.

⊕ Stopping in an emergency

In normal conditions, a good driver shouldn't need to brake really hard.

However, emergencies can happen – for instance, when a child runs into the road in front of you – so you must know how to stop quickly under control. Stopping in an emergency increases the risk of skidding.

Remember, even when stopping quickly, follow the rule of progressive braking – pushing the brake pedal harder as the vehicle slows down.

A quick reaction is crucial in an emergency. The sooner you start braking, the sooner you'll stop!

Practise the following routine

- Keep both hands on the steering wheel. You need as much control as possible.
- Avoid braking so hard that you lock any of the wheels. A skid may cause serious loss of control.

- Don't press down the clutch pedal until just before you stop. This helps with your braking and stability. For vehicles fitted with ABS, read the owner's manual. The manufacturer may advise a different technique to get the best out of its system.
- Don't use the parking brake while the vehicle is moving. Most parking brakes work on the back wheels only. Extra braking here can cause skidding.

Unless you're moving off again straightaway, put the parking brake on and the gear lever into neutral.

If it's safe, practise braking to judge the correct pressure and remember to take into account road and weather conditions.

If the road is dry you should apply firm pressure, but on a wet road or loose surface you should avoid using too much. This means you'll need to reduce speed and increase your separation distance from the vehicle in front.

When braking in an emergency

- Don't signal – you need both hands to control the steering.
- Don't make a special point of looking in the mirror – if you've been using your mirror regularly you should know what's behind.

- Stop as quickly and safely as possible, keeping your vehicle under full control.
- Look all round before moving off again.

Defensive driving

- Try to avoid the emergency arising.
    - Look well ahead.
    - Watch for children playing.
    - Remember school times.
    - Look out for pedestrians.
    - Look for clues, such as reflections.

- Always drive at such a speed that you can stop safely in the distance you can see to be clear. If it's not clear, slow down.
- Prepare for the unexpected.

Anti-lock braking systems

If your vehicle is fitted with ABS brakes, the system activates automatically under conditions of harsh braking.

ABS employs wheel-speed sensors to anticipate when a wheel is about to lock under extreme braking. Just before the wheels begin to lock, the system releases the brakes momentarily before automatically reapplying them. This cycle is repeated several times a second to maximise braking performance, sending a pulsing sensation through the brake pedal. You may find this a little disconcerting the first time it occurs and you may be tempted to respond by relaxing the pressure on the brake pedal. However, it's important that maximum pressure is maintained.

ABS doesn't necessarily reduce your stopping distance, but because the wheels are prevented from locking you can continue to steer – something you wouldn't be able to do if the wheels were locked. Reducing the pressure or pumping the brake pedal reduces the effectiveness of the system. The pressure on the brake pedal must be maintained until the hazard is safely avoided.

Knowing ABS will help you stop safely shouldn't encourage you to drive less carefully. ABS can't overcome the laws of physics; it's still possible for one or more of the tyres to skid because of

- poor road contact
- surface water
- a loose road surface.

⊙ Skidding

Skids don't just happen. They're caused by a driver asking too much of the vehicle for the amount of grip the tyres have on the road at that time.

A skid happens when your vehicle changes speed or direction so suddenly that its tyres can't keep their grip on the road.

There's a greater risk of skidding when

- slowing down
- speeding up
- driving around a corner or bend
- driving uphill or downhill.

The risk increases on a slippery road surface.

Drivers of vehicles equipped with anti-skid technology (for example, ESC – see page 100) should refer to the vehicle handbook for the manufacturer's advice on getting the best out of its anti-skid system.

Skids caused by braking

Harsh and uncontrolled braking is one of the chief causes of skidding. Brakes have their greatest stopping power when they're nearly, but not quite, locked.

The weight of the car is thrown forward when braking. The heavier the braking, the more weight goes to the front and the less there is on the rear wheels.

The less weight there is on the rear wheels, the more likely they are to lock.

Skidding on dry roads
Skids can happen on dry roads, even with good tyres, if you brake harshly.

A lot of the weight is thrown forward and it's impossible to keep the vehicle straight. It begins to swing and only has to touch something to be in danger of turning over.

Anti-lock brakes

ABS brakes help you to continue steering while braking, but on wet or slippery roads this will be less effective. The brakes are only as good as the tyres' grip on the road.

Don't assume that ABS brakes will reduce the stopping distance.

Skids caused by steering

These are caused by steering too sharply for the speed at which you're travelling.

Skids caused by acceleration

Sudden or harsh acceleration while cornering, particularly in the lower gears, may cause the driving wheels to spin on the road surface. Unless you ease off the accelerator very quickly, the vehicle could go into a skid because of the wheelspin.

Skids caused by braking and steering

If you brake harshly while turning, the combined forces can quickly overcome your tyres' grip, leading to a skid.

You may skid if your tyres are only just gripping while you're cornering and you start braking.

You could also skid if you're braking when you start cornering.

The answer is simple: adjust your speed to the conditions and give yourself plenty of space. If the road is wet or icy, your tyres have much less grip.

Avoiding skids

There's no better protection against skids than driving in a way that will avoid them. Skids are caused by drivers; they don't just happen. Take note of the following.

- On very slippery surfaces your stopping distance can be as much as **10 times** longer than on a dry road.
- Look out for signs of slippery roads. Any wet road, even in summer, is likely to be slippery. Be wary of rain, ice, packed snow, frost, wet mud, loose surfaces and wet leaves. Diesel and oil spillages will also make the road slippery, as will patches of new tarmac.
- If you suspect the road is slippery, keep your speed down. When your tyre grip is poor, braking is more likely to cause a skid.
- Use engine braking. Change down in good time.

Anti-skid technology

Electronic stability control (ESC) is a computer-controlled system that combines the functions of ABS and traction control. It detects loss of traction and automatically makes corrective adjustments to prevent loss of control. When the system operates, the driver may be unaware of how close the car is to its handling limits. To alert the driver, the ESC indicator lamp will flash on when the ESC operates.

 ESC can't overcome the laws of physics; if the driver is travelling too fast, there's a risk of losing control.

ESC is fitted to all new cars sold in the EU, but some manufacturers give it a different name; for example, Electronic Stability Programme (ESP®). Refer to your vehicle handbook for details.

REMEMBER, drivers have a responsibility to be able to stop in the distance they can see to be clear, and not to rely on manufacturers' safety devices to overcome bad driving.

Dealing with skids if your vehicle isn't fitted with anti-skid technology

If your car is skidding, there are a number of things you should do.

- Release the brake pedal fully. Drivers often instinctively do the opposite, keeping their right foot hard down on the brake pedal throughout the skid. This makes matters worse, so keep off the brakes.
- If the skid is more than a slight slide, to bring the wheels into line again, ease right off the accelerator and turn into the skid. That is
  - if the rear of the vehicle is going left, you should steer left to bring the front wheels into line with the direction of the back wheels
  - if the rear of the vehicle is going right, steer to the right. Be careful not to overcorrect with too much steering. Too much movement of the front wheels will lead to another skid in the opposite direction.

If the front wheels are sliding instead of, or as well as, the back wheels, release the accelerator and don't try to steer until the wheels regain some of their grip.

Too much power on a front-wheel-drive vehicle can produce the same problem. Again, ease off the accelerator.

101

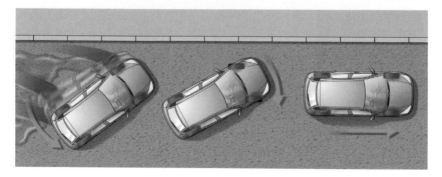

Remember

- adopt safe driving techniques that avoid the build-up to a skid

- adjust to the conditions and give yourself time to react safely

- if your vehicle is fitted with anti-skid technology, you should follow the manufacturer's instructions.

⊙ The parking brake

You should normally apply the parking brake whenever the vehicle is stationary.

Apply the parking brake according to the instructions in your vehicle's handbook and put the gear lever into neutral when you're stopped at traffic lights or queuing behind other vehicles, unless the wait is likely to be very short.

Your foot could easily slip off the footbrake if, for example, your shoes are wet or if you're bumped from behind. You could then be pushed into another vehicle or a pedestrian.

Always leave a safe gap between your vehicle and the vehicle in front while queuing, especially on a hill. This will give you room to manoeuvre should the vehicle in front roll back.

In vehicles fitted with automatic transmission, the use of the parking brake is even more important. The parking brake will help avoid

- the possibility of the vehicle creeping forward
- the vehicle surging forward if the accelerator is pressed accidentally while in 'D' (Drive).

 Steering

When you're learning to drive, practise steering your vehicle (at low speed at first) while keeping about 1 metre (3 feet) from the kerb.

Look well ahead, not just at the front of your vehicle. Keep your movements steady and smooth. Never make a sudden or jerky action while steering.

Steering with one hand

When you can steer a straight course with both hands on the steering wheel, try steering with only one hand.

The reason for practising steering with one hand isn't so that you can always drive like that. It's because there are times when you'll only have one hand free for

steering – for example, when you're changing gear or operating a control.

Stiffen your arm slightly to help you steer a straight course without pulling the wheel down or swerving. Practise with each hand.

⊙ Changing gear

To drive safely, you must combine the skill of knowing how to change gear with knowing when to change gear, as well as which gear to select. These are skills which take time – and practice – to acquire.

The gear positions

You need to know the various positions of the gear lever without having to look down.

You can practise and get to know the gear position with the clutch disengaged and the engine switched off. A light but firm touch should be all you need to move from one gear to another. Never force the gear lever.

On some gearboxes you might require slight pressure to select some gears.

First to second
You might need to put a little pressure to the left on the gear lever when you change up from first to second gear. This is to prevent the lever slipping into fourth while passing through neutral.

Down to first
You may need to put slight pressure to the left when you change down from third or second gear to first.

Up to fifth or sixth
You'll need to put pressure to the right when you change up to fifth or sixth gear.

Don't force the gear lever
If you feel resistance, don't force the gear lever into any position.

Don't
* rush gear changes
* take your eyes off the road when you change gear
* coast with the clutch pedal pressed in, or the gear lever in neutral
* hold the gear lever longer than necessary.

Changing up

When to change up
You need to change gear in order to match the engine speed and load to the speed of the vehicle. This will vary with the vehicle you're driving and whether you're moving on the level, uphill or downhill. As a general rule, change up as the road speed increases.

Listening to the engine helps to determine when to change up. You'll become more familiar with this as you practise, and will soon learn to recognise the appropriate level of sound at which to change gear.

To change up

- place your left hand on the gear lever
- press the clutch pedal right down at the same time as you ease off the accelerator pedal. Don't take your foot off the accelerator altogether
- move the gear lever to the next highest position required
- let the clutch pedal come up smoothly and, at the same time, press the accelerator gradually
- put your left hand back on the steering wheel.

Matching engine and road speed
Releasing the accelerator when changing up lets the engine speed drop to match the higher gear to give you a smooth gear change.

Being able to judge when it's time to change up comes with experience.

Changing down

When to change down
You'll need to change down to a lower gear

- if you've slowed down and the gear you're in doesn't provide enough power for driving at the lower speed
- if you're going uphill in too high a gear and your engine labours or struggles to give enough power
- to increase the effect of the engine braking – for example, when on a long downhill gradient.

Driving in a high gear at low speed makes engine performance sluggish, and is bad driving practice.

Unless you intend to stop, you'll need to change to a lower gear once you've slowed down.

As a general rule, use the brakes to reduce speed before changing down to the most suitable gear for the lower speed.

In the early stages of learning to drive, it may help you to become familiar with the gearbox if you change down through each of the gears in turn. Be guided by your instructor.

When changing down, you might need to

- raise the engine speed to get a smooth change, or
- keep a light pressure on the footbrake to stop the vehicle gathering speed on a downhill slope.

To change down

- place your left hand on the gear lever
- press the clutch pedal right down and, at the same time, keep a little pressure on either the accelerator pedal or the footbrake, whichever is appropriate to the road and traffic conditions
- move the gear lever to the most suitable lower gear for the speed
- let the clutch pedal come up smoothly. Return to the accelerator or continue braking as necessary
- put your left hand back on the steering wheel.

Never rush gear changes. Smooth, even movements are best.

How much pressure is needed on the accelerator or footbrake when changing down will depend on

- the road and traffic conditions
- the speed of your vehicle at the time the clutch pedal is released.

The sound of the engine will help you judge this.

Finding the right gear

To change gear, you need to anticipate and assess the situation well in advance. Ask yourself if the gear you're in is correct for that particular situation.

Overtaking

You should consider changing to a lower gear to overtake. A lower gear can give you the extra acceleration to pass safely.

Try to avoid changing gear while you're actually overtaking. It's preferable to keep both hands on the wheel during the manoeuvre.

Your engine is more responsive in a lower gear and will therefore give you better vehicle control.

Going downhill

When descending a steep hill a lower gear gives more engine braking and control, particularly on a bend.

General rule

You should change down

- to accelerate more quickly
- if your speed drops.

Smooth gear changing

Smooth gear changes are a mark of good driving. Take your time and think ahead.

Selective/block gear changing

Missing out gears

The flexibility of modern engines and the efficiency of braking systems and gearboxes often makes it unnecessary to change into every gear when changing up and down the gearbox.

Missing out gears at the appropriate time will give you more time to concentrate on the road ahead and allow you to keep both hands on the steering wheel for longer.

Changing down

As a general rule, it's preferable and safer to brake to the desired speed and then change down into the appropriate gear. It might be necessary to maintain a light pressure on the footbrake while changing down.

Changing up

There are many occasions when missing out gears while changing up is desirable; however, don't accelerate too fiercely or for too long in the lower gears.

This

- uses much more fuel
- could damage your engine
- could cause wheelspin and loss of control.

How many gears to miss out

It depends on the individual vehicle and the road and traffic conditions.

It's possible to miss out various gears but the most common examples when changing down are

- fifth to third
- fourth to second
- third to first.

The most common examples when changing up are

- first to third
- second to fourth
- third to fifth.

See also section 17 on ecosafe driving.

Coasting

Coasting means that, although the vehicle is moving, it's not being driven by the engine. This occurs either when the clutch pedal is held down or when the gear lever is in the neutral position.

Coasting for any distance is wrong because

- it reduces the driver's control of the vehicle
- you might have difficulty engaging a gear if something unexpected happens
- it almost certainly leads to the vehicle gathering speed when travelling downhill. It means harder braking and it removes the assistance of engine braking in a low gear.

Each time you change gear you coast a little; this is unavoidable, but it should be kept to a minimum.

Over-run

If there's only light pressure on the accelerator pedal when the vehicle is travelling at speed, the engine may not appear to be 'driving' the vehicle.

This is known as travelling on the over-run and shouldn't be confused with coasting. There's no loss of control, because the vehicle is still in gear and either engine braking or acceleration are available immediately.

Slipping the clutch

This is holding the clutch pedal partially down so that the clutch isn't fully engaged. This allows the engine to spin faster than if it were fully engaged and is often necessary when manoeuvring at slow speeds.

Slipping the clutch to compensate for being in too high a gear at a low speed is bad driving practice and should be avoided. This can result in excessive wear of the clutch.

Judgement

As you become more proficient, you'll be able to judge exactly the gear you need for the speed you intend and the manoeuvre you're planning.

⊙→ Signalling

Signals are normally given by direction indicators and/or brake lights. There are occasions when an arm signal can be helpful.

It's important that you use the correct signal.

Use signals

- to let other road users, including pedestrians, know what you intend to do
- in good time and for long enough to allow other road users to see the signal and act upon it.

Signalling too soon can confuse rather than help – for example, when there are several side roads very close together.

Signalling too late can cause vehicles behind you to brake hard or swerve.

Watch out for situations that call for special timing in signalling. For example, when you signal to pull up on the left, make sure there isn't a junction just before the place you intend to stop. If you signal left too soon, a driver waiting at that junction might think you intend to turn left. Delay signalling until you're in a position where your signal can't be misunderstood.

Flashing your headlights

Flashing the headlights has the same meaning as sounding the horn and can be used in situations where the horn might not be heard or at a time when the horn shouldn't be used.

Avoid flashing your headlights to

- instruct other drivers
- reprimand another road user
- intimidate a driver ahead.

Sometimes you may need to move around an obstruction where the view ahead is restricted. Flashing your headlights as you pass can help any approaching driver to see you.

Other drivers flashing their headlights

Some drivers flash their headlights for a variety of reasons, including

- inviting you to pass before them
- thanking you for your courtesy
- warning you of some fault with your vehicle
- telling you your headlights are dazzling them.

When other drivers flash their headlights, the signal

- might not mean what you think
- might not be intended for you.

Make sure you know their intention before you act on the signal.

> **REMEMBER**, flashing of headlights might not be an invitation. The other driver might have flashed someone else or have flashed accidentally.

⊕ Moving off at an angle

Use the same steps as for moving off straight ahead – see 'Moving off', earlier in this section.

Before moving off, ask yourself these questions

- At what angle should I move out?
- How far will this take me into the road?

Your decision will depend on

- how close you are to the vehicle or object in front
- how wide the vehicle ahead is
- oncoming traffic.

Your window pillar can obstruct your view ahead. Make sure there's nothing in the area hidden by this obstruction.

Watch out for other vehicles behind and signal, if necessary, then

- look over your right shoulder
- release the parking brake as you ease the clutch pedal up. The vehicle will begin to move. Tight clutch control is needed, so keep the clutch pedal at or just above the biting point
- give yourself time to complete the amount of steering you need to clear the vehicle in front
- release the clutch pedal smoothly when your vehicle is clear of the obstruction
- if you're steering around a vehicle, allow room for someone to open a door
- move out slowly, straighten up, and be ready to brake; a pedestrian might step out from the other side of the parked vehicle
- check your mirrors when you've moved off.

➡ Moving off on hills

Moving off uphill

Your vehicle will want to roll back. To avoid this you must use the accelerator, clutch and parking brake together.

Much of the drill for moving off uphill is the same as for moving off on the level.

- With your left foot, press the clutch pedal down and hold it down.
- Move the gear lever into first.
- With your right foot, press the accelerator further than you would when starting on the level and hold it perfectly steady. The amount will depend on how steep the hill is.
- Bring the clutch pedal up to the biting point, which will be slightly higher than when you're moving off on the level.
- Make your safety checks, use your mirrors and look round over your right shoulder to check the blind spot.
- Signal if necessary.
- Look round again if necessary.
- Lift the parking brake and release the button while you press the accelerator a little more. How much acceleration you need depends on the steepness of the hill.
- Let the clutch up a little more, until you feel and hear the engine trying to move the vehicle.
- Release the parking brake smoothly.
- Gradually press the accelerator as the vehicle begins to move, and bring up the clutch pedal smoothly.

Some vehicles are fitted with hill-start controls that are designed to stop a car from rolling away when on a gradient. If your vehicle is fitted with such a device, consult your vehicle handbook and follow the manufacturer's guidelines.

Controlling the parking brake and clutch

This requires good timing. If you release the parking brake too soon, the vehicle will roll back.

The vehicle will stall if

- you release the parking brake too late
- you bring up the clutch too quickly or too far
- you don't use enough acceleration.

Practise the steps until you've mastered the technique. Then practise moving off uphill from behind a parked vehicle and at an angle without rolling backwards.

REMEMBER

- Allow a safe gap in any traffic because your vehicle will be slower pulling away and building up speed.
- Don't cut across or block traffic coming uphill.

Moving off downhill

This routine is simpler than moving off uphill because the weight of the vehicle helps you to move away.

The aim is to prevent the vehicle from rolling forward down the hill while moving away.

- Press the clutch pedal down fully.
- Engage the appropriate gear for the steepness of the hill. (This could be second gear.)
- Apply the footbrake.
- Release the parking brake, keeping the footbrake applied.
- Check mirrors. Look round just before you move off to cover the blind spots.
- Signal if necessary.
- Only move away when you're sure it's safe to do so.
- Look round again if necessary.
- Release the footbrake and release the clutch pedal smoothly as the vehicle starts to move.

REMEMBER

- Use the right gear for the steepness of the hill to give you more control.
- Drivers coming downhill will need more time to slow down or stop. Again, leave a large enough gap before pulling away.

Section six

⊙ Traffic signs

This section covers

- The purpose of traffic signs
- Signs giving orders
- Signs giving warning
- Signs giving directions and other information
- Waiting restrictions
- Road markings
- Traffic lights
- Traffic calming
- Level crossings

⊕ The purpose of traffic signs

Signs are an essential part of any traffic system. They tell you about the rules you must obey and warn you about the hazards you may meet on the road ahead.

Signs can be in the form of words or symbols on panels, road markings, beacons, bollards or traffic lights.

To do its job, a sign must give its message clearly and early enough for you to see it, understand it and then act safely on it.

This section deals with the various types of traffic signs and their meaning. For more information, refer to **Know Your Traffic Signs**, which illustrates and explains the vast majority of traffic signs.

Symbols

Symbols are used as much as possible because they're

- more easily recognised and understood
- mainly standardised, particularly throughout Europe.

What are the basic rules when it comes to recognising signs?

You'll recognise traffic signs more easily if you understand some basic rules. The shapes and colours of the main groups are:	
	Circular signs These give orders. Blue circles tell you what you **MUST** do, while signs with red rings tell you what you **MUST NOT** do.
	Triangular signs These warn you of something, such as a junction.

	Rectangular signs These inform and give directions.
KEEP CLEAR	**Road markings** These inform, give directions and give orders.
STOP	**Other shapes** A few signs are a different shape altogether as they're very important and need to stand out.

⊙ Signs giving orders

Signs that give orders can be

• mandatory signs: these tell you what you **MUST** do
• prohibitory signs: these tell you what you **MUST NOT** do.

Mandatory signs

These signs are mostly circular, with white symbols and borders on a blue background; for example

• mini-roundabout
• keep left
• turn left.

In addition

- 'stop – children' sign (lollipop) carried by a school-crossing patrol. This is circular with black lettering on a yellow background
- 'stop' in white on a red background, often manually controlled at roadworks
- 'stop' and 'give way' signs appear at junctions and are very important for everyone's guidance and safety.

'Stop' signs

These are octagonal, with white lettering on a red background, and are usually found at a junction with a limited zone of vision. The design is deliberately unique so you can tell it apart from other signs. 'Stop' signs are always accompanied by a stop line marked on the road. The line tells you how far forward you should go before stopping to look, assess and decide whether it's safe to proceed.

What you MUST do at 'stop' signs

- Stop (even if you can see the road is clear).
- Wait until you can enter the major road without causing other drivers to change speed or direction.

'Give way' signs

These are made up of

- a red triangle pointing downwards
- black lettering on a white background.

They're always accompanied by road markings. However, some junctions only have the 'give way' lines. This is usually where there's relatively little traffic.

'Give way' signs and/or road markings show you that traffic on the road you want to enter has priority.

The double broken lines across the road show you where to stop, if necessary, to take your final look.

What you **MUST** do at 'give way' signs

- Give way to traffic already on the major road.
- Wait until you can enter the major road without causing any traffic already on the road to change speed or direction.

REMEMBER Look, assess, decide and act.

The 'give way' sign is unique, being the only sign that's a downwards-pointing triangle. This is to ensure that it can be recognised and obeyed, even if you can't see it fully.

Prohibitory signs

These tell you what you **MUST NOT** do.

They're easy to recognise by their circular shape and red border. The message is given by symbols, words or figures, or a combination of these. The exceptions are

- 'no entry' sign (circular with white border and red background)
- 'bus lane' sign.

Speed-limit signs

A red circle with a number on a white background shows the speed limit.

A white disc with a black diagonal line cancels the previous speed limit, but you mustn't exceed the national speed limit for the type of road you're on or the vehicle you're driving. If you're driving a light van of over 2 tonnes maximum laden weight, the national speed limit for goods vehicles of up to 7.5 tonnes maximum laden weight applies.

Speed limits

Type of vehicle	Built-up areas* mph (km/h)	Single carriage-ways mph (km/h)	Dual carriage-ways mph (km/h)	Motorways mph (km/h)
Cars and motorcycles (including car-derived vans up to 2 tonnes maximum laden weight)	30 (48)	60 (96)	70 (112)	70 (112)
Cars towing caravans or trailers (including car-derived vans and motorcycles)	30 (48)	50 (80)	60 (96)	60 (96)
Buses, coaches and minibuses (not exceeding 12 metres in overall length)	30 (48)	50 (80)	60 (96)	70 (112)
Goods vehicles (not exceeding 7.5 tonnes maximum laden weight)	30 (48)	50 (80)	60 (96)	70† (112)
Goods vehicles (exceeding 7.5 tonnes maximum laden weight) in England and Wales	30 (48)	50 (80)	60 (96)	60 (96)
Goods vehicles (exceeding 7.5 tonnes maximum laden weight) in Scotland	30 (48)	40 (64)	50 (80)	60 (96)

*The 30 mph limit usually applies to all traffic on all roads with street lighting unless signs show otherwise.
†60 mph (96 km/h) if articulated or towing a trailer.

Be aware that large vehicles may have speed limiters – buses and coaches are restricted to 62 mph and large goods vehicles to 56 mph.

Repeater signs are a smaller form of the original speed-limit sign and are situated at intervals to remind you of the speed limit. In areas where there are regularly spaced street lights, you should assume that the 30 mph (48 km/h) speed limit normally applies, unless there are repeater signs showing a different speed limit.

Test your knowledge of signs by taking the quiz on the Safe Driving for Life website.

safedrivingforlife.info/signsquiz

⊕ Signs giving warning

Usually, this type of sign is a red triangle pointing upwards, with a symbol or words on a white background. These warn you of a hazard you might not otherwise be able to recognise in time; for example, a bend, hill or hump bridge. The sign will make clear what the hazard is. You must decide what to do about it.

Narrowing roads

These signs tell you from which side the road is narrowing (sometimes both sides), and should warn you against overtaking until you've had a chance to assess the hazard.

Children

The warning here is: watch out for children, especially at school start and finish times. Plates may be used with the sign to give extra information, such as 'School', 'Playground' or 'Patrol'. As well as children, look out for school-crossing patrols and obey their signals.

Low bridge sign

Even if you're not in a high vehicle, be aware that an oncoming vehicle might have to use the centre of the road to make use of any extra headroom there.

Junctions

These tell you what type of junction is ahead: T-junction, crossroads, roundabout, staggered junction and so on. The priority through the junction is indicated by the broader line.

Sharp change of direction

Chevrons or roadside posts with reflectors may be used where

- the road changes direction sharply enough to create a hazard
- to reinforce a warning sign on a particularly sharp bend.

Other hazards

If there's no special sign for a particular hazard, a general hazard warning sign is used: a red triangle with an exclamation mark on a white background. There'll be a plate underneath it telling you what the hazard is – for example, a hidden dip.

⊙ Signs giving directions and other information

These help you find and follow the road you want. They can also direct you to the nearest railway station, car park, or other facility or attraction. The colours of these signs vary with the type of road. For example

- motorways – blue with white letters and border
- primary routes, except motorways – green with white letters and border, route numbers shown in yellow
- other routes – white with black letters and black border.

All these roads may also display tourist signs, which are brown with white letters and border.

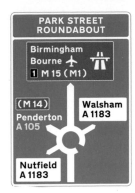

Signs giving directions on primary routes

Advance direction signs
You'll see these before you reach the junction. They enable you to decide which direction to take and to prepare yourself.

Direction signs at the junction
These show you the route to take as you reach the junction.

Route confirmatory signs
Positioned after the junction, these confirm which road you're on. These signs also tell you places and distances on your route. If the route number is in brackets, it means that the road leads to that route.

Information signs
These tell you where to find parking places, telephones, camping sites, etc, or give information about such things as no through roads.

Signs for traffic diversions

In an emergency, when it's necessary to close a section of motorway or other main road to traffic, a temporary sign may advise drivers to follow a diversion route. This route guides traffic around the closed section, bringing it back onto the same road further along its length.

To help drivers follow the route, black symbols on yellow patches may be permanently displayed on existing direction signs, including motorway signs. An initial sign will alert road users to the closure, then the symbol is shown alongside the route that drivers should follow.

A number of different symbols may be used, as in some places there may be more than one diversion operating. The range of symbols used is shown here.

Drivers and riders should follow signs showing the appropriate symbol. These may be displayed on separate signs, or included on direction signs, giving the number of the road to follow

⊙ Waiting restrictions

These are indicated by signs and road markings. Yellow lines along the road parallel to the kerb indicate that restrictions apply.

Small yellow plates may be mounted on walls, posts or lampposts nearby. These give more precise details of the restriction that applies. If there are double yellow lines painted on the road but no plates nearby, there's no waiting at any time.

Controlled parking zones

In controlled parking zones, the times of operation of the zone will be shown on the entry signs. Yellow lines show where waiting is prohibited or restricted, but yellow plates aren't normally provided in these zones.

White bay markings and upright signs indicate where parking is allowed.

Clearways

Some areas and main roads are designated as 'no stopping' zones or clearways. This means no stopping on the main carriageway at any time, not even to pick up or set down passengers.

On urban clearways there's no stopping during the hours of operation except for as long as necessary to set down or pick up passengers.

Loading and unloading

'Loading' is defined as when a vehicle stops briefly to load or unload goods that are so heavy or bulky it isn't easy to carry them any distance, and more than one trip may be involved. Picking up items that can be carried, such as shopping, doesn't constitute loading.

You may be allowed to load and unload in places where waiting is restricted. Yellow markings on the kerb show that loading and unloading is prohibited. The times when this is prohibited are shown on the nearby upright signs. There may also be special bays marked by broken white lines and the words 'Loading only' marked on the road and upright signs.

Red Routes

On many roads in larger cities in the UK, Red Route signs and red road markings have been introduced to replace the yellow-line restrictions (see section 18). For more information on Red Routes, visit **tfl.gov.uk/redroutes**

⊕ Road markings

Markings on the road give information, orders or warnings. They can be used either with signs on posts or on their own.

Their advantages are

- they can often be seen when other signs are hidden by traffic
- they can give a continuing message as you drive along the road.

As a general rule, the more paint, the more important the message.

Lines across the road

'Give way' lines

Double broken white lines across your half of the road show that traffic on the road you want to enter has priority. The lines show where you should stop, if necessary, to take your final look. These may also be found on a roundabout where traffic on the roundabout is required to give way to those joining.

A single broken line is normally found at the entrance to a roundabout. This tells you that traffic coming from your immediate right has priority and you **MUST** give way.

Single 'stop' lines

A single continuous line across your half of the road shows where you **MUST** stop

- at junctions with 'stop' signs
- at junctions controlled by traffic lights
- at level crossings and emergency vehicle access points
- at swing bridges or ferries.

Lines along the road

Double white lines

Double white lines have rules for

- overtaking

- parking.

Overtaking

When the line nearest you is continuous, you **MUST NOT** cross or straddle it except when the road is clear and you want to

- enter or leave a side road or entrance on the opposite side of the road

- pass a stationary vehicle

- overtake a pedal cycle, horse or road maintenance vehicle, if they're travelling at 10 mph (16 km/h) or less.

If there isn't room to leave enough space when passing, you should wait for a safe opportunity. Don't try to squeeze past.

If there's a broken white line on your side and a continuous white line on the other side, you may cross both lines to overtake, as long as it's safe to do so. Make sure you can complete the manoeuvre before reaching a solid line on your side.

Arrows on the road indicate the direction you should pass double white lines or hatch markings. Don't begin to overtake when you see them.

Parking
You **MUST NOT** stop or park on a road marked with double white lines, even if one of the lines is broken, except to pick up or drop off passengers or to load or unload goods.

Hatch markings
There are dangerous areas where it's necessary to separate the streams of traffic completely, such as a sharp bend or hump, or where traffic turning right needs protection. These areas are painted with white chevrons or diagonal stripes and the tarmac areas between them may also be a different colour (for example, red).

In addition, remember

- where the boundary line is solid, don't enter except in an emergency
- where the boundary line is broken, you shouldn't drive on the markings unless you can see that it's safe to do so.

Single broken lines
Watch out for places where the single broken line down the centre of the road gets longer. This means that there's a hazard ahead.

Lane dividers
Short broken white lines are used on wide carriageways to divide them into lanes. You should keep between them unless you're

- changing lanes
- overtaking
- turning right.

Lanes for specific types of vehicle

Bus and cycle lanes are shown by signs and road markings. In some one-way streets these vehicles are permitted to travel against the normal flow of traffic. These are known as contraflow lanes.

Bus lanes

Only vehicles shown on the sign may use the lane during the hours of operation, which are also shown on the sign. Outside those periods all vehicles can use the bus lane. Where there are no times shown, the bus lane is in operation for 24 hours a day. Don't park or drive in bus lanes under any circumstances when they're in operation.

Cycle lanes

Don't drive or park in a cycle lane marked by a solid white line during the times of operation shown on the signs. If the cycle lane is marked by a broken line, don't drive or park in it unless it's unavoidable. If you park in a cycle lane at any time, you make it very dangerous for any cyclist who's using that lane.

High-occupancy vehicle lanes

You **MUST NOT** drive in these lanes during their period of operation unless your vehicle contains the minimum number of people indicated on the sign.

Reflective road studs

These may be used with white lines.

- Red studs mark the left-hand side of the road.
- White studs mark the lanes or middle of the road.
- Amber studs mark the right-hand edge of the carriageway on dual carriageways and motorways.
- Green studs mark the edge of the main carriageway at lay-bys and slip roads.

At roadworks, fluorescent green/yellow studs may be used to help identify the lanes in operation.

Box junction markings

Yellow crisscross lines mark a box junction. Their purpose is to keep the junction clear by preventing traffic from stopping in the path of crossing traffic.

You **MUST NOT** enter a box junction unless your exit road is clear. But you can enter the box when you want to turn right and you're only prevented from doing so by oncoming traffic.

If there's a vehicle already on the junction waiting to turn right, you're free to enter behind it and wait to turn right – providing that you won't block any oncoming traffic wanting to turn right.

If there are several vehicles waiting to turn, it's unlikely you'll be able to proceed before the traffic signals change.

Words on the road

Words painted on the road usually have a clear meaning, such as 'Stop', 'Slow' or 'Keep clear'.

When they show a part of the road is reserved for certain types of vehicle – for example, buses, taxis or ambulances – don't park there.

Schools

Yellow zigzags are often marked on the road outside schools, along with the words 'School – keep clear'. Don't stop (even to set down or pick up children) or park there. The markings are to make sure that drivers who are passing the area and children who are crossing the road have a clear, unrestricted view of the crossing area.

Destination markings

Near a busy junction, lanes sometimes have destination markings or road numbers painted on the road.

These enable drivers to get into the correct lane early, even if advance direction road signs are obscured by large vehicles.

Lane arrows

These tell you which lane to take for the direction you want.

Where the road is wide enough, you may find one arrow pointing in each direction

- left in the left-hand lane
- straight ahead in the centre lane
- right in the right-hand lane.

Some arrows might be combined, depending on how busy the junction is. If the road is only wide enough for two lanes, arrows might have two directions combined

- straight ahead and left in the left-hand lane
- straight ahead and right in the right-hand lane.

Left- and right-turn arrows are placed well before a junction to help you get into the correct lane in good time. They don't indicate the exact point at which you should turn. It's especially important to remember this at right turns.

Speed reduction lines

Raised yellow lines may be painted across the carriageway at the approach to

- roundabouts
- reduced speed limits
- particular hazards.

The purpose of these lines is to make drivers aware of their speed after a period of driving at higher speeds. Reduce your speed in good time.

⊕ Traffic lights

Traffic lights have three lights – red, amber and green – that change in a set cycle

- red
- red and amber together
- green
- amber
- red.

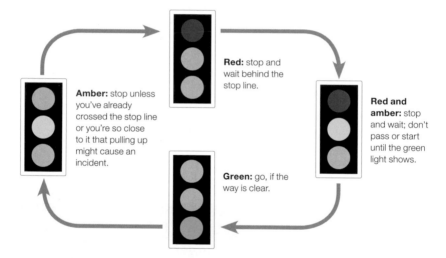

Red: stop and wait behind the stop line.

Red and amber: stop and wait; don't pass or start until the green light shows.

Green: go, if the way is clear.

Amber: stop unless you've already crossed the stop line or you're so close to it that pulling up might cause an incident.

What the colours mean

- Red – stop and wait at the stop line.
- Red and amber – stop and wait. Don't go until green shows.
- Green – go if the way is clear.
- Amber – stop, unless
  - you've already crossed the line
  - you're so close to it that pulling up might cause an incident.

Approaching traffic lights

Use the Mirrors – Signal – Manoeuvre (MSM) and Position – Speed – Look (PSL) routines as you approach the lights. Pay attention to lane markings and get into the correct lane in good time. Keep your speed down and be prepared to stop.

If the lights are showing green, don't speed up to 'beat the lights'. Be ready to stop, especially if the lights have been green for some time.

Green filter arrow

A green arrow in a traffic light means you can filter in the direction the arrow is pointing, even if the main light isn't showing green. Don't enter this lane unless you want to go in the direction shown by the arrow. When turning left or right at traffic lights, take special care and give way to pedestrians already crossing.

If traffic lights fail

If the traffic lights fail, proceed with caution. Treat the situation as you would an unmarked junction.

Advance stop lines

At some traffic lights there are advance stop lines to allow cyclists to position themselves ahead of other traffic.

When the lights are amber or red you should stop at the first white line and avoid the marked area, which is reserved for cyclists only. However, if you've crossed the first white line at the time that the signal changes to red, you must stop at the second white line even if you're in the marked area. Allow cyclists time and space to move off when the lights change to green.

In some areas there are bus advance areas. These should be treated in the same way as those provided for cyclists.

Special traffic lights

These are often used to control traffic where low-flying aircraft pass over the road, or at swing or lifting bridges, or other special sites such as fire stations.

They may either be

- normal traffic lights (red, amber and green) – follow the normal rules
- double red flashing lights – stop when the red lights are flashing.

School-crossing warning

At some busy locations, two amber lights flashing alternately warn traffic of a school-crossing point ahead.

Keep your speed down and proceed with great care.

⊙ Traffic calming

Traffic-calming measures are used to encourage people to drive at a lower speed than they might otherwise do. They're used in particularly sensitive areas where it's considered that a reduction in speed would benefit the immediate community.

Various features can be provided to slow down traffic, such as

- road humps
- road narrowings, central islands and chicanes
- mini-roundabouts.

20 mph zones

Some traffic-calmed areas are indicated only by a 20 mph (32 km/h) speed-limit sign.

This speed-limit sign, in addition to advising the maximum speed, indicates that there may be traffic-calming features within the signed zone; these may not be individually signed.

You should drive at a steady speed within the speed limit, and avoid frequent acceleration and deceleration within these areas.

Road humps

These may be round- or flat-topped humps laid across the carriageway. They may be used on roads where there's a speed limit of 30 mph (48 km/h) or less.

In some areas the humps are in the form of 'cushions', which cover only part of the lane and are designed so that larger vehicles, especially buses, can straddle them.

If road humps or cushions are provided outside 20 mph (32 km/h) zones, there will normally be

- warning signs at the beginning of the section of road where the hump or series of humps is installed
- triangle and edge line markings at each hump.

Road narrowings

Roads may be narrowed by the use of 'build-outs' on one or both sides of the road.

If these are provided outside 20 mph (32 km/h) zones, there will normally be

- warning signs indicating on which side of the road the narrowing occurs
- 'give way' road markings on one side of the road, accompanied by signs advising priority for oncoming vehicles.

If these are on your side of the road, you **MUST** always give way to drivers approaching from the other direction.

If priority isn't given in either direction, then all drivers should ensure that they can pass through the narrowing without endangering vehicles approaching from the other direction. You shouldn't accelerate as you approach the narrowing, but be prepared to slow down or give way to approaching traffic.

Hold back and allow cyclists and motorcyclists room to pass through; don't try to squeeze through at the same time.

Mini-roundabouts

Mini-roundabouts are often used as part of traffic-calming schemes to break up a long road into shorter sections and allow traffic to join from minor roads.

Methods of dealing with mini-roundabouts are given in section 8.

Psychological traffic calming

Increasingly, urban planners are choosing to remove road furniture such as kerbs, traffic lights, signs, white lines and other road markings to create 'naked roads'. The theory is that removing the sense of security provided by road furniture causes the driver to exercise more caution. There's evidence that this approach reduces speed and accidents, and encourages drivers to be more considerate to pedestrians.

⊕ Level crossings

At a level crossing, the road crosses railway lines. Approach and cross with care. Never

- drive onto the crossing unless the road is clear on the other side, or drive over it 'nose to tail' with another vehicle
- stop on or just after the crossing
- park close to the crossing.

Most crossings have full or half barriers, although some have no gates or barriers. If you stop at a level crossing and your wait is likely to be more than a few minutes, consider switching off your engine, as this can save fuel and cut down on pollution.

Railway telephones

If there's a telephone, you **MUST** use it to contact the signal operator to get permission to cross if you're

- driving a large or slow-moving vehicle, or one with limited ground clearance
- herding animals.

Remember to telephone the signal operator again once you're clear of the crossing.

Automatic barriers

Crossings with lights

A steady amber light followed by twin flashing red lights warns of an approaching train. An audible alarm to warn pedestrians will also sound once the lights show.

You **MUST** obey the lights' signals.

Don't

- move onto the crossing after the lights show
- zigzag round half barriers
- stop on the crossing if the amber light or audible alarm starts to operate – keep going if you're already on the crossing.

If the train goes by and the red lights continue to flash, or the audible alarm changes tone, you **MUST** wait because another train is approaching.

Crossings without lights

At crossings with no lights, stop when the gates or barriers begin to close.

Open crossings

The sign in the shape of a cross shown in the following image is used at all level crossings without either gates or barriers.

Crossings with lights

Automatic open level crossings have flashing road traffic signals and audible warnings similar to those on crossings with barriers.

Crossings without lights

At an open crossing with no gates, barriers, attendant or traffic signals, there will be a 'give way' sign.

Look both ways, listen and make sure there's no train coming before you cross.

User-operated crossings

These crossings are normally private and should be used by authorised users and invited guests only.

Crossings with signals

Some crossings with gates or barriers have 'stop' signs and small red and green lights. Don't cross when the red light is on because this means that a train is approaching. Cross only when the green light is on.

If you're crossing with a vehicle

- open the gates or barriers on both sides of the crossing
- check the green light is still on and cross promptly
- close the gates or barriers when you're clear of the crossing.

Crossings without signals

Some crossings have gates but no signals. At these crossings, stop, look both ways, listen and make sure that no train is approaching.

If there's a railway telephone you **MUST** contact the signal operator to make sure it's safe to cross.

Open the gates on both sides of the crossing and check again that no train is coming before crossing promptly.

Once you've cleared the crossing, close both gates and, if there's a telephone, inform the signal operator.

Always give way to trains – they can't stop easily.

See the Network Rail guide to using level crossings safely.

networkrail.co.uk/level-crossings

Incidents or breakdowns

If your vehicle breaks down, or you're involved in an incident on the crossing

- get everyone out of the vehicle and clear of the crossing
- if there's a railway telephone, use it **immediately** to inform the signal operator; follow any instructions you're given
- **if there's time** and if it's possible, move the vehicle clear of the crossing
- if the alarm sounds, or the amber light comes on, **get clear of the crossing at once – the train won't be able to stop.**

Crossings for trams

Look for traffic signs that show where trams cross the road.

Treat them in the same way as normal railway crossings.

REMEMBER, modern trams move quietly. Take extra care and look both ways before crossing.

Section seven
⊙➔ On the road

This section covers

- Awareness and anticipation
- Road positioning
- Bends
- Stopping distance
- Separation distance
- Overtaking
- Obstructions
- Pedestrian crossings
- Driving on hills
- Tunnels
- Trams or LRT systems

⊕ Awareness and anticipation

In any traffic situation there are some things that are obviously going to happen and some things that **might** happen.

To anticipate is to consider and prepare for something that will or might happen.

You can anticipate what might happen by making early use of the available information on the road.

Ask yourself

- What am I likely to find?
- What are other road users trying to do?
- Should I speed up or slow down?
- Do I need to stop?

Changing and difficult conditions

Traffic conditions change constantly and you need to

- check and recheck what's going on around you
- be alert all the time to changes in conditions, and think ahead.

How much you need to anticipate varies according to the conditions.

You'll find it more difficult to decide what might happen when

- the light is poor
- it's raining, snowy or foggy
- the traffic is heavy
- the route is unfamiliar.

Types of road

The type of road will also affect how much you can anticipate.

It's easier in light traffic to anticipate what other drivers might do. It's more difficult on a busy single carriageway, dual carriageway or motorway, where there are more possibilities to consider.

Driving ahead

Look well ahead to anticipate what might happen. You need to be alert and observant at all times.

Assess the movement of all other road users, including pedestrians, as far as you can see along the stretch of road on which you're travelling.

Take in as much as possible of the road

- ahead
- behind
- to each side.

You should

- observe the middle distance and far distance, as well as the area immediately in front of you
- glance frequently in the mirror to see what's happening in the area you've just passed
- scan the area in your view.

Observation

If you're a new driver, you'll tend to give most of your attention to controlling the vehicle.

Practise 'reading' the road (looking for important details). You don't have to be driving to do this; you can also do it as a passenger in a car or on a bus. Things to look for include

- other vehicles and pedestrians
- signals given by other drivers
- road signs and markings
- the type and condition of the road surface

- large vehicles, which sometimes need extra space to manoeuvre – for example, at roundabouts and other junctions
- movements of vehicles well ahead of you, as well as those immediately in front
- side roads or hills ahead
- buses signalling to move out from bus stops.

Clues

Look out for clues to help you act safely on what you see.

Watch for details in built-up areas where traffic conditions change rapidly. Be aware of the actions and reactions of other road users.

Reflections in shop windows can often give important information where vision is restricted or when you're reversing into a parking space.

A pedestrian approaching a zebra crossing might step out into the road sooner than you think.

Looking over, under and through parked vehicles may help you to see a pedestrian who is otherwise hidden from your view. This can enable you to anticipate and respond to the hazard in good time.

Take care approaching parked vehicles, especially if someone is in the driving seat.

Watch out for a driver stopping to set down or pick up a passenger. You may find they move off without warning, without checking in the mirrors or looking around.

When following a bus, watch for passengers standing up inside: the bus will probably stop shortly.

> **REMEMBER,** try to anticipate the actions of other road users.

Be aware

How much you can see depends on how well you can see.

Your eyesight can change without you being aware of it. Have regular eyesight checks.

Your sense of hearing can also make you aware of what's happening around you. For example, if you're waiting to pull out at a junction and your view is restricted, you may hear an approaching vehicle before you can see it.

At works entrances and schools you should expect an increased number of pedestrians, cyclists and vehicles. Watch for vehicles picking up and setting down at school start and finish times – buses as well as cars.

School buses will also be picking up and setting down passengers where there may not be normal bus stops.

Emergency vehicles

Look and listen for emergency vehicles. As well as the usual emergency services – police, fire and ambulance – others, such as coastguard, bomb disposal, mountain rescue and the blood transfusion service, may use blue flashing lights. Doctors attending emergencies may use green flashing lights.

HM Coastguard

Bomb disposal

Blood transfusion

Mountain rescue

You should try to keep out of the way of any emergency vehicle. Check where they're coming from: behind (using your mirrors), ahead or across your path.

Don't panic. Watch for the path of the emergency vehicle and take any reasonable – and legal – action possible to try to help it get through. They won't expect you to break the law; only to make a reasonable and safe attempt to help clear the way for them so that they can do the rest.

Look well ahead and choose a sensible place to pull into the side of the road, but don't endanger yourself or other road users or risk damage to your car.

Try to avoid stopping before the brow of a hill, a bend or a narrow section of road where the emergency vehicle may have difficulty getting through, and don't

- put yourself in a position where you would be breaking the law – for example, by crossing a red traffic light or using a bus lane during its hours of operation
- break the speed limit to get out of the way
- risk damaging your tyres, wheels or steering by driving up kerbs.

Emergency vehicles are normally travelling quickly and it's important to clear their path to allow them to do so. However, ambulances may need to travel slowly, even if they have blue lights flashing, when a patient is being treated inside. In this case, it's important for them to have a smooth ride, so don't drive in a manner that would cause the ambulance to brake or swerve sharply.

Watch the Blue Light Aware video to find out more about how to help emergency vehicles get through traffic.

motoringassist.com/bluelightaware

Driving in busy areas

When driving in busy areas, you should be especially alert to all possible hazards.

You should also be particularly aware of your speed and always drive at a speed appropriate to the conditions.

The speed limit is the absolute maximum and doesn't mean that it's always safe for you to drive at that speed. For example, in a narrow residential street with cars parked on either side, you'll need to drive more slowly than you would on a clear street that has the same speed limit.

When driving in queues, try to leave junctions and entrances clear. This allows other drivers to turn into or out of the opening and can prevent unnecessary congestion.

⊕ Road positioning

You should normally keep to the left when driving in Great Britain.

However, keep clear of parked vehicles, so that you can respond safely to

- doors opening into the road
- pedestrians stepping out between vehicles
- children, who may be difficult to see and who might run into the road.

Don't

- drive too close to the kerb, particularly in streets crowded with pedestrians
- weave in and out between parked vehicles. It's unnecessary and confusing to other drivers.

When necessary, ease over to the left to let a faster vehicle overtake.

The correct position

You should always be in the correct position for the route you're going to take.

- Keep to the left if you're going straight ahead or turning left.
- Keep as close to the centre of the road as is safe when you're turning right.

Your position is important not only for safety, but also to allow the free flow of traffic. A badly positioned vehicle can hold up traffic in either direction.

Before turning right, position your vehicle just to the left of the centre of the road.

One-way streets

In one-way streets, all traffic flows in one direction. Position your vehicle according to whether you intend to go ahead, turn left, or turn right.

- To turn left, keep to the left-hand lane.
- To turn right, keep to the right-hand lane, provided there are no obstructions or parked vehicles on the right-hand side of the road you're in.
- To go ahead, be guided by the road markings. If there's no specific lane for ahead, select the most appropriate lane, normally the left, in good time.

Follow the road markings, get into the correct lane as soon as possible and stay in this lane. Watch for drivers making sudden lane changes without using the Mirrors – Signal – Manoeuvre (MSM) routine. Sometimes their positioning or hesitant driving is a clue that they're unsure of their route and may make a sudden decision to change lane.

Traffic in one-way streets often flows freely. Be aware that vehicles may pass on either side of you.

Lane discipline

You should always follow lane markings, which are there for two reasons.

* They make the best possible use of road space.
* They provide route directions for drivers.

Position yourself in good time
If you find you're in the wrong lane, don't try to change by cutting across other drivers. Carry on in your lane and find another way back to your route.

Changing lanes
Select the lane you need as soon as it's safe to do so. Always check your mirrors and, if necessary, take a quick sideways glance to be sure that you won't cause another road user to change course or speed. When it's safe to do so, signal in good time and, when clear, move out.

* Never weave from lane to lane.
* Never drive along straddling two lanes.
* Never change lanes at the last minute.
* Always stay in the middle of your lane until you need to change.

In heavy and slow-moving traffic
Don't

* change lanes suddenly or unnecessarily
* straddle lanes

- switch from lane to lane in an attempt to get through traffic more quickly
- obstruct 'keep clear' markings.

Allow for

- pedestrians crossing
- cyclists riding past on the left
- large vehicles needing to straddle lanes before turning
- motorcyclists filtering between lanes
- doors opening.

Driving ahead
Keep to the left-hand lane wherever possible. Don't use the right-hand lane just because you're travelling at speed.

On a carriageway with four or more lanes, peak-time 'tidal flow' systems might permit or forbid the use of some lanes on the right, depending on the time of day. Only use the lanes on the right when signs or markings allow you to do so.

Bus and cycle lanes
These are separate lanes shown by signs and road markings. Don't enter these lanes unless permitted by the signs.

You'll find more information on lane discipline in section 11, which covers driving on motorways.

Approaching a road junction

Look well ahead for signs and markings.

If you have two lanes in your direction and

- you intend to turn left, stay in the left-hand lane
- you intend to go straight ahead, stay in the left-hand lane unless otherwise indicated
- you intend to turn right, move to the right-hand lane in good time.

Don't try to gain an advantage by using an incorrect lane. Trying to change back to the proper lane at or near the junction can be dangerous.

If you have three lanes in your direction and you intend to

- turn left, stay in the left-hand lane
- go straight ahead, use the left-hand lane (unless there are left filter signs) or the middle lane, or be guided by road markings
- turn right, use the right-hand lane.

Slip road

Some junctions also have a slip road.

Get into the left-hand lane in good time before entering the slip road. You'll be able to slow down to turn left without holding up other traffic.

 Bends

To deal effectively and safely with bends, you should look well ahead and try to assess accurately

- how severe the bend is
- the speed at which you need to be travelling to negotiate the bend under control.

Where vision is restricted, be prepared for

- oncoming vehicles
- obstructions such as broken-down or slow-moving vehicles
- pedestrians walking on your side of the road.

You should

- use the footbrake to control your speed on approach to the bend
- choose the right gear for the speed at which you're now driving
- use the accelerator carefully
- steer to hold the correct line through the bend.

REMEMBER, a bend can feel like a sharp corner if you approach it too fast, and you'll find it more difficult to keep your vehicle under control.

Positioning on bends

Left-hand bend

Keep to the centre of your lane as you approach.

Don't move to the centre of the road to improve your view round the bend. This could put you too close to oncoming traffic.

Right-hand bend

Keep to the left to improve your view of the road, but don't let a clear view tempt you to enter the bend at too high a speed.

Speed when approaching bends

Judging the correct road speed as you approach bends and corners takes practice and experience.

The correct speed is the one that allows you to drive your vehicle around the bend under full control.

That speed will depend on the

- type and condition of the road
- sharpness of the bend
- camber of the road
- visibility
- weather conditions.

Camber

The camber of a road is the angle at which the road normally slopes away from the centre to help drainage.

Adverse camber

Here the road slopes down towards the outside of the corner and the forces acting on your vehicle could cause it to leave the road more easily than on a normal corner.

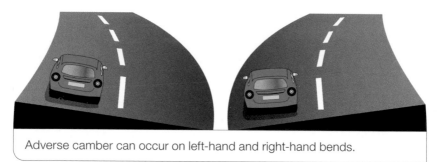

Adverse camber can occur on left-hand and right-hand bends.

Banking

On a few bends, such as some motorway slip roads, the outward force may be partly counteracted by banking. This is where the road slopes up towards the outside of the bend.

Adjusting your speed going into a bend

Don't go into a bend too fast. If necessary, reduce speed before you enter the bend.

You can reduce your speed by taking your foot off the accelerator and

- allowing your speed to fall naturally, or by
- using the footbrake progressively and, if necessary, changing to a lower gear.

Your speed should be at its lowest before you begin to turn.

Braking on a bend

Try to avoid braking harshly on a bend. This can make your vehicle unstable.

The sharper the bend, the greater the effects of braking while cornering and the more likely the vehicle is to skid.

Acceleration

Don't confuse 'using the accelerator' with 'accelerating', which means going faster. When dealing with bends, 'using the accelerator' means using it just enough to drive the vehicle around the bend.

The correct speed at a corner or bend will depend on a number of things, including

- how sharp it is
- whether there are any static or moving hazards.

You'll have to judge

- the position you should be in
- the best speed for the corner or bend
- the gear most suitable for that speed.

Make sure that

- your speed is at its lowest before you start the turn
- you use the accelerator so that the engine is doing just enough work to drive the vehicle round the bend without going faster.

Too much acceleration can cause the wheels to lose their grip and skid, resulting in the vehicle swinging off course. This is particularly true on rear-wheel-drive vehicles.

Only increase your speed after you've straightened as you leave the bend.

Gears

Make sure you select the correct gear before you enter the bend. You need both hands on the steering wheel as you're turning.

Steering

Every vehicle 'handles' differently. It's very important that you get to know how the vehicle you're driving behaves when you're steering round a bend.

Some vehicles 'understeer': they respond less than you would expect in relation to the amount of steering you use.

Others 'oversteer': they respond more than you would expect in relation to the amount of steering you use.

When a car understeers, the front tyres lose grip on the road. The car continues to travel in the same direction it was moving at the moment the tyres lost grip.

When a car oversteers, the rear tyres lose grip on the road and the rear of the car slides out. In severe cases this can lead to the car spinning and a serious loss of control.

To negotiate a bend, corner or junction safely, you must be able to judge how much steering to use.

Load

Any significant change in the centre of gravity of the vehicle or the weight it's carrying will affect its handling on bends, compared with when it's lightly loaded.

This change may be caused by

- extra passengers
- heavy objects in the boot
- objects on the roof rack.

Tyre pressures

Incorrect tyre pressures can also affect steering. Low pressure and excess pressure can both affect road holding and tyre wear.

Low pressure produces a heavier feel and in severe cases can cause the tyres to overheat.

Excess pressure can affect road holding on bends and increases the risk of skidding.

Negotiating the bend

Look ahead

Look well ahead for any indications, such as road signs, warnings and road markings, which will tell you

- the type of bend
- the direction the road takes
- how sharp the bend is
- whether the bend is one of a series.

Assess the situation

Ask yourself

- How dangerous does it seem? Remember, if the word 'slow' is painted on the road, that means there's a hazard and you need to respond to it safely.
- What if there's an obstruction on the bend, such as a slow-moving or parked vehicle?
- Are there likely to be pedestrians on your side of the road? Is there a footpath?
- Is there an adverse camber? Remember that on a right-hand bend an adverse camber could make your vehicle veer to the left.

Always drive so you can stop safely within the limit of your vision. Where your view is restricted, adjust your speed accordingly.

Approach with care

As you approach, follow the Mirrors – Signal – Manoeuvre (MSM)/Position – Speed – Look (PSL) routine. Before you reach the bend

- take up the best position for the type of bend
- adjust your speed, if necessary, and select the most suitable gear.

Entering the bend

As you enter the bend, press the accelerator just enough to keep

- the wheels gripping
- the vehicle under full control.

After you begin to turn

Avoid heavy braking, except in an emergency.

Stopping on a bend

Avoid stopping on a bend, except in an emergency.

If you have to stop, do so where following traffic can see you. This is especially important on left-hand bends, where vision can be more limited.

If you can, stop clear of a continuous centre line and give clear warning of any obstruction to other traffic. Use hazard warning lights and, if you have one, an advance warning triangle (or any other permitted warning device); see section 15.

At night

On unfamiliar roads, the lights of oncoming traffic may help you to plan ahead. However, negotiating bends at night has its own hazards.

* Anticipate hazards around the bend.
* Be prepared to be affected by the lights of oncoming traffic, especially on right-hand bends. Don't be taken by surprise.
* Dip your headlights in advance for oncoming traffic approaching the bend, especially on left-hand bends.

For more information on cornering techniques and bend analysis, advanced drivers may wish to refer to the TSO/Police Foundation publication **Roadcraft**.

A series of bends

Double and multiple bends are almost always signed. Take note of

* road signs
* double white lines
* arrows directing you to move to the left.

For example, if the second bend follows closely after the first and you haven't taken notice of the road sign or markings, you could find yourself speeding up when you should be slowing down.

On a winding road, selecting the appropriate gear will help you to

* drive at a safe speed
* keep the right amount of load on the engine and the right amount of grip on the road.

Where there's a series of bends, they often turn in alternate directions. As soon as you've negotiated one, you have to prepare for the next. Look well ahead for changes in the camber of the road, which could affect your control.

Defensive driving

Always be on the lookout for other vehicles creating dangerous situations, such as

- a vehicle overtaking too close to a bend
- a vehicle approaching a bend too fast
- oncoming vehicles straddling the centre lines
- oncoming vehicles skidding in bad weather
- a vehicle waiting to turn into a concealed entrance.

Limit points

Understanding limit points, and learning how to use them to improve your driving ability, is an important skill to master.

Simply put, the limit point is the furthest uninterrupted view of the road surface ahead, or the point at which the two verges – left and right – appear to meet.

If the limit point is rushing towards you, then you should slow down and allow yourself more time and space in which to stop.

If the limit point appears to be a constant distance away from you, this indicates that your speed on approach to the bend is correct, providing you can still stop in the distance you can see to be clear.

If the limit point is moving away from you, this indicates that you may start to accelerate as the bend opens out.

The following diagram illustrates the point.

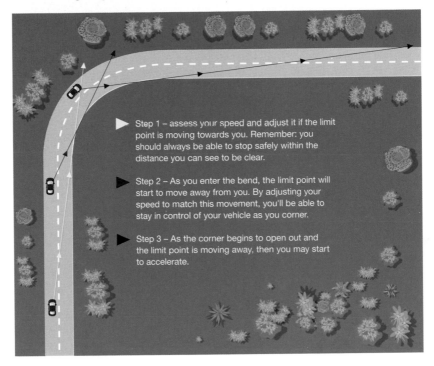

Step 1 – assess your speed and adjust it if the limit point is moving towards you. Remember: you should always be able to stop safely within the distance you can see to be clear.

Step 2 – As you enter the bend, the limit point will start to move away from you. By adjusting your speed to match this movement, you'll be able to stay in control of your vehicle as you corner.

Step 3 – As the corner begins to open out and the limit point is moving away, then you may start to accelerate.

⊙ Stopping distance

This is the distance your vehicle travels

• from the moment you realise you must brake

• to the moment the vehicle stops.

You need to leave enough space between you and the vehicle in front so that you can pull up safely if it slows down or stops suddenly.

To do this, you must be able to judge your overall stopping distance.

Practise judging distance while you're walking. Pick out something ahead and estimate how far away it is. Check your estimate by walking the distance and measuring it against your stride. (One good stride is roughly a metre.)

Stopping distance depends on

- how fast you're going
- whether you're travelling on the level, uphill or downhill
- the weather and the state of the road
- the type and age of your vehicle (normally, older vehicles need a longer stopping distance)
- the condition of your brakes and tyres
- the size and weight of your vehicle
- your ability as a driver, especially your reaction times when applying the brakes.

Stopping distance divides into

- thinking distance
- braking distance.

What are the usual stopping distances?

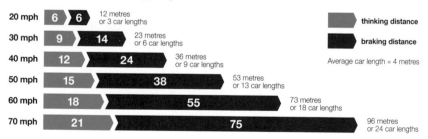

Distances are measured in metres and are approximate only.

Thinking distance

This depends on how quickly you react. It takes well over half a second for most people to react.

If you're tired or unwell, it may take longer.

Braking distance

This depends mainly on the speed of your vehicle, although other factors can also play a part.

Allow double the normal stopping distance on wet roads and 10 times the normal distance when the roads are icy.

Your tyres will have less grip on the road where

- the road surface is loose
- any diesel is spilt on the road.

In these conditions, you'll need more time and room to stop the vehicle.

Thinking distance
(distance travelled in the time it takes to react to a situation)

+

Braking distance
(distance travelled from when you start to use the brakes to when your car completely stops)

=

Stopping distance

⊕ Separation distance

Road traffic incidents can be caused by drivers getting too close to the vehicle in front.

It's essential that every driver is able to judge a safe separation distance in all road, traffic and weather conditions.

How far should you keep from the vehicle in front? Ideally, you should be no closer than the overall stopping distance that corresponds to your speed.

In heavy, slow-moving urban traffic that might not be realistic, as you could be wasting valuable road space. However, even then, the gap should never be less than your thinking distance – and much more if the road is wet and slippery.

A reasonable rule to apply in good, dry conditions is a gap of one metre for each mph of your speed. For example, at 55 mph (88 km/h) a gap of 55 metres would be appropriate. In bad conditions, leave at least double the distance.

A useful technique for judging one metre per mph is to use the 'two-second rule'.

> **REMEMBER,** your overall stopping distance is the only really safe ⚠ gap and anything less is taking a risk.

The two-second rule

In good, dry conditions, an alert driver, who's driving a vehicle with good tyres and brakes, needs to be at least two seconds behind the vehicle in front.

In bad conditions, double the safety gap to four seconds or even more.

How to measure

Choose an obvious stationary point ahead, such as a bridge, a tree or a road sign.

When the vehicle ahead passes the object, say to yourself, 'Only a fool breaks the two-second rule.' If you reach the object before you finish saying it, you're too close to the vehicle in front and need to drop back.

Driving too close to the vehicle in front is a major factor in crashes. You can avoid such incidents by looking well ahead, keeping your distance and giving yourself time to react.

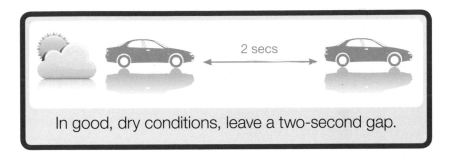

In good, dry conditions, leave a two-second gap.

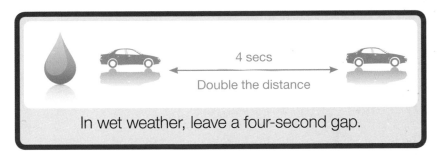

In wet weather, leave a four-second gap.

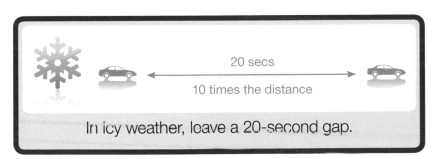

In icy weather, leave a 20-second gap.

When a vehicle behind is driving too close to you, ease off the accelerator very gradually and increase the gap between you and the vehicle in front. This will give you more time to react if the driver ahead should slow down or stop suddenly.

⊕ Overtaking

Overtaking can be a risky manoeuvre, as it can put you on a collision course with approaching traffic.

Overtaking at the wrong time or in the wrong place is extremely dangerous. It's vital to choose your time and place carefully.

Before overtaking you must be certain you can return to your side of the road safely without getting in the way of

- vehicles coming towards you
- vehicles you're overtaking.

Overtaking a moving vehicle

Don't overtake unless it's necessary. For example, don't rush to get past someone only to turn off that road shortly afterwards. Ask yourself whether it's really necessary. If you decide it is, you need to find a suitable place.

You **MUST NOT** overtake where to do so would cause you to break the law. Details are shown in The Highway Code.

In addition, some places are never suitable. For example, **don't** overtake

- if your view ahead is blocked
- if there's too little room
- if the road narrows
- if you're approaching a bend or junction
- if there's 'dead ground' – a hidden dip in the road where an oncoming vehicle can be out of sight.

Judging speed and distance

The speed of the vehicle you're overtaking is very important. When you're closing up behind a moving vehicle, it will cover quite a distance before you can actually pass it – probably much more than you think.

It could take you quite a long time to overtake. For example, if you're doing 30 mph (48 km/h), it could take a quarter of a mile (400 metres) just to catch up with a vehicle 200 yards (180 metres) ahead that's travelling at as little as 15 mph (24 km/h).

On the other hand, if you're travelling at 55 mph (88.5 km/h) and an oncoming vehicle is doing the same, both vehicles are actually approaching each other at 110 mph (177 km/h) or 50 metres per second.

Overtaking takes time. The smaller the difference between your speed and the speed of the vehicle you're overtaking, the longer the stretch of clear road you'll need.

Overtaking large vehicles

If you're considering overtaking a large vehicle, you need to keep well back to ensure that you

- get the best view of the road ahead
- allow the driver to see you in their mirrors. Remember, if you can't see their mirrors, they can't see you. Be especially aware that left-hand-drive lorries have different blind spots from right-hand-drive vehicles.

Leave a good space while waiting to overtake. If another car fills the gap, drop back again.

If possible, you should also note whether the vehicle you intend to overtake is loaded or unloaded. The speed of large vehicles varies greatly when they're going up and down hills. A loaded vehicle might crawl slowly uphill and then pick up speed surprisingly quickly on the downhill run.

Always remember these possible changes in speed when you're thinking of overtaking. Avoid driving alongside a large vehicle; you may be in its blind spot and the driver may not be able to see you.

Overtaking slow-moving vehicles

There are several types of slow-moving vehicle that you may encounter on the roads. These include farm machinery, tractors, roadworks vehicles and refuse collection vehicles. Most will have flashing amber beacons.

Tractors and farm machinery will often pull in to the left when it's safe, or if there's space to do so, to let a queue of traffic pass. However, they're not always able to do so.

Travelling behind a slow-moving vehicle can be frustrating, but be patient. Wait until the road ahead is completely clear of oncoming traffic and you're sure it's both safe and legal to overtake. Remember also that there may be workers in the road – for example, around roadworks vehicles or refuse collection trucks.

Don't overtake on the approach to bends, before the brow of a hill or where there are dips in the road ahead which could hide an oncoming vehicle. In rural areas, there may also be hidden entrances to farm properties from which vehicles may suddenly emerge.

Only overtake if your view of the road ahead is completely clear and unobstructed, and you're sure there's no oncoming traffic. Also check behind, to make sure no other vehicle is trying to overtake at the same time.

Leave plenty of room when overtaking and allow plenty of time for your manoeuvre. Some vehicles, especially those towing farm machinery, may be wider or longer than expected.

Overtaking on a hill

Uphill

Give yourself time and room to return to your side of the road well before the brow of the hill. Your zone of vision will get shorter as you approach the brow of the hill. Don't forget that oncoming vehicles will be travelling downhill and could be approaching very quickly.

Downhill

It's more difficult to slow down when going downhill. If you overtake going downhill, you may find yourself travelling faster than you intended. Be careful not to lose control of your vehicle.

Overtaking on long hills

On some long hills, double white lines divide the road so that there are two lanes for traffic going uphill, but only one downhill.

If the line is broken on the downhill side, this means you can overtake going downhill if it's safe to do so.

Overtaking on three-lane roads

Some roads are divided into three lanes, where the middle lane can be used for overtaking in either direction. These roads can be particularly dangerous. Before overtaking, you must make sure the road is clear far enough ahead. If in doubt, **wait**.

Some three-lane roads have double white lines marked on the road to allow vehicles travelling uphill to overtake.

Before overtaking

Many danger spots are marked with double white lines along the road. Look out for arrows directing you to move over to the left as you're approaching these areas.

Junction signs and hatch markings in the middle of the road alert you to the possibility of turning traffic. Don't overtake as you approach a junction, and look for traffic

- waiting to turn right
- slowing to turn left
- crossing your path
- queuing.

Watch the vehicle in front

Before overtaking, decide what the driver in front is likely to do by watching both them and the road ahead for a while. They might

- decide to overtake
- continue to drive at the speed of the vehicle ahead of them
- intend to turn off soon
- have seen something ahead which you haven't.

Vehicles turning right

Research has shown that most overtaking incidents are caused by the overtaking driver hitting a vehicle that's turning right. To avoid this type of collision you should

- check the indicators of the vehicle you're about to overtake
- assume that a vehicle that's slowing down is about to turn.

Following through

Never automatically follow an overtaking vehicle without being able to see for yourself that the way is clear. The vehicle in front obscures your view and hides you from the view of oncoming traffic.

Always make your own decisions about overtaking, based not only on what you see but also on what **you** know.

Be patient. If in doubt, hold back. There might not be enough time for both of you to overtake at once.

Steps to overtaking

To overtake, you might have to use some or all of these steps several times before the right moment arrives. For example, if someone overtakes you just as you're about to overtake, you'll need to start all over again.

Use the MSM/PSL routine

M – Mirrors

Check your mirrors to assess the situation behind and look well ahead.

S – Signal Give a signal if it will help

- drivers behind
- the driver you're overtaking
- drivers coming towards you.

M – Manoeuvre

Use the PSL routine

P – Position

Be near enough to the vehicle ahead to overtake smoothly when you're ready, but not so close that you can't get a good view of the road ahead.

S – Speed

Be fast enough to keep up with the vehicle in front and with enough reserve power to pass it briskly.

You might need to change down to get extra acceleration when you're ready to start overtaking.

L – Look

Assess the whole situation

- the state of the road
- what the driver ahead is doing or might be about to do
- any hazards
- the speed and position of oncoming vehicles
- the speed difference between you and oncoming vehicles.

Make a final check in front and behind. Check especially for motorcyclists as they may be approaching quickly and could have been hidden from view previously. Be aware of, and check, any blind spots by taking a quick sideways glance if necessary before deciding to pull out to overtake. If it's safe, steer out gradually, then

- overtake as quickly as you can
- steer gradually back to the left and avoid cutting in.

Never begin to overtake if another vehicle is overtaking you or is about to do so. Overtake only when you're sure it's safe to do so.

Allow plenty of room

When overtaking cyclists, motorcyclists or horse riders, give them plenty of room – move out as far as you would if you were overtaking a car. Never attempt to overtake them just before you turn left or if you would have to stop or slow down soon after.

If they look over their shoulder it could mean that they intend to pull out, turn right or change direction, so give them time and space to do this.

Overtaking on the left

You should never overtake on the left unless

- the vehicle in front is signalling to turn right, and you can safely overtake on their left. Take care if there's a road to the left; oncoming traffic turning right into it may be hidden by the vehicle you're overtaking
- traffic is moving slowly in queues, and vehicles in the lane on your right are moving more slowly than you are.

Passing on the left

In addition, you can go past on the inside of slower traffic when

- you're in a one-way street (but not a dual carriageway) where vehicles are allowed to pass on either side
- you're in the correct lane to turn left at a junction.

Overtaking on dual carriageways

Overtake only if you're sure you can do so safely.

You should normally stay in the left-hand lane and only use the right-hand lane for overtaking or turning right. If you use the right-hand lane for overtaking, you should move back to the left-hand lane as soon as it's safe to do so.

Plan well ahead and use the appropriate parts of the MSM/PSL routine.

For example

M – Mirrors

Use your mirrors to assess the speed and position of following traffic. On a high-speed dual carriageway, start the checks in plenty of time.

S – Signal

Give a signal if it will help the driver you're overtaking and other drivers further ahead. Be aware that on a dual carriageway, a vehicle in the right-hand lane signalling right may be slowing to turn right through the central reservation.

P – Position

Keep well back from the vehicle you're going to overtake to give you a good view of the road ahead.

S – Speed

Make sure you have enough speed in reserve to overtake briskly without breaking any speed limits.

L – Look

Look ahead and assess

- the condition of the road
- what the vehicle ahead is doing
- any hazards.

Check behind again to reassess the situation; check especially for motorcyclists as they can approach very quickly. Don't begin to overtake if another vehicle is about to overtake you.

If it's safe, change lanes by steering gradually across to the right-hand lane and overtake briskly. Make sure you're well clear of the vehicle you've overtaken before moving back to the left. Don't cut in.

Overtaking on the left

You mustn't overtake on the left unless traffic is moving slowly in queues, and the queue on your right is moving more slowly than you are.

Never move to a lane on your left to overtake.

Defensive driving

Never accelerate when someone is overtaking you. If necessary, ease off to help them pass you.

> **REMEMBER,** if in doubt, don't overtake. Overtaking often takes longer than you think, especially if you're overtaking a large vehicle.

Keep well back from any vehicle that's too close to the vehicle in front and swinging in and out. Be patient, in case they do something hasty.

Be considerate. Don't block faster vehicles that might want to overtake you, even if they're breaking the speed limit.

⊛ Obstructions

The way to deal with any obstruction is to look and plan well ahead, and to use the MSM/PSL routine.

The decision to wait or to go around the obstruction will depend on

- the type and width of the road
- whether the obstruction is on
  - your side of the road
  - the other side of the road
  - both sides of the road
- whether there's approaching traffic
- the behaviour of following drivers
- the room available.

As a general rule, if the obstruction is on your side of the road, approaching traffic will have priority.

Don't assume that you have priority if the obstruction is on the other side of the road. Always be prepared to give way and remember that the obstruction could conceal something such as a pedestrian.

Driving around an obstruction

Look well ahead to identify the obstruction in good time before using the routine.

M – Check your mirrors to assess the speed and position of following traffic.

S – Signal if necessary.

P – Decide on your position. Avoid keeping so far to the left that you have to steer past the obstruction at the last minute; a gradual change of course is required. If you have to stop and wait, keep well back from the obstruction in a position that allows you to see ahead clearly without blocking the approaching traffic.

S – Adjust your speed as necessary. This will depend on the situation, but aim to regulate your speed so that you can steer a steady course.

L – Finally, look and assess the situation before you decide whether it's

- necessary to wait
- safe to proceed.

Obstructions on hills

These need special care. Give yourself the time and space you need, remembering that you may need to brake earlier than normal.

If you're travelling downhill and the obstruction is on the other side of the road, don't take your priority for granted. If it's safe, be prepared to give way to traffic coming uphill, especially heavy vehicles. Your consideration will be appreciated.

Roadworks

These areas make the usable width of the road much narrower. They can be controlled either by temporary traffic lights or by workers with 'stop/go' boards.

Obey all lights and signs, slow down and look out for workers who may be walking on or near the road.

More information on negotiating roadworks areas and contraflow systems can be found in section 11.

Large, slow-moving vehicles

These vehicles include

- machines working along the verge, such as mowers or hedge cutters
- agricultural vehicles
- vintage vehicles
- plant and machinery used for road maintenance
- escorted wide, long or heavy loads
- refuse collection vehicles.

You may see a temporary sign alerting you to slow vehicles operating in the area. There may also be clues, such as bins awaiting collection, freshly cut grass or hedge cuttings in the road. If you come across a large, slow vehicle, be patient and hold back so that you have a good view past it. If you're in a queue and the vehicle in front overtakes, don't blindly follow it. Look out for workmen in the road and only pass when you can see it's safe to do so.

Drive so that you can respond safely should you unexpectedly come across a large, slow vehicle. Remember – the drivers of these vehicles can't move out of the way quickly.

Defensive driving

Don't follow through behind the vehicle in front without being able to see for yourself that the way ahead is clear.

Keep a safe distance from the obstruction and the approaching traffic. Where space is limited, reduce your speed and take extra care. The smaller the gap, the lower your speed needs to be.

⊕ Pedestrian crossings

The driver and pedestrian crossings

People on foot have certain rights of way at pedestrian crossings.

Some rules and advice apply to all types of crossing.

- You **MUST NOT** park
    - on a crossing; this blocks the way for pedestrians
    - within the area marked by zigzag lines; this obstructs both the pedestrian's view of approaching vehicles and an approaching driver's view of the crossing.
- You **MUST NOT** overtake
    - the moving vehicle nearest to a crossing
    - the leading vehicle that has stopped to give way to a pedestrian.
- Even if there are no zigzag lines, never overtake just before a crossing.
- Give yourself more time to stop if the road is wet or icy.
- Keep crossings clear when queuing in traffic, stopping before the crossing if you can see that you won't be able to clear it.
- You should take extra care where the view of either side of a crossing is blocked by queuing traffic. Pedestrians may be crossing between these vehicles, incorrectly thinking they've stopped to allow pedestrians to cross.
- Always allow pedestrians plenty of time to cross, especially if they're older or disabled, and don't try to hurry them by revving your engine or edging forward.
- Watch out for pedestrians who try to rush across at the last minute.

Also, on all signal-controlled crossings you should

- give way to anyone still on the crossing even if the signal for vehicles has changed to green
- proceed with extreme caution if the signals aren't working.

There are additional rules for different types of crossing.

Zebra crossings

Zebra crossings have flashing yellow beacons on both sides of the road and black and white stripes on the crossing. They also have white zigzag markings on both sides of the crossing and a 'give way' line about a metre from the crossing, which marks the place for drivers to stop when necessary. When pedestrians are waiting to cross at a zebra crossing, check your mirrors and stop if you can do so safely.

Be aware also of pedestrians approaching the crossing. They may suddenly start to move onto the crossing, so be ready to stop for them.

You **MUST** give way to anyone who

* is already crossing
* has stepped onto the crossing.

Don't wave people across. There could be another vehicle coming in the other direction and you can't be sure what other drivers might do.

REMEMBER, some zebra crossings are divided by a central island. Each half is a separate crossing.

Pelican crossings

These are light-controlled crossings where the pedestrian uses push-button controls to control the lights. They have no red-and-amber phase before the green light. Instead, they have a flashing amber light, which means you must give way to pedestrians on the crossing but may drive across if the crossing is clear.

The crossing area is shown by studs and a 'stop' line marks the place for drivers to stop when it's necessary.

Pelican crossings may be

- **straight**
  A pelican crossing that goes straight across the road is one crossing, even if there's a central refuge. You must wait for people coming from the other side of the refuge

- **staggered**
  If the crossings on each side of the central refuge aren't in line, the crossings are separate.

Puffin crossings

These are user-friendly, 'intelligent' crossings where electronic devices automatically detect when pedestrians are on the crossing and delay the green light until the pedestrians have reached a position of safety.

Unnecessary delays in traffic flow are reduced by these devices.

- If the pedestrians cross quickly, the pedestrian phase is shortened.
- If the pedestrians have crossed the road before the phase starts, it will automatically be cancelled.

The light sequence at these crossings is the same as at traffic lights (see section 6).

Toucan crossings

These are shared by pedestrians and cyclists. Cyclists are permitted to cycle across.

The light sequence at these crossings is the same as at traffic lights.

Equestrian crossings

These are for horse riders and may be alongside those for pedestrians and cyclists. They have wider crossing areas, pavement barriers and either one or two sets of controls, one being set at a higher position.

School-crossing patrols

Watch out for these patrols and obey their signals.

At particularly dangerous locations, two amber lights flashing alternately give advance warning of the crossing point.

Don't overtake when you're approaching a school crossing. Always keep your speed down so you're ready to slow down or stop if necessary.

Defensive driving

Always look well ahead to identify pedestrian crossings early. Look for the flashing yellow beacons, traffic lights, zigzag markings, etc.

Use the MSM routine and keep your speed down.

Brake lights can't be seen by the pedestrians at the crossing or by approaching drivers, so if you're the leading vehicle you should consider using an arm signal when slowing down or stopping at a zebra crossing.

⊕ Driving on hills

You need to understand how driving uphill and downhill can affect your control of the vehicle.

- Going uphill, your engine has to use more power to overcome gravity and drive the vehicle up the hill.
- Going downhill, gravity will cause the vehicle to increase speed. The steeper the hill, the greater this effect.

In each case, the effect on the controls is different from driving on the level.

Going uphill

When going uphill

- you'll find it more difficult to maintain or increase speed. The engine has to work harder to make the vehicle go faster
- your brakes will slow the vehicle down more quickly
- you might need to change to a lower gear to maintain your speed. If you release the accelerator or push the clutch pedal down, your speed will drop more quickly than it would on the level. Changing to a lower gear should be done without hesitation, so you don't lose too much speed
- remember to apply the parking brake before you release the footbrake when stopped, otherwise you might roll back.

Look for signs

On steeper hills, you'll see warning signs telling you how steep the upward slope is. The figures usually measure the gradient in percentage terms (or very occasionally as a ratio): the higher the percentage, the steeper the hill.

You may see another rectangular sign telling you the length of the hill and further information.

Watch out for slow-moving, heavy vehicles. They may be travelling much more slowly than other traffic and their large size can make them difficult to overtake safely.

Assess the hill

If the hill is very steep, think ahead and consider changing to a lower gear. If you do need to change gear, make sure you do so in good time.

Don't stay in a high gear to try to keep your speed up. Your vehicle will climb better in a lower gear.

> Turning and climbing at the same time is hard work for the engine. If the road bends sharply, you'll find it safer and easier on the engine to change down before the bend.

Separation distance

Keep well back from the vehicle ahead.

- If you don't hold back and the vehicle ahead suddenly slows or stops, you may have to brake harshly.
- Holding back may enable you to keep going gently while the vehicle ahead regains speed. This is safer and can also help to avoid congestion.

Overtaking

It's usually more difficult to overtake when travelling uphill. Oncoming traffic may be travelling faster than usual and may take longer to slow down or stop.

On a dual carriageway, overtaking is easier because there's no danger from oncoming traffic. Here you should keep a lookout for others following behind you who can overtake with ease. Don't block their progress.

Going downhill

When going downhill

- you'll find it more difficult to slow down and the brakes will have less effect
- it's harder for the engine to hold the vehicle back. In higher gears it won't do so at all
- you should avoid coasting, either out of gear or with the clutch pedal down, because you'll have no engine braking. Without engine braking your vehicle will pick up speed more easily, and this could result in you having less control of the vehicle

- try to avoid braking on a bend
- get into a lower gear in good time, particularly if there's a bend ahead. This will increase the engine braking and help to control the vehicle's speed
- use the correct combination of lower gear and careful use of the footbrake to keep control of your speed.

Look for signs

The steep hill (downwards) warning sign will give you the gradient of the downward slope.

You might also see a rectangular sign advising use of a low gear. The steeper the hill, the lower the gear.

Assess the hill

Use the sign to help you think ahead. If the route is unfamiliar, or a bend limits your view of the road, change down before you begin to descend. Change smoothly and without hesitation.

Separation distance

Always keep the correct separation distance from the vehicle ahead.

If you don't hold back and the vehicle ahead suddenly slows down or stops, you'll have to brake very hard. The driver behind will get very little warning.

If you hold back, you'll have time to reduce your speed more gradually.

Adjust your speed

On steep hills, you'll normally need to reduce speed. Change down to a lower gear to give yourself more braking power and control.

By selecting a lower gear, you should be able to avoid using your brakes too much. Excessive braking on hills can result in 'brake fade' and loss of control. Brake fade is a loss of braking power caused by the heat generated by continuous use of the brakes.

Look for 'escape lanes', which are designed to stop runaway vehicles.

Overtaking

It's only safe to overtake downhill where

- there are no bends or junctions
- your view of the road ahead is clear.

You should be absolutely **certain** that you can overtake without causing oncoming traffic to slow down or change course.

Remember that the vehicle you're overtaking may build up speed, and you'll find it more difficult to slow down for oncoming traffic. They'll find it more difficult to get out of your way.

Look out for road markings, especially continuous white lines along the centre of the road.

Hills in towns

Take particular care in towns, where pedestrians may be crossing at junctions on hills.

Traffic speeds are generally lower and vehicles closer together. As a result, your view will often be reduced.

Pay attention to your distance from the vehicle ahead.

You'll find traffic lights, school-crossing patrols and pedestrian crossings are sometimes situated on a hill. Where this is the case, it adds to the importance of

- using your mirrors
- leaving a suitable gap when you stop
- using your parking brake effectively
- making sure you're in the right gear for the situation.

You'll be doing these things in towns already, but on hills they have additional importance.

⊕ Tunnels

When approaching a tunnel

- switch on your dipped headlights
- don't wear sunglasses
- observe the road signs and signals
- keep an appropriate distance from the vehicle in front.

Many tunnels, particularly the longer ones in Europe, are equipped with radio transmitters so that drivers can be warned of any incidents, congestion or roadworks. If this applies to the tunnel you're approaching, switch on your radio and tune in to the indicated frequency.

When entering a tunnel, your visibility will be suddenly reduced. Be prepared for this change in conditions and make sure that you can stop within the distance you can see to be clear. Increase the distance between you and the car in front if necessary.

If tho tunnel is congested

- switch on your warning lights
- keep your distance, even if you're moving slowly. If you have to stop, leave at least a five-metre gap between you and the vehicle in front

- if possible, listen out for messages on the radio
- follow any instructions given by tunnel officials or variable message signs.

For action to take in the event of a breakdown or incident, see section 16.

⊙ Trams or LRT systems

Light rapid transit (LRT) systems, or 'metros', are being introduced in many large towns and cities to provide a more efficient and environmentally friendly form of public transport.

Tram systems are common throughout Europe and there are plans to introduce them to more cities in the UK.

Trams may operate completely separately from other traffic or they may run on roads open to other traffic. As they run on rails, they're fixed in the route they follow and can't manoeuvre around other road users. The vehicles may run singly or as multiple units, and may be up to 60 metres (about 200 feet) long. Remember that trams are quiet, move quickly and can't steer to avoid you.

The area occupied by a tram is marked by paving or markings on the road surface. This 'swept path' must always be kept clear. Anticipate well ahead and never stop on or across the tracks or markings except when in queuing traffic or at traffic lights.

Take extra care when you first encounter trams until you're accustomed to dealing with the different traffic system.

Crossing points

Deal with these in exactly the same way as normal railway crossings.

Also bear in mind the speed and silent approach of trams.

Reserved areas

Drivers mustn't enter 'reserved areas' for the trams, which are marked with white line markings, a different type of surface, or both.

The reserved areas are usually one-way, but may sometimes be two-way.

Hazards

The steel rails can be slippery whether it's wet or dry. Try to avoid driving on the rails and take extra care when braking or turning on them, to avoid the risk of skidding.

Take care also where

- the tracks run close to the kerb to pick up or set down passengers
- the lines move from one side of the road to the other.

Tram stops

Where a tram stops at a platform, either in the middle or at the side of the road, follow the route shown by road signs and markings. If there's no passing lane signed, wait behind the tram until it moves off.

At stops without platforms, don't drive between a tram and the left-hand kerb when the tram has stopped to pick up or set down passengers.

Warning signs and signals

Obey all warning signs or signals controlling traffic. Where there are no signals, always give way to trams.

Diamond-shaped signs or white light signals give instructions to tram drivers only.

Do

- watch out for additional pedestrian crossings where passengers will be getting on and off the trams. You must stop for them
- make allowances for other road users who may not be familiar with tram systems
- be especially aware of the problems of cyclists, motorcyclists and moped riders. Their narrow tyres can put them at risk of slipping on or getting stuck in the tram rails.

Don't

- try to race a tram where there isn't enough road space for both vehicles side by side; remember the end of the vehicle swings out on bends
- overtake at tram stops
- drive between platforms at tramway stations. Follow the direction signs
- park so that your vehicle obstructs the trams or would force other drivers to do so. Remember that a tram can't steer round an obstruction.

Section eight
⊕ Junctions

This section covers

- Approaching a junction
- The junction routine
- Turning
- Emerging
- Lanes at junctions
- Types of junction
- Junctions on hills
- Junctions on dual carriageways
- Roundabouts

⊙ Approaching a junction

A junction is a point where two or more roads meet. Junctions are hazards, where there's a significant risk of an incident occurring. Treat them with great care, no matter how easy they look.

Advance information

Look for information about the junction ahead, and the level of difficulty, such as

- the type of junction
- the amount of traffic
- warning signs
- road markings
- direction signs
- 'give way' and 'stop' signs
- traffic lights
- a break in the line of buildings
- changes in the road surface.

Priority

Usually, road signs and markings indicate priority. Where no priority is shown at a junction, take care and don't rush.

⊛ The junction routine

At every junction, use a routine such as Mirrors – Signal – Manoeuvre (MSM)/ Position – Speed – Look (PSL).

M Check in your mirrors to assess the speed and position of vehicles behind.

S Signal clearly and in good time.

M Manoeuvre – use PSL.

P Position your vehicle correctly and in good time. Early positioning lets other road users know what you're going to do.

S Adjust your speed as necessary.

L Look for other traffic when you reach a point from which you can see.

- Assess the situation.
- Decide whether to go or wait.
- Act accordingly.

If the road has lane markings

Use the correct lane for the direction you intend to take, and move into it as soon as you can.

Defensive driving

Where your path crosses or joins the path of other road users, there's an increased risk of a collision if you don't look and assess the situation correctly.

Check your mirrors, particularly for cyclists and motorcyclists, when turning at junctions. These road users can approach very quickly from behind and are less easy to see than a larger vehicle.

 Turning

Turning left

Use the MSM/PSL routine on approach.

Road position
Your road position should be well to the left.

Speed on approach
Left turns into minor roads are often sharper than right turns.

Make sure you

- slow down sufficiently
- select the correct gear

or you could swing wide of the corner and finish up on the wrong side of the road.

Other vehicles
Watch out for vehicles

- stopping to park, or parked, just before a left-hand junction
- parked around the corner and close to the junction
- approaching in the side road.

Pedestrians and cyclists

You should

- give way to pedestrians already crossing when you turn – they have priority
- keep a special lookout for cyclists coming up on your left
- take special care when crossing a cycle track, bus lane or cycle lane
- hold back and allow a cyclist to clear the junction before you turn. Don't overtake and then immediately turn across their path.

Avoid steering too early or too sharply; your nearside rear wheel might mount the kerb.

After the turn

- Check in your mirrors so you know what's following you on the new road.
- If it's safe to do so, increase your speed as you leave the junction.
- Make sure your signal has cancelled.

Turning right

Use the MSM/PSL routine on approach.

Road position

- Move into position early before turning right. It helps other drivers know what you intend to do.
- Position yourself as close to the centre of the road as is safe, so that vehicles can pass on your left if there's room. Take into account any parked vehicles or obstructions on the right-hand side of the road.
- In a one-way street, move to the right-hand side of the road when appropriate.

Speed of approach

- Adjust your speed in good time.
- Approach at a safe speed.

Oncoming traffic

- Watch out for oncoming traffic, especially motorcycles and bicycles, which are less easily seen.
- Watch particularly for vehicles overtaking oncoming traffic.
- Stop before you turn if you have any doubt about being able to cross safely.

Emerging vehicles

- Watch for vehicles waiting to emerge from the minor road.

Pedestrians

- Give way to pedestrians already crossing the minor road. They have priority.

Obstructions

- Look carefully for anything that could prevent you entering the minor road safely and leave you exposed on the wrong side of the road.

- You **MUST NOT** cross to the other side of the centre line until you're sure you can enter the minor road safely.

Turning

Check your mirrors for overtaking traffic one final time before you turn. Don't

- cut the corner

- accelerate fiercely. Your engine should be just pulling as you turn.

Missed turn

If you miss a turning, don't cause a problem by stopping suddenly. Go past the junction and turn round at the next safe opportunity.

⊕ Emerging

'Emerging' is when a vehicle leaves a minor road to join, cross or turn onto a major road.

You'll have to judge the speed and distance of any traffic on the road you intend to join or cross, and only emerge when it's safe to do so. This needs care and sometimes patience as well.

Assess the junction. Check road signs and markings and use the MSM/PSL routine.

'Give way' sign or lines

A 'give way' sign and lines across the road mean that you must give way to traffic which is already on the road you intend to enter.

If you can emerge without causing drivers or riders on that road to alter speed or course, you can do so without stopping. Otherwise, you must stop.

'Stop' sign

You must always stop at the stop line accompanying a 'stop' sign. The view at these junctions is limited and it will be impossible to safely assess the traffic on the road you intend to enter unless you stop as directed.

Move off only when

- you have a clear view

- you're sure it's safe.

Junctions without signs or road markings

Treat these with great care.

Don't assume you have priority at an unmarked junction.

MSM/PSL routine

M Look in your mirrors to assess what's behind.

S Signal left or right, as appropriate, in good time.

M Manoeuvre – use PSL.

P When turning left, keep well to the left. When turning right, position yourself, in good time, as close to the centre of the road as is safe. In a one-way street, move to the right-hand side of the road or the right-hand lane in good time.

S Reduce your speed. Be prepared to stop; you must give way to traffic on a major road.

L Look in all directions as soon as you can see clearly. Keep looking as you slow down or stop, if necessary, until you're sure it's safe to enter the major road.

Other traffic

Bends and hills could make it more difficult to see traffic coming towards you.

If the vehicle approaching from your right is signalling to turn left into your road, wait until you're sure the vehicle is turning and not just pulling up on the left beyond your road.

Motorcyclists are especially vulnerable at junctions. Look out for them

- coming from behind as you approach the junction
- travelling along the road you're joining, as they can be very difficult to see and their speed and distance can be difficult to judge.

When to go

You have to decide when to wait and when it's safe to go. That decision depends largely on your zone of vision.

Your zone of vision is the area you can see from your vehicle. It's determined by

- buildings and hedges
- bends in the road or contours in the land
- moving and parked vehicles
- obstructions
- available light and the weather.

As you approach a junction, your zone of vision into the other road usually improves. The last few metres are critical.

You can only decide whether to wait or go on when you've put yourself in a position where you can see clearly.

Watch out for cyclists, motorcyclists, powered wheelchairs/mobility scooters and pedestrians, as they're not always easy to see.

Sometimes parked vehicles interfere with your zone of vision, so that you have to inch carefully forward to see more. If another vehicle or a pedestrian isn't in your zone of vision, you're not usually in theirs.

Looking means that you need to assess the situation, decide whether it's safe and act accordingly.

An approaching vehicle, particularly a bus or a lorry, can easily mask another moving vehicle which may be overtaking.

After emerging

- Accelerate to a safe speed for the road and conditions as soon as possible.
- Make sure your indicator is cancelled.
- Use your mirrors to check the speed and position of traffic behind you.
- Keep a safe distance from the vehicle in front.
- Don't attempt to overtake until you've had time to assess the new road.

Defensive driving

When turning right, even though there might be little traffic approaching from the right, don't be tempted to move out and drive down the centre of the road hoping to fit into a gap in the traffic. If the road narrows, or if there are junctions or bollards, you'll have nowhere to go.

When turning left or right into a major road (see the advice earlier in this section), it takes time to complete the steering manoeuvre safely.

You need to accurately assess the speed of approaching traffic.

If in doubt, wait.

⊕ Lanes at junctions

When you approach a junction

- do so in the correct lane for the direction you intend to take; don't switch lanes to gain advantage
- look well ahead and watch for traffic and direction signs
- look out for signals from drivers who want to change lanes
- look out for drivers suddenly changing lanes without signalling.

Articulated or long vehicles

Stay clear of large vehicles at junctions. They need much more room than smaller vehicles and may be in a position that seems incorrect to you.

The driver often needs to swing out to the right before turning left, and to the left before turning right.

Be ready for them to stop if their way is blocked.

Passing minor roads

Look out for road signs indicating minor roads, even if you're not turning off.

Watch out for emerging vehicles; the driver's view is often reduced at narrow junctions and they might pull out in front of you.

If this happens, and you're not sure that the driver has seen you, slow down. Be prepared to stop.

Be tolerant and don't sound your horn aggressively or drive too close to the other vehicle.

Overtaking

Don't overtake at, or when approaching, a junction. A left-hand signal from the vehicle in front isn't an indication for you to pull out and pass.

The road surface

Be aware of the road surface: look for slippery surfaces or loose chippings. Avoid braking while you're turning. Plan ahead and brake well before the junction.

Adjust your overall speed when passing a series of minor roads so you can stop within the distance you can see to be clear.

⊙ Types of junction

There are five main types of junction

- T-junctions
- Y-junctions
- staggered junctions
- crossroads
- roundabouts.

Each type of junction can have many variations.

What you intend to do at the junction determines how you approach each type.

T-junctions

This is where a minor road joins a major road.

Normally, the road going straight ahead, along the top of the 'T', has priority.

The minor road may have

- a 'stop' sign and road markings

- a 'give way' sign and road markings
- 'give way' lines only
- no road sign or markings.

If you're emerging from the minor road, follow the procedure described earlier in this section.

Driving on the major road
If you want to go straight ahead

- take note of any road signs and markings
- watch out for vehicles emerging to turn left or right
- look for stopped vehicles waiting to turn into the minor road
- avoid overtaking any vehicle on the approach to a junction.

Hatch markings
On busier roads the major road is often split before and after the junction, with a turn-right filter lane protected by white diagonal hatch markings (or chevrons), surrounded by a broken or unbroken white line.

Join and leave the major road at these junctions exactly as you would a dual carriageway.

Areas of hatch markings painted on the road

- separate streams of traffic
- protect traffic waiting to turn right.

Where the boundary line is solid, don't enter except in an emergency.

Where the boundary line is broken, you shouldn't drive on these markings unless you can see it's safe to do so.

T-junctions on bends

Look well ahead for traffic signs and road markings indicating priority.

These junctions need extra care, especially when turning right from a major road that bends to the left, because

- your field of vision might be limited
- traffic might be approaching quickly from the other direction
- you'll need time to manoeuvre safely.

Your position before you turn mustn't endanger either oncoming traffic or yourself.

Wait until there's a safe gap in the traffic before turning.

Unmarked T-junctions

Never assume priority over another road if there are no road signs or markings. What's obvious to you might not be obvious to drivers on the other road.

Watch carefully for vehicles

- approaching the junction on the other road
- waiting at the junction
- emerging from the junction to join or cross your path.

Any vehicle crossing

- might assume priority and expect you to give way
- might not assume priority, but might have misjudged your speed or might not have seen you.

Such a vehicle creates a hazard. You should respond in a safe and sensible manner. Anticipate and adjust your speed accordingly to avoid a collision.

Defensive driving
Adjust your overall speed when passing a series of side roads on the left, and be prepared for vehicles emerging onto the major road.

Y-junctions

Y-junctions can be deceptive because they often call for little change in direction.

Normally, the road going straight ahead has priority and joining roads have either 'give way' or 'stop' signs. However, there are many exceptions. Watch out for oncoming vehicles positioned incorrectly. The drivers might have misjudged the junction.

Going straight ahead on the major road
- Look well ahead for road signs and markings.
- Watch out for vehicles emerging to turn left or right.
- You mustn't overtake when approaching any junction.

Emerging from a minor road
If the angle of approach to the major road is very sharp and from the right, the view to your left might be restricted.

If you position your vehicle towards the major road at a right angle as you approach the 'stop' or 'give way' lines, you'll improve your view.

This is especially important if your vehicle has no rear side windows – a van, for example.

Staggered junctions

These are junctions where roads join from both the right and the left, but not directly opposite each other, so that the path from one side road to the other is staggered.

Driving on the major road

Look well ahead for road signs and markings. Use the MSM/PSL routine.

Adjust your speed as necessary and prepare to stop, especially if your view is limited or if another driver's view of you might be limited.

Watch for vehicles

- emerging from either minor road to turn left or right
- on the major road turning into a minor road on the left or right
- driving across the main road from one minor road into the other.

Emerging

When emerging from a minor road to cross the major road and enter the other minor road, watch out for traffic approaching from both directions.

When it's safe to emerge, drive to the centre of the major road opposite the minor road you intend to enter and check the traffic again before entering the minor road.

If you're travelling only a short distance from one minor road to another one almost opposite, take extra care and make sure the gap in traffic is wide enough in both directions.

Look, assess, then decide. Either go if it's safe, or wait.

Crossroads

The procedure when turning at a crossroads is much the same as at any other junction.

You'll need to assess the crossroads as you approach, so look well ahead and check for road signs and markings that might indicate priority.

Driving on the major road

- Watch for road signs and markings.
- Watch for emerging traffic. Be especially careful of vehicles trying to cut across, using gaps in the traffic. They may misjudge your speed.
- Adjust your speed approaching the crossroads.

Turning right

Getting your position and speed right is vital. Look out for traffic on the road you're joining, as well as on the road you're leaving.

Check your mirrors before starting to turn, especially if you've had to wait.

Turning right when an oncoming vehicle is also turning right

When two vehicles approaching from opposite directions both want to turn right, there are two methods that can be used. Either method is acceptable, but it will usually be determined by

* the layout of the crossroads
* what course the other driver decides to take
* road markings.

Turning offside to offside

The advantage of this method is that both drivers can see oncoming traffic.

In congested traffic conditions, leave a space for approaching traffic to turn right.

Turning nearside to nearside

This method is less safe because the view of oncoming vehicles isn't clear. Watch out for oncoming traffic hidden by larger vehicles. Motorcyclists and cyclists are particularly vulnerable, as they can be hidden by any type of vehicle.

Be ready to stop for oncoming vehicles.

Road markings sometimes make this method compulsory.

Approaching on a minor road

If you approach a crossroads on a minor road and want to turn onto a major road, as long as the minor road opposite is clear, you should treat it as if you're emerging from a T-junction.

If you want to turn onto the major road, and another vehicle is approaching the crossroads from the minor road opposite, then

- if you're turning left or going straight on, you should proceed with extra caution and make sure no vehicle from the opposite direction is going to cross your path

- if you're turning right and the other vehicle is going ahead or turning left, you should normally wait for the other vehicle to clear the junction before you make your turn. Otherwise, you'd be cutting across their path

- if you're turning right and the other vehicle is turning right, you should try to make eye contact with the other driver to establish who should proceed, as neither of you has priority.

Defensive driving

Try to make eye contact with the driver of the approaching vehicle to determine which course is best. Your speed should allow you to stop if the other driver pulls out across your path.

Unmarked crossroads

Treat unmarked crossroads with extreme caution, since neither road has priority. Never assume you have priority if there are no signs or markings.

Drivers approaching on other roads might also assume they have priority, and an incident could result.

Proceed only when you're sure it's safe to do so.

Remember **LADA** – you must **L**ook, **A**ssess and **D**ecide, before you **A**ct.

Take extra care when your view is restricted by vehicles, walls, hedges or other obstructions.

⊙ Junctions on hills

Take care when negotiating junctions on hills.

Downhill junctions

- Moving into the correct position at a safe speed is essential when you're approaching a downhill junction.
- Make early use of the junction routine MSM/PSL, using brakes, gears and steering to get into position.
- Choose a point with a good all-round view before you look, assess, and decide to go or wait if necessary.

- Oncoming traffic may be travelling slowly because of the gradient. If you need to cross its path, don't move from your 'look' position until it's safe to do so.
- Don't block oncoming traffic and cause a hold-up.

Uphill junctions

Judge your position and speed accurately when climbing towards a junction. Your position is particularly important to drivers following you.

- If you intend to turn right, position your vehicle just to the left of the centre of the road. This allows following traffic to pass on your left if there's room.
- If you stop too far to the left, you could obstruct following drivers, causing them to stop unnecessarily.

Joining a hill at a junction
It's relatively easy to judge the speed of vehicles coming uphill.

Turning left at a T-junction into a road where you'll be driving uphill is reasonably easy. You don't have to cross traffic and it's easier to judge the flow of traffic coming uphill.

Turning right at a T-junction into a road where you'll be driving uphill is more difficult. You have to cross fast-moving traffic coming downhill. At the same time, you have to fit into the flow of traffic coming up from the left without blocking it.

⊕ Junctions on dual carriageways

On a dual carriageway, lanes in one direction are separated from lanes in the other direction by a central reservation. There may be a safety barrier along this central reservation.

Some dual carriageways are very similar to motorways, with slip roads to join and leave. However, motorway regulations don't apply and you may come across slow-moving traffic such as cyclists or farm tractors.

Emerging from a side road

To turn left

If there's no slip road, emerge as you would to turn left on to a major road (see the advice earlier in this section). If there's a slip road

- Use the slip road to adjust your speed to that of traffic on the main carriageway.
- Look for a gap in the traffic and then move into the left-hand lane.
- A quick sideways glance might be necessary to check the position of other vehicles.

- Stay in the left-hand lane until you get used to the speed of the traffic in the other lanes.
- Don't emerge unless you're sure you won't cause traffic to alter speed or course.

To turn right

You need to cross the first carriageway before you can join the carriageway you want.

- Assess whether the central reservation is deep enough to protect the full length of your vehicle.

- If the central reservation is deep enough, cross the first carriageway when it's safe and then wait within the central reservation for a gap in the traffic on the second carriageway.
- If the central reservation can't contain the length of your vehicle, you mustn't begin to cross until the dual carriageway is clear in both directions.
- Don't emerge unless you're sure you won't cause traffic on the major road to alter speed or course. This is particularly important if you're driving a longer vehicle, or towing a caravan or trailer.

Defensive driving

Watch out particularly for motorcyclists at these junctions. They can be difficult to see due to their narrow profile and their speed can be difficult to judge. They may also be hidden behind slower-moving traffic if they're overtaking.

After you join the carriageway

- Check your mirrors.
- Cancel any indicator signal.
- Drive in the left-hand lane.
- Accelerate as soon as you can to a suitable and safe speed for the new road.
- Don't overtake until you're used to the conditions on the new road.

Always look for signs that might indicate a higher speed limit on the dual carriageway. Allow for this when you assess the speed of oncoming traffic.

Leaving a dual carriageway

Turning left from a dual carriageway

If there's no slip road, use the same procedure you would for turning left into a side road.

- Use the MSM/PSL routine and get into the left-hand lane in plenty of time.
- Signal left much earlier than you would on ordinary roads because of the higher speeds involved.
- Reduce your speed in good time.

If there's a slip road on the left, use the same procedure as you would for leaving a motorway (see section 11).

Turning right from a dual carriageway

The central reservation sometimes has gaps for turning right. Watch out for special approach lanes.

- Use the MSM/PSL routine.
- Signal right and move into the right-hand lane much earlier than you would on normal roads because of the higher speeds involved.
- Observe any lane markings.
- Reduce your speed in good time.

Take particular care when turning. You might have to cross the path of fast oncoming traffic in two or more lanes. If in doubt, wait.

⊕ Roundabouts

Roundabouts allow traffic from different roads to merge or cross without necessarily stopping.

Priority

Before you enter a roundabout, you normally give way to any traffic approaching from your immediate right. However, you should keep moving if the way is clear.

In a few cases, traffic on the roundabout has to give way to traffic entering. Look out for 'give way' signs and road markings on the roundabout.

Some roundabouts have traffic lights (sometimes part-time) which determine priority.

Always use the MSM/PSL routine on approach.

Approaching a roundabout

Always look well ahead for the advance warning sign. At large or complex roundabouts, in particular, this will give you a clear picture of the layout of the roundabout, together with route directions.

The sign will enable you to select the most suitable lane in which to approach the roundabout.

Watch out also for advance warnings of appropriate traffic lanes at the roundabout. These are often backed up by road markings, which may include route numbers.

- Get into the correct lane in good time.
- Don't straddle lanes.
- Avoid changing lanes at the last moment.

Where possible, it's a good idea to look across the roundabout and identify the exit you want to take. This will help you to plan the safest course through the roundabout.

Procedure when entering/leaving a roundabout

Adopt the following procedures unless road signs or markings indicate otherwise.

Going left

- Indicate left as you approach.
- Approach in the left-hand lane.
- Keep to that lane on the roundabout.
- Maintain a left turn signal through the roundabout.

Going ahead

- No signal is necessary on approach.
- Approach in the left-hand lane. If you can't use the left-hand lane (because, for example, it's blocked), use the lane next to it.
- Keep to the selected lane on the roundabout.
- Check your mirrors, especially the nearside exterior mirror.
- Indicate left after you've passed the exit just before the one you intend to take.

Going right or full-circle

- Indicate right as you approach.
- Approach in the right-hand lane.
- Keep to that lane and maintain the signal on the roundabout.
- Check your mirrors, especially the nearside exterior mirror.
- Indicate left after you've passed the exit just before the one you intend to take.

More than three lanes

Where there are more than three lanes at the approach to the roundabout, use the most appropriate lane on approach and through the roundabout, unless road signs or markings tell you otherwise.

> **REMEMBER,** when using the right-hand lane to go ahead or turn right, be aware of traffic in the lane to your left.

Defensive driving

Always keep an eye on the vehicle in front as you're about to enter the roundabout.

Don't assume that the driver will keep going, as they may stop while you're still looking to the right. Many rear-end collisions happen this way. Make sure the vehicle has actually moved away.

Always check the vehicle in front before moving off.

Hazards

Roundabouts can be particularly hazardous areas. While negotiating the roundabout, you should be especially aware of

- pedestrians: in many areas, zebra crossings are located near the entrances to and exits from roundabouts. Even if there are no formal crossings, pedestrians may attempt to cross the road at these junctions. Always be aware of pedestrians who may be trying to cross the road

- cyclists and horse riders: they often keep to the outside of the roundabout even when intending to turn right. Take extra care and allow them plenty of room

- motorcyclists and cyclists: it's often difficult to see them on a roundabout

- long vehicles: because of their length, they might take a different course or straddle lanes as they approach the roundabout and as they go round it. Watch out for their signals and allow for the path the rear of their vehicle follows

- all vehicles: be prepared for vehicles to cross your path to leave at the next exit. Always be on the lookout for their signals

- the road surface: this can become polished and slippery, especially when wet. Avoid harsh braking and acceleration when on the roundabout.

Mini-roundabouts

Approach these in the same way as a roundabout: slow down and be prepared to give way to traffic from the right. Remember, however, there's less space to manoeuvre and less time to signal. For example, you may not have time to signal left when leaving. Also

- vehicles coming towards you might want to turn right. Give way to them
- be sure any vehicle on the roundabout is going to leave it before you join the roundabout
- beware of drivers who are using the roundabout for a U-turn
- you must pass round the central markings unless you're driving a large vehicle or towing a trailer which is physically incapable of doing so.

Try to avoid using a mini-roundabout to make a U-turn, but be aware that other drivers may do this.

Double mini-roundabouts
- Treat each roundabout separately and give way to traffic from your right.
- Take careful all-round observation before you enter.

Spiral roundabouts

Spiral roundabouts differ from normal roundabouts in that the lanes spiral outwards from the centre of the roundabout and each lane has a designated exit. Road markings are used to keep vehicles in the correct lane, and to guide them towards the appropriate exit.

When you encounter a spiral roundabout

- make sure you're in the correct lane when approaching and joining the roundabout
- follow the road markings for your lane to the relevant exit
- beware of drivers who may wish to join your lane from another.

If you need to change lanes, make sure you check it's safe before you do so and signal if necessary.

On a spiral roundabout, following the lanes and road markings will lead you to the appropriate exit.

Multiple roundabouts

At some complex junctions, a large roundabout can incorporate a series of mini-roundabouts at the intersections.

While each mini-roundabout follows the normal rules, with traffic travelling clockwise around them, traffic moving around the central roundabout travels in an anti-clockwise direction. Lanes, signs and road markings give directions, but these are complicated intersections requiring care and concentration.

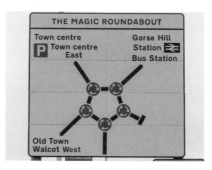

Look and assess
Keep a good lookout and assess the situation at each mini-roundabout. Look for direction signs well in advance.

Section nine
→ Manoeuvring

This section covers

- Before manoeuvring
- Reversing
- Turning around
- Parking

⊙ Before manoeuvring

You need to make choices based on legality, safety and convenience before manoeuvring. Your knowledge of The Highway Code, road signs, road markings and common sense will help you decide.

Ask yourself

- Is this a safe place?
- Is the manoeuvre within the law here?
- Is it a convenient place?

You must also ask yourself

- Will I be able to control my vehicle here?

You alone can answer that question. For example, an experienced driver might have no difficulty reversing downhill but, if you've not attempted it before, you might feel unsure of yourself. Only when you can say 'Yes' to all four questions can you be sure the place is suitable.

Other road users

Avoid inconveniencing other road users. Another driver or road user shouldn't have to slow down or change course.

Decide whether it's safe or whether it would be better to wait. Watch for other road users approaching, but avoid being too hesitant.

When other vehicles stop for you
Other drivers or riders may stop out of courtesy. However, you must satisfy yourself that they're actually stopping for you and not for some other reason. Check it's clear in all directions before you act upon any signal.

Use of the accelerator

Whichever manoeuvre you carry out, use the accelerator smoothly and keep close control. This saves fuel and cuts down on noise.

⊖ Reversing

Reversing needs practice until you become confident. Start by reversing in a straight line, then go on to reversing round corners and more complicated manoeuvres.

Your vehicle will respond differently in reverse gear. You can't feel the car turning with the steering as you would in forward gears, and you have to wait for the steering to take effect.

Move your vehicle slowly while in reverse. This way, you'll be able to respond accurately and safely to the steering movements.

How to sit

Turn slightly in your seat. If you're reversing straight back or to the left, hold the steering wheel near the top – at 12 o'clock – with your right hand, and low on the wheel with your left hand.

If this position is uncomfortable, you might find it easier to hold the wheel at 12 o'clock with your right hand. Your left arm can rest on the back of your seat or the back of the front passenger seat.

Seat belts

You may remove your seat belt while carrying out a manoeuvre that involves reversing. Don't forget to refasten it before driving off.

How to steer

When to begin steering?

Avoid turning the steering wheel while the vehicle is stationary ('dry' steering). It could cause damage to the tyres and increased wear in steering linkages.

As soon as you start moving, turn the steering wheel the way you want the rear of the vehicle to turn.

In reverse, it's often helpful to begin turning or straightening up sooner than seems necessary.

Remember, reverse slowly and you'll have time for

- unhurried control of the vehicle
- checks to the front, side and rear.

What to check

All-round observation is just as important when you're reversing as it is when you're going forward.

- Check for other road users before you reverse; motorcycles, cyclists and pedestrians are more difficult to see.
- Check to the rear, particularly for children playing behind the vehicle.
- Check all round – forward, behind, over both shoulders and in all mirrors. Do this before you reverse.

- If in doubt, get out and check.
- Keep checking all the time you're moving backwards, particularly behind you and to the sides, and especially at the point of turning.

Always be ready to stop.

Reverse-assist technology

Two main reverse-assist technologies are available in modern cars

- ultrasonic parking sensors that bleep when you approach an object such as a wall
- rear-facing cameras, where the image from the camera is shown on a screen on the dashboard.

Don't rely on these technologies alone. You should still observe all around you and throughout the manoeuvre.

⊛ Turning around

There are three methods of turning around

- using a side road
- turning in the road
- making a U-turn.

It's usually safest to use a side road. Alternatively, you could drive round a block of side streets.

On narrow or busy roads
It's normally safer to

- find a side road on the left or right, and use a turning off that road into which you can reverse
- go into the side road and use forward and reverse gears to turn around.

Remember also

- never to reverse into a main road from a side road
- to make sure it's safe to reverse, even if that means getting help
- not to reverse for a long distance, for your own safety and for that of other people. It's an offence to reverse further than necessary
- to always be ready to give way and stop.

Driveways
Another place you may need to reverse is when you're using your driveway.

You should reverse into your driveway, so you can drive out forwards onto the road.

If you need to turn around, don't use other people's driveways. You should drive on until you find a suitable side street.

Reversing into a side road on the left

After selecting a safe side road, use the Mirrors – Signal – Manoeuvre (MSM) routine as you approach the corner.

If a signal is necessary, don't indicate too early that you intend to pull up on the left after the corner. You could mislead the traffic behind you or anyone waiting to emerge. Your brake lights will tell the traffic behind you that you're slowing down.

Stop your vehicle reasonably close to the kerb and parallel to it. The sharper the corner, the further away from the kerb you need to be. Apply the parking brake and select neutral.

Observation and starting the manoeuvre

Turn slightly in your seat. You'll find control easier.

Assess the position of your vehicle in relation to the kerb through the rear window. When you've finished reversing into the side road, the vehicle should be the same distance from the kerb as when you started.

Select reverse gear. Set the engine revs to a steady hum. Bring the clutch pedal to the biting point and check all round.

When you're sure it's safe, start reversing.

As a general rule

Keep the clutch pedal at, or near, the biting point. Keep the vehicle moving slowly enough by making proper use of the accelerator, clutch and brakes. The combination of controls you use will depend on the slope of the road.

You should relate the position of the rear nearside wheel (just behind the back seat on most cars) to the edge of the kerb. Try to keep that wheel parallel to the kerb.

Start to turn left as the rear wheels reach the beginning of the corner. As a general guide, you should be able to follow the kerb as it disappears from view in the back window and reappears in the side window.

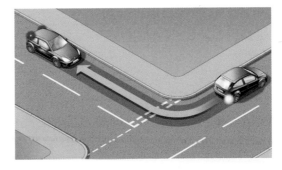

The amount of steering needed depends on how sharp the corner is. Remember to keep the vehicle moving slowly.

Continuous observation

Keep a good lookout throughout, but particularly before you start to turn. The front of your vehicle will swing out as you turn, and it's at this point that it will present the greatest hazard to any passing traffic.

Remember to check all blind spots before you start to turn. If any other road users are likely to be affected by your actions, pause until it's safe to continue.

Completing the manoeuvre

When you begin to see into the side road, be ready to straighten up the wheels.

Where there's a kerb in the new road, you can use the kerb to help you determine when to straighten up.

Try to keep the vehicle about the same distance from the kerb as when you started, and parallel to it.

> **REMEMBER,** keep on the lookout for other road users, particularly
>
> - pedestrians about to cross behind you
> - cyclists and motorcyclists
> - vehicles approaching from any direction.

Reversing into a side road on the right

A useful manoeuvre where

- there isn't a side road on the left
- you can't see through the rear window
- your view to the sides is restricted – for example, in a van or a loaded estate car.

It actually involves two manoeuvres.

Moving to the other side of the road after passing the junction

For this part of the manoeuvre you'll need to make

- full use of your mirrors
- a proper judgement of position and speed
- a proper assessment of the side road as you pass it.

Reversing into the side road itself

When doing this you'll need to

- stop your vehicle reasonably close to and parallel with the kerb – the sharper the turn, the further out you'll need to be
- sit so that you have a good view over your right shoulder and are still able to see forward and to the left.

All-round observation is even more important on a right-hand reverse because you're on the wrong side of the road, in the path of oncoming traffic.

- When you're sure it's safe, start reversing. Don't rush, but keep the vehicle moving by using the controls as for a left-hand reverse.
- It's easier to judge your distance from the kerb because you can look directly at it.
- Make sure that you reverse far enough back so that you can join the left-hand side of the road before emerging.

Throughout the manoeuvre, keep a good lookout for other road users, particularly

- pedestrians about to cross behind you
- cyclists and motorcyclists
- vehicles approaching from any direction.

Turning in the road

You'll find this manoeuvre useful for turning when you can't find a side road or an opening.

Keep the vehicle moving slowly while steering briskly during this manoeuvre. Close control of the clutch is essential.

Before you turn

Choose a place where

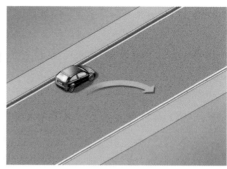

- you have plenty of room
- there's no obstruction in the road or on the pavement.

Stop on the left. Avoid lampposts or trees near the kerb.

Select first gear and prepare to move.

Check all round, especially your blind spots. Give way to passing vehicles.

Turning across the road

Move forward slowly in first gear, turning your steering wheel briskly to full right lock. Your aim is to get the vehicle at a right angle across the road.

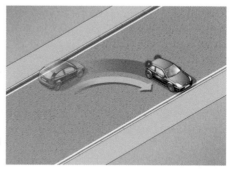

Just before you reach the opposite kerb, still moving slowly, begin to steer briskly to the left. Your wheels will then be ready to reverse left.

As you near the kerb, push the clutch pedal down and use the footbrake to stop. It may be necessary to use the parking brake to hold the vehicle if there's a camber in the road.

To reverse

Select reverse gear.

Check the way is clear all round. Look through the rear window over your left shoulder to start with. Reverse slowly across the road, turning the steering wheel as far to the left as possible (full left lock).

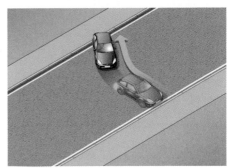

Look round over your right shoulder as the vehicle nears the rear kerb. At the same time, turn your steering wheel briskly to the right.

Push the clutch pedal down and use the footbrake to stop.

Your wheels should be pointing to the right, ready to drive forward again.

To drive forward again

Apply the parking brake if necessary, and select first gear.

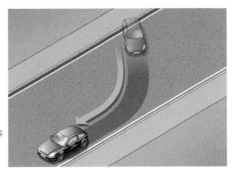

Check that the road is clear and drive forward when it's safe to do so.

You might have to reverse again if the road is narrow or your vehicle is difficult to steer.

Straighten up on the left-hand side of the carriageway.

If your vehicle is likely to overhang the kerb at any point, first make sure there are no pedestrians nearby or any street furniture (lampposts, bins, signs) or trees that you might hit.

REMEMBER, all-round observation is essential throughout the manoeuvre.

Making a U-turn

A U-turn means turning the car right round without any reversing.

You may have to cross lines of opposing traffic to complete a U-turn.

If you need to make a U-turn, consider carrying out the manoeuvre in a wide, quiet road or at a large roundabout.

Never make a U-turn

- on a motorway

- in a one-way street

- wherever a road sign forbids it.

Before making a U-turn

Always ask yourself

- Is it safe?

- Is it legal?

- Is it convenient?

- Is the road wide enough?

If in doubt, don't attempt it.

Observation

Good all-round observation is particularly important before a U-turn.

It's essential to check your blind spot just before starting to turn.

Be aware that other drivers won't be expecting you to make a U-turn.

Avoid mounting the kerb.

 Parking

Whenever possible, park off the road or in a car park. If you have to park on the road, choose a safe place.

Ask yourself

- Is it safe?
- Is it convenient?
- Is it legal?

Road signs and markings

These will help you recognise places where you shouldn't park your car, such as

- the approach to pedestrian crossings
- school entrances
- near junctions
- other restricted places.

Road signs and markings will also tell you if there are restrictions

- at certain times of the day
- on particular days of the week.

In general, The Highway Code lists places where you should not or must not park. Make sure you know these.

Never use your hazard warning lights as an excuse for stopping where you shouldn't.

Never copy another driver's bad example. It won't excuse you from any penalties.

Parking on the road

Always use the MSM routine and signal, if necessary, before you park.

Try not to touch the kerb when you park. Scraping your tyres can weaken them, possibly with serious results.

Don't park so near to other vehicles that it will be difficult for you and them to get out. This is especially important if the other vehicle is displaying a Blue Badge. Allow room for a wheelchair to be manoeuvred or loaded in these cases. As a general rule, park parallel with, and close to, the kerb.

Always switch off the engine and headlights (and fog lights) when you park. Before you leave the vehicle, make sure that it's in gear and the parking brake is applied firmly.

Remember that unless your vehicle is parked in an authorised parking place, it could cause an obstruction. Never leave your vehicle where it could prevent emergency vehicles passing, particularly in narrow residential roads where vehicles often park on both sides of the road.

You'll acquire better parking skills with practice.

When parking you should

- take care to plan your parking
- always manoeuvre your vehicle slowly
- never park in a space reserved for a Blue Badge holder unless you, or the passenger you're carrying, are the holder of a Blue Badge.

You should also make sure that you won't hit another road user, or cause another driver or rider to swerve, when you open your car door. Look out particularly for bicycles and motorcycles. Make sure any passengers do the same and also that they don't hit pedestrians on the pavement when opening their door.

Consideration

Always consider other road users when you park. Don't park where you would cause an obstruction – for example, where the kerb has been lowered for disabled access, or across a driveway or entrance.

Don't park on the pavement, as this could obstruct or seriously inconvenience pedestrians, people in wheelchairs or with visual impairments, and people with prams or pushchairs. In London, it's illegal to park either partially or wholly on the pavement.

In some areas, where the local authority wants to keep the road free from parked cars, signs will indicate that you're permitted to park on the verge or footway. This is an exception; parking on verges or footways anywhere else could lead to a fine.

Parking on hills

If you park your vehicle on a hill, remember the following.

Parking facing uphill

- Stop your vehicle as close as you can to the nearside kerb, if there is one.
- Leave your steering wheel turned to the right. If the vehicle rolls backwards, the front wheels will be stopped by the kerb.
- If there's no kerb, leave your steering wheel turned to the left. If the vehicle rolls backwards, it won't roll across the road.
- Leave the vehicle in first gear, with the parking brake firmly applied.

Parking facing downhill

- Leave your steering wheel turned to the left. The kerb should stop any forward movement.
- Leave your vehicle in reverse gear, with the parking brake firmly applied.

Leaving a gap

Parking on a hill is more difficult than on the flat and can take more room. You should leave a bigger gap to allow extra space for manoeuvring. A larger gap will help both you and others.

Vehicles with automatic transmission

When you park facing either uphill or downhill in a vehicle with automatic transmission, make sure your vehicle is stationary and the parking brake is firmly applied before using the selector setting 'P' (Park).

If your vehicle has no 'P' setting

* turn your front wheels to the kerb
* make sure your parking brake is firmly applied.

Reverse parking

This makes use of the vehicle's manoeuvrability in reverse gear to park in a restricted space.

Remember, while you're carrying out this manoeuvre, you could be a hazard to other road users.

Position and observation

Good all-round observation is essential throughout this manoeuvre.

Don't start to manoeuvre if you're likely to endanger other road users.

Other drivers might not be aware of your intentions, so before you pull up at the place where you've chosen to park, remember to carry out the MSM routine.

Positioning your vehicle

Stop your vehicle reasonably close to, and parallel with, the parked vehicle ahead of the gap.

Your vehicle should be about level with, or slightly ahead of, the parked vehicle. This will depend on the size of the gap and the length of your vehicle.

You can start practising using only one parked car. When you've mastered the technique, you should be able to park between two vehicles.

The gap should be at least one-and-a-half times the length of your own vehicle.

Manoeuvring into the gap

Apply the parking brake, if necessary. Show your brake lights by pressing the footbrake. Select reverse gear to show the reversing light(s). This warns other road users of your intentions. Check all round.

Bring the clutch up to biting point and, if it's still safe, release the parking brake if you applied it. Ease the clutch pedal up just enough to start to move.

Hold the clutch pedal steady at, or just above, the biting point. Reverse slowly using left lock, but watch the corner of the parked vehicle.

> **REMEMBER,** keep a good lookout for other road users throughout this manoeuvre, particularly
>
> • pedestrians
>
> • oncoming vehicles
>
> • passing traffic.

Don't forget to look round as you begin to reverse into the space. The front of your vehicle could swing out into the path of passing traffic.

Try lining up the rear offside (right-hand side) of your vehicle with the nearside headlight of the vehicle behind the space you're entering.

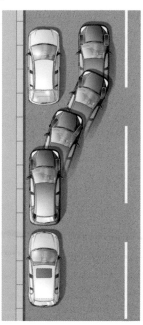

Straightening up in the gap

Straighten up by taking off the left lock. Keep a careful eye on the position of your vehicle. There's a danger of 'clipping' the vehicle in front at this point.

When you're sure the front of your vehicle is clear of the parked vehicle, use sufficient right lock to gradually bring your vehicle parallel with, and reasonably close to, the nearside kerb. Straighten up by taking the right lock off and adjust the position of your vehicle as necessary.

Defensive driving

Other road users may not understand your intention. Showing your reversing lights should help. If another vehicle pulls up close behind, move on and park somewhere else.

Parking-assist technology

Some modern vehicles are fitted with technology which assists drivers in parking their vehicle.

The technology uses a variety of sensors to detect obstacles and is controlled by instruments on the dashboard.

This vehicle technology shouldn't be relied upon solely and good observation should be used at all times.

Car parks

Arrow markings and signs show you which lanes to take inside the car park. Follow these. Don't drive against the traffic flow.

Indoor car parks
Use dipped headlights in multi-storey, underground or other indoor car parks. This helps other drivers and pedestrians to see you.

Parking
Unless there's space at the end of the row, you'll have to fit in between two other vehicles.

Check that there's

- enough space for you to centre your vehicle
- enough room to open the doors safely.

Whether you're reversing in or going forward, move slowly so the steering has the maximum effect and gives you time to make corrections.

Reverse parking
Unless other cars are badly parked, you'll nearly always find it best to reverse into a parking space. You'll have a better view when you drive away, especially with back-seat passengers or at night.

You can line up by

- driving forward past the space and then turn as you reverse into the parking space, or
- turning as you approach the space, so that you're in a position from which you can reverse into the space.

Choose whichever method suits the configuration of the car park or a combination of both.

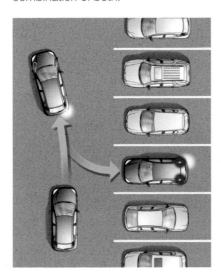 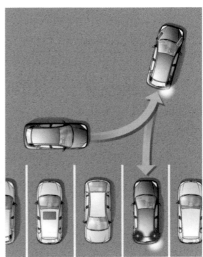

Park squarely in the marked spaces

Always try to park squarely in the marked spaces, otherwise the car next to you might have to squeeze in, or there might not be enough room for its doors to be opened.

Parking forwards

Some car parks are designed for you to park forwards to make it easier to load shopping. In these cases take extra care as you reverse out of the parking space because pedestrians and vehicles may be passing behind.

You might also find it more difficult to drive out because your wheels may be at the wrong angle when you reverse to leave.

If you haven't enough room to go forward all the way into a tight space, you might need to nose in then back out and straighten up to move into the space.

Remember the following when parking.

- Before entering the car park, use your mirrors and signal.
- Look at the layout, markings and signs to guide you. Choose a space.
- Use your mirrors and signal again if necessary.
- Check your position and keep your speed down. Look out for pedestrians.
- Make sure your vehicle is parked squarely between the white lines in one space.

Find out more about parking at

britishparking.co.uk

Take great care when reversing out of a parking space. Check for pedestrians and vehicles behind you.

Section ten

➡ Defensive driving

This section covers

- Defensive driving
- Observation
- Signalling
- Hazards
- Lighting and weather conditions
- Other road users

⊕ Defensive driving

The roads today are busier than they've ever been, and they're getting busier all the time.

As well as heavy traffic, the driver often has to cope with unpredictable, irrational, offensive and sometimes dangerous driving behaviour. In such conditions, drivers need to learn and practise a suitable strategy.

That strategy is called 'defensive driving', sometimes known as 'planned driving'.

Defensive driving is based on effective observation, good anticipation and control. It's about always questioning the actions of other road users and being prepared for the unexpected, so as not to be taken by surprise.

Defensive driving involves

- awareness
- planning
- anticipating
- staying in control

and driving with

- responsibility
- care
- consideration and courtesy.

Safety

You should put safety above all else. This means having real concern not only for your own safety but also for that of other road users, including the most vulnerable – those walking or riding.

Expect other people to make mistakes, and be ready to slow down or stop – even if you think you have priority.

Never assume that other road users will follow the rules. They may break them, either deliberately or accidentally. Your safety lies mainly in your own hands. The better your control of your vehicle and road space, the safer you'll be.

A good example

Your driving should always set a good example to other road users, and any passengers you may have.

Your good example could make a deep impression on another driver, especially a learner or inexperienced road user, and perhaps save lives in the future. Good driving practice could also have a positive effect on your passengers – especially children.

Reducing hostility

With defensive driving, you'll show patience and anticipation. This will help to reduce the number of incidents which result in

- open hostility
- abusive language
- threats
- physical violence.

Avoid the kind of driving that

- causes offence to other road users
- provokes reaction
- creates dangerous situations.

Never drive in a spirit of competition on a public road. Competitive or aggressive driving is the opposite of defensive driving. It increases the risks to everyone.

Make allowances

Make allowances if someone pulls out or turns in front of you: hold back and increase the distance between you and them. That way, if they brake suddenly, you've given yourself a greater safety margin.

When you check in the mirrors, look and then act sensibly on what you see.

If someone else is driving recklessly, keep calm and don't be tempted to retaliate.

⊕ Observation

Look at other road users and assess their

- speed
- driving behaviour
- possible intentions.

At junctions, there's no point in just looking if your view is obstructed by, for example, parked vehicles. You must move carefully into a position where you can see, without moving into the path of passing traffic. Remember LADA

- **L**ook
- **A**ssess and
- **D**ecide before you
- **A**ct.

That's what effective observation is all about.

Observing what's ahead

As a defensive driver you'll constantly watch and interpret what's happening ahead, to the side and, through frequent use of the mirrors, behind you.

You'll always drive at a speed that allows you to stop safely within the distance you can see to be clear.

Approaching a bend

Ask yourself

- Can I see the full picture?
- How sharp is the bend?
- Am I in the right position?
- Is my speed right?
- What might I meet?
- Could I stop if I had to?

Approaching a junction

Ask yourself

- Have I seen the whole junction?
- Can other drivers see me?
- Am I sure they've seen me?
- Have I got an escape route if they haven't?

Left-hand-drive vehicles

If you're driving a left-hand-drive vehicle, be aware of how this affects your field of view and make full use of your mirrors.

Zone of vision at a junction

Your zone of vision is what you can see as you look forward and to the side from your vehicle. As you approach a junction, your zone of vision into the other road usually improves.

You may need to get very close before you can look far enough into another road to see whether it's safe to proceed. The last few metres are often crucial.

Sometimes, parked vehicles restrict your view so much that you need to stop and creep forward for a proper view before you emerge.

- Look in every direction before you emerge.
- Keep looking as you join the other road.
- Be ready to stop.
- Use all the information available to you; for example, look through the windows of parked vehicles.
- Where your view is restricted, it can help to use the reflections in shop windows to see approaching traffic.

Screen pillar obstruction
Windscreen pillars can cause obstructions to your view of the road. You should be aware of this effect, particularly when

- approaching junctions and bends
- emerging from junctions.

Road users such as motorcyclists, cyclists and pedestrians may be completely obscured by the pillar.

You should be aware that some vehicles have larger blind spots than others, and groups of pedestrians, a motorcyclist or even a small car can be hidden from view. You may need to move around in your seat to overcome the effect of these blind spots.

If you can't see the driver's face, they won't be able to see you.

Other road users

It can be difficult to see some other road users, especially when you're emerging from a junction. Those who are particularly at risk are

- pedestrians – they frequently cross at junctions and may find it difficult to judge the speed and course of approaching traffic
- cyclists – they can be difficult to see, as they may be obscured by trees and other objects, especially if they're riding close to the side of the road. They might be approaching faster than you expect
- motorcyclists – like cyclists they're often less easy to see than other traffic, but they're likely to be moving much faster than cyclists.

Always make sure it's safe before emerging from a junction.

Never rely solely on a quick glance – give yourself time to take in the whole scene.

If another vehicle or a pedestrian isn't in your zone of vision, you're not usually in theirs.

Making eye contact with other road users helps you to know whether they've seen you.

Observing traffic behind you

Before you move off, change direction or change speed, you need to know how your action will affect other road users, including those behind you.

You must also be aware of traffic likely to overtake.

Using your mirrors

Using your mirrors regularly enables you to keep up to date with what's happening behind you **without** losing sight of what's going on in front.

Look as far behind in your mirrors as you look ahead through the windscreen. By looking only at the following vehicle you might miss important information that could help you to plan your manoeuvre.

Your mirrors must be clean and properly adjusted to give a clear view.

When should you use your mirrors?

Before you signal or make any manoeuvre. For example, before

- moving off
- changing direction
- turning right or left
- overtaking
- changing lanes
- slowing or stopping
- opening a car door.

Looking around

You should look around to check your blind spot before moving off.

A quick sideways glance

This is helpful, for example, to check your blind spot

- before you change lanes, especially on a motorway or dual carriageway
- where traffic is merging from the left or right.

Take great care in looking around while on the move, particularly when driving at high speeds. In the time you take to look around, you could lose touch with what's happening in front of you.

Remember that a vehicle travelling at 70 mph (112 km/h) covers around 30 metres (about 100 feet) every second. Even if it only takes half a second to look around, you'll still have travelled 15 metres (about 50 feet) in that time.

Just looking isn't enough

You must act sensibly on what you see. Take note of the speed, behaviour and possible intentions of traffic behind you.

Another driver's blind spot

Avoid driving in another driver's blind spot for any longer than necessary. This is a particular problem with left-hand-drive lorries, as the driver may not be able to see you and may think it's safe to change lane or overtake.

Approaching green traffic lights

Ask yourself

- How long have they been on green?
- Are there many vehicles already waiting at either side of the junction? (If there's a queue, the lights are probably about to change.)
- Do I have time to stop?
- Can the vehicle behind me stop? If it's a large goods vehicle, it might need a greater distance in which to pull up.

Don't

- try to beat the traffic signals by accelerating
- wait until the last moment to brake. Harsh braking can cause skids and loss of control.

Sometimes, drivers anticipate the change of signals and move away while the lights are still showing red and amber. This isn't a safe practice and could result in a collision. Safety cameras are placed at some traffic lights and these record how drivers behave at the lights – including when they move away too soon.

Traffic signals not working

Where traffic signals aren't working, treat the situation as you would an unmarked junction and proceed with great care.

⊕ Signalling

Signal to warn others of your intention and to help other road users. Remember that people could be using the road in a variety of ways.

Road users include

- drivers of other motor vehicles
- drivers of large or slow-moving vehicles
- motorcyclists
- users of powered mobility vehicles
- cyclists
- pedestrians
- horse riders
- crossing supervisors
- road workers
- persons directing traffic.

Signal clearly and in good time.

Give only the signals shown in The Highway Code.

Direction indicator signals

Help other road users to understand your intention by

- signalling in good time, so that they have time to see and react to your signal
- positioning yourself correctly and in good time for the manoeuvre you intend to make.

Conflicting signals

A signal with the left indicator means 'I am going to turn left' **or** 'I am going to stop on the left'.

Avoid using your left indicator before a left-hand junction if you intend to stop on the left just after the junction. A driver waiting at that junction might think you're turning left and drive out into your path.

- Wait until you've passed the junction, then indicate that you intend to stop.

- Reduce speed by braking gently, so that your brake lights warn drivers behind you.

If you're waiting to emerge and a vehicle seems to be indicating its intention to turn left, wait until you can see that it's actually going to turn before you pull out. Otherwise, you might drive into its path.

REMEMBER, roundabouts often have several lanes of traffic, with vehicles changing speed and direction. It's important that you give any signals correctly and at the right time.

Warning signals

The horn

There are very few situations in which you'll need to use the horn.

Using the horn doesn't

- give you priority
- mean you don't have to drive safely.

Sound it only if

- you think someone may not have seen you
- you want to warn other road users of your presence; for example, at blind bends or junctions.

Avoid using a long blast on the horn, as this can alarm pedestrians. If a pedestrian doesn't react to a short signal on the horn, it could mean they're deaf. If possible, avoid sounding the horn near animals; it may increase the danger because their reaction will be unpredictable.

Never use your horn to signal your unhappiness at another driver's actions. Don't use it to attract the attention of someone at the side of the road, to signal your arrival to someone, or as a farewell.

Unless a moving vehicle poses a danger, it's illegal to use your horn

- when stationary
- when driving at night (11.30 pm to 7.00 am) in a built-up area.

Flashing your headlights

This is an alternative to the horn and has the same meaning: to warn others that you're there.

Don't flash your headlights at anyone to indicate that they should go ahead or turn.

If someone flashes their headlights at you

Before you act on the signal, make sure

- you understand what they mean
- the signal is meant for you.

Never assume it's a signal to proceed.

Ask yourself

- What's the other driver trying to tell me: 'Stop', 'Go', 'Turn', 'Thank you'?
- If I move, will it be safe?
- Is the signal intended for me or for another road user?
- Am I causing a hold-up by staying where I am?
- Is the other driver really signalling, or were those headlights flashed accidentally?

Take your time and watch for other road users who may think the signal was for them.

On motorways and dual carriageways

If you think a warning is necessary, flashing your headlights is usually better than using your horn. Be alert for such warnings from other drivers.

If a driver behind starts flashing their headlights and driving dangerously close

- stay calm
- don't be intimidated.

Move back to the left as soon as you can do so safely, without cutting in on vehicles that you've overtaken.

> **REMEMBER,** the only official meaning for the flashing of headlights is to let other road users know you're there – the same as using the horn.

⊕ Hazards

A hazard is any situation that could require you to adjust your speed or change course. Hazards can be either static or moving.

To identify a static hazard, you must look well ahead for clues such as

- road signs
- changes in road conditions
- parked vehicles
- junctions.

Moving hazards include all road users, such as

- other vehicles
- motorcyclists
- users of powered mobility vehicles
- cyclists
- pedestrians
- horses and riders
- road workers
- persons directing traffic
- loose animals.

Remember, as soon as you've recognised a hazard, you must assess

- how to deal with it safely
- how your actions will affect other road users.

Allowing time and space

Always leave yourself enough time and space to cope with what's ahead.

- Scan the road ahead, in the far and near distance – especially in town, where things change quickly.
- Check your mirrors frequently so that you always know what's happening behind you.
- Watch for clues about what's likely to happen next.

For example, a parked car is a potential hazard if the driver is sitting in it, or you see vapour from the exhaust in cold weather. This could indicate that

- a door might open suddenly
- the car might pull out without warning.

If you can see underneath a parked vehicle and notice someone's feet at the other side, remember that the pedestrian might not be able to see you and could step into the road.

Effective observation and anticipation are your main defence.

Always keep a good separation distance between you and the vehicle in front. Leave a gap of at least one metre or yard for each mph of your speed, or use the two-second rule.

In bad conditions, leave at least double the distance or a four-second time gap.

Tailgating

When a vehicle behind is too close to you, ease off the accelerator very gradually and increase the gap between you and the vehicle in front. This will give you a greater safety margin. If another road user pulls into the space in front of you, drop back until you've restored your safety margin.

Large vehicles

Take extra care when following large vehicles, especially at roundabouts, junctions and entrances.

The driver might have to take a course that seems incorrect to you; for example, moving out to the right before turning left.

In wet weather, large vehicles throw up a lot of spray. This can make it difficult for you to see the road ahead, so drop back until your view improves.

Keep well back from any large vehicles that are in the process of manoeuvring to the left or right.

Be patient and don't try to pass while they're manoeuvring.

Large vehicles can also block your view. Your ability to see and plan ahead will be improved if you keep back.

REMEMBER, if you're following a large vehicle too closely, the driver might not be able to see you in their mirrors. If you can't see their mirrors, the driver can't see you.

Recognising hazards

Events can happen at the same time, or in quick succession. In the illustration above, the driver of the blue car must pull out to pass the stationary coach, but

- is the green car really going to turn left? (The driver might have forgotten to cancel the indicator from a previous turn)
- if the green car does turn, will the pedestrian with the briefcase decide to cross?
- when will the driver of the blue car notice the red car, which may want to turn left?

If you're travelling too fast, you're unlikely to be able to cope with all the events at once. This is how other road users, who might not be doing anything wrong, can turn a straightforward piece of driving into a hazardous situation.

REMEMBER, the defensive driver is always

- in the correct position
- travelling at the correct speed for the road, traffic and weather conditions
- in the right gear
- anticipating and prepared for the next change in the traffic situation.

The action you need to take will vary from one hazard to another. Any action that involves a change of speed or course is called a manoeuvre.

A manoeuvre can vary from slowing slightly to turning on a very busy road.

Approaching any hazard

Follow the MSM/PSL routine every time you recognise a hazard.

Mirror(s)

Check the position of traffic following you.

Signal

If necessary, signal your intention to change course or slow down. Signal clearly and in good time.

Manoeuvre

Carry out the manoeuvre if it's still safe to do so. Manoeuvre has three phases – Position, Speed, Look.

Position

Get into the correct position in good time to negotiate the hazard. This helps other road users to anticipate what you intend to do.

Positioning yourself too late can be dangerous. Ask yourself

- Can I see and be seen?
- What are my options?

Don't do anything that would obstruct another driver or rider.

If lanes are closed or narrow because of roadworks, obey the temporary road signs and move into the correct lane in good time.

- Don't reduce your safety margin by responding at the last moment.
- Don't overtake and squeeze in later on – you'll only increase the frustration of drivers already waiting.

Speed

Ask yourself

- Could I stop in time if the vehicle in front braked suddenly?
- Am I going too fast for the road conditions?
- Am I in the right gear to keep control?

Slow down as you approach a hazard. Always be ready to stop.

Look

Keep looking ahead to assess all possible dangers. This is particularly important at a junction. Look in all directions, even if you're not turning.

If you're joining a road, keep looking as you turn from one road to the other. Watch out for

- traffic turning across your path
- motorcyclists, as they're more difficult to see and can easily be hidden behind other vehicles
- pedestrians.

Country roads

FACTS Deaths are disproportionately likely to occur on rural roads: in 2013, these roads carried 53% of traffic, but accounted for around two-thirds of road deaths.

Take extra care and reduce your speed as you approach bends and junctions.

Bends and junctions

Bends can often be sharper than you think they're going to be. They may also obscure other, more vulnerable road users, such as pedestrians, horse riders and cyclists, or larger slow-moving farm vehicles which may take up the whole width of the road.

Junctions, especially minor junctions or entrances to farm premises, aren't always signed and may be partially hidden.

Other road users

Many roads in country areas have no pavements or footpaths. Where this is the case, pedestrians are advised to walk on the right-hand side of the road so they can see oncoming traffic. However, you should always be prepared to find people walking or jogging on your side of the road.

Horse riders and cyclists are also often found on country roads. Give them plenty of space, always be patient and wait until it's safe before overtaking, especially on narrow or winding roads.

Narrow roads with passing places

On single-track roads, look well ahead and be prepared to stop. If you see an oncoming vehicle

- pull into the passing place if it's on the left
- be prepared to reverse into a passing place if necessary
- wait opposite a passing place on the right.

Avoid driving onto the verge; it may be soft, with drainage ditches or gulleys that could damage your vehicle's suspension.

If your view ahead is restricted by hedges or bends, reduce your speed so that you can stop safely if necessary.

If another driver wishes to overtake, pull into or stop opposite a passing place to allow them to do so.

> See the Don't Risk It website for advice on driving on country roads.
>
> **dontriskit.info/country-roads**

⊕ Lighting and weather conditions

Driving at night

You can't see as far ahead at night, so try to get help from

- illuminated signs
- reflective signs
- reflectors between white lines
- the glow of vehicle headlights on trees and buildings, indicating a corner or junction.

Be aware of the hazards of driving at night. In particular

- it can be difficult to judge distance and speed from the headlights of approaching vehicles
- bright lights on some vehicles make it difficult to see less bright lights, such as those of cyclists or low-powered motorcycles
- keep a good lookout for pedestrian crossings, traffic lights and other road users, and don't let shop and advertising signs distract you.

More information about driving at night can be found in section 13.

Weather conditions

Many different weather conditions can make driving more difficult.

Rain and wet roads can create hazards at any time of year.

Rain

Rain makes headlights less effective at night. On dark and poorly lit roads, slow down and watch for unlit objects such as roadworks, builders' skips or parked cars. Drive more slowly and carefully in rain. Match your speed to the conditions.

Wet roads

Stay alert to the road surface because you might have to brake. Ask yourself

* Is the road slippery?
* Is it a good surface on which to brake?

If the surface is wet, allow more time to stop.

A wet road means

* less efficient braking
* a longer distance needed to stop
* a greater risk of skidding.

On wet roads, take the conditions into account and reduce your speed.

Don't splash pedestrians as you drive through puddles. This is an offence and you could be prosecuted.

At night, wet roads can

* increase distracting reflected light
* make unlit objects very difficult to see.

More information about driving in different weather conditions can be found in section 12.

⊕ Other road users

You, as a driver, aren't the only person using the road. Most other types of road user are more vulnerable than you are because they're less well protected in the event of a collision.

Cyclists

Make allowances for cyclists. They have every right to be on the road, but they're vulnerable. The younger the cyclist, the more vulnerable they're likely to be.

Allow cyclists plenty of room; they might

- glance round, showing they could be about to move out or turn
- veer suddenly into your path
- be carrying items that may affect their control and balance
- weave about, slow down, or stop on uphill gradients
- swerve around potholes or drain covers or to avoid being hit by carelessly opened vehicle doors
- have problems in bad weather, particularly when there are strong side winds
- have difficulty on poor road surfaces or where tramlines are set into the road.

Look out for them particularly when you're

- in slow-moving traffic
- emerging from a junction
- negotiating a roundabout.

They could be travelling faster than you first think, so never rely solely on a quick glance.

Don't assume that cyclists will always adopt a position on the left of the road or use cycle lanes; it's sometimes safer for them to adopt a more central position in the road. Don't drive aggressively or try to intimidate them.

When travelling at low speeds, such as at junctions, cyclists are likely to be more unstable and therefore more vulnerable. Give them plenty of room.

FACTS Pedal cyclists accounted for 11% of all road casualties in 2013: 6% of all road accident fatalities, 15% of all serious injuries and 10% of all slight injuries.

Motorcyclists

Make allowances for motorcyclists.

Much of what has been said about cyclists also applies to motorcyclists. They're very vulnerable because, like cyclists, they're much smaller than other vehicles, with a narrow profile that makes them difficult to see. They can also appear to be further away than they actually are, making it difficult to judge when it's safe to emerge in front of them or turn across their path. However, motorcyclists travel much faster than cyclists, so situations can develop much more quickly than those involving cyclists.

Many road traffic incidents happen because drivers fail to notice motorcyclists, so look out for them when

- emerging from junctions. The motorcyclist may be travelling along the major road and may be hidden behind other traffic. They may also be hidden by signs, trees, street furniture, etc

- turning into a road on your right. The motorcyclist may be following, overtaking or approaching you. Oncoming motorcyclists may be particularly difficult to see if they're being followed by a larger vehicle

- changing lanes or moving out to overtake slower-moving or parked vehicles.

> **REMEMBER,** motorcyclists and cyclists are harder to see than other vehicles and are exposed to bad weather, slippery roads and uneven surfaces. Look out for them, especially at junctions.

Think once

Think twice

Think bike!

Pay special attention to motorcycles and scooters displaying L plates. The riders of these machines may be riding on the road with very little experience, so they're particularly vulnerable.

Motorcycles in windy weather

Windy weather has a big effect on motorcyclists; they can be blown into your path, so

- if you're overtaking a motorcyclist, allow extra room
- if a motorcyclist in front of you is overtaking a high-sided vehicle, keep well back, as they could be blown off course
- be particularly aware of motorcyclists where there are side-wind warning signs.

Powered vehicles used by disabled people

These small vehicles (also known as invalid carriages) can be used on the pavement and on the road. They're extremely vulnerable when they're on the road because of

- their small size
- their low speed – they have a maximum speed of 8 mph (12 km/h).

Their small size means they're not easy to see. On a dual carriageway where the speed limit exceeds 50 mph (80 km/h) they should be displaying an amber flashing light, but on other roads you may not have that advance warning.

Buses and coaches

Look well ahead when you see buses and coaches at a bus stop. Be aware of

- people getting off the bus or coach. They may not look properly before they cross the road – and even if they do look, their view is often restricted
- buses and coaches pulling away from the bus stop. If they're signalling to move out, give way to them if you can do so safely.

REMEMBER, always think of the other road user, not just of yourself.

Pedestrians

Always drive carefully and slowly in areas where there are likely to be pedestrians, such as residential areas and town centres.

Be particularly careful in Home Zones and Quiet Lanes, where people could be using the whole of the road for a range of activities.

Always look out for pedestrians when

- turning from one road into another – give way to people who are crossing the road into which you're turning
- approaching pedestrian crossings. Never overtake on the approach to a crossing
- driving past a bus or tram stop, as pedestrians may walk out into the road.

Keep your speed down when driving in an area where there are pedestrians, especially children. If a pedestrian is in collision with a car, the survival rate of the pedestrian reduces drastically the faster the car is travelling.

Older people

Several factors make older people more vulnerable.

If they have poor eyesight or hearing, they might not be aware of approaching traffic. They might not be able to judge the speed of approaching traffic when crossing the road. Even when they do realise the danger, they may be unable to move quickly, or they may become flustered.

They may also take longer to cross the road. Be patient and don't hurry them by revving your engine or edging forwards.

People with disabilities

Take special care around people with disabilities.

Visually impaired people may not be able to see you approaching. They may carry a white cane or use a guide dog. The guide dog has a distinctive loop-type harness. Remember, the dog is trained to wait if there's a vehicle nearby.

A person with hearing difficulties isn't easy to identify, so take extra care if a pedestrian fails to look your way as you approach. Remember they may not be aware of your presence. They may have a guide dog wearing a distinctive yellow or burgundy coat.

Those who are deaf and blind may carry a white cane with a red band or may be using a guide dog with a red and white harness. They may not see or hear instructions or signals.

Children
Take extra care where children might be around, particularly in residential areas and near schools and parks.

Drive carefully and slowly past schools, especially during school start and finish times. Be aware that

- two amber lights, flashing alternately, are used to alert drivers to a school crossing patrol ahead
- a school-crossing patrol may stop you to escort children across the road
- children may be getting on or off a bus showing a 'school bus' sign.

Children are impulsive and unpredictable. Therefore, drive slowly in narrow roads where parked cars obscure your view.

Look out for parked ice-cream vans. Children are usually more interested in ice cream than they are in traffic and they may forget to look before running across the road.

Animals

Animals are easily frightened by noise and vehicles coming close to them. You should

- drive slowly and quietly; don't sound the horn
- keep your engine speed low; don't rev your engine or accelerate rapidly once you've passed them
- always watch out for animals on unfenced roads, as they may step out in front of you. You should always be able to stop safely within the distance you can see to be clear, especially at night when your lights are dipped.

Give animals as much room as possible.

People in charge of animals

If someone in charge of animals signals to you to stop, do so and switch off your engine.

Horses

Be particularly careful when approaching horses, especially those being ridden by children.

As a driver you should

- look out for horses being led or ridden on the road
- take extra care and keep your speed down at left-hand bends, especially on narrow country roads
- slow down when you see a horse rider on the road.

Be aware that at roundabouts and at junctions where a horse rider is turning right, they may signal right but keep to the left-hand side of the road (and the outside lane round the roundabout) for safety.

As you approach a horse rider from behind

- slow down, give them plenty of room and be prepared to stop
- don't sound your horn or rev your engine. Horses can be easily scared by noise and may panic around fast-moving vehicles
- look out for signals given by the riders and heed a request to slow down or stop.

Always pass horses slowly, giving them plenty of room.

Take special care when meeting what appears to be a riding-school group. Many of the riders might be inexperienced. Horses are potential hazards and you should always take great care when approaching or passing them.

Also look out for horse-drawn vehicles and treat them in a similar way to horses being ridden.

See the Think! road safety advice about horses on the road.

http://think.direct.gov.uk/horses.html

Wild animals

Over 2 million deer live wild in Great Britain. Increases in the deer population, combined with a rise in traffic volumes, have resulted in a large number of road traffic incidents involving deer each year.

Incidents happen throughout the year, but they're more likely during May, and from October through to January. The risks increase around dawn and dusk, when deer activity peaks, coinciding with rush hours.

To minimise the risk of collisions with deer

- Pay attention to deer warning signs.
- Keep your speed down.
- Take extra care at dawn and dusk, when deer activity is at its highest.
- Use your headlights on full beam if there's no traffic, so you can see any deer. Dip them if you see a deer, otherwise it may freeze in your path.
- Be aware that many deer could be in the area – not just the ones you spot.

Report any collisions with deer to the police non-emergency number, 101, so that a deer warden can attend. If the animal is dead, then you should report it to the local authority so they can remove it.

Section eleven

⊙ Motorway driving

This section covers

- Driving on motorways
- Motorway signs and signals
- Joining a motorway
- On the motorway
- Lane discipline
- Smart motorways
- Overtaking
- Leaving a motorway
- Weather conditions
- Stopping on motorways
- Motorways at night
- Roadworks
- Traffic officers
- The novice driver

⊙ Driving on motorways

Motorways differ from ordinary roads in that they're designed to help traffic travel faster and in greater safety.

Motorways are statistically safer than other roads in relation to the number of incidents occurring. However, when they do happen, motorway incidents usually occur at higher speed and involve more vehicles. As a result, injuries are usually more serious – and are more likely to result in loss of life.

Because traffic travels faster, conditions change more rapidly. You need to be alert and have total concentration.

Before you drive on a motorway

- You must hold a full driving licence.
- You should have a thorough knowledge of all rules within The Highway Code, but particularly those dealing with motorways.
- You need to know and understand motorway warning signs and signals.

Concentration

You need to be fit and alert to drive anywhere, but particularly so on motorways. Never use the motorway if you feel tired or unwell.

General guidelines on dealing with fatigue are given in section 1 but the problems when driving on motorways tend to be greater because of the long distances involved and the monotony of the journey.

Research has found that fatigue accounts for 15–20% of incidents on monotonous roads (especially motorways). These tend to result in more serious injury than the average collision because of the high speed of the impact (there's often no braking beforehand).

If your journey seems monotonous and you feel drowsy, keep a window open until you reach a service area. Plan plenty of rest stops, especially at night.

Parking is forbidden except at service areas. If you need rest, you'll sometimes have to travel a long distance before an exit or a service area. Remember it's an offence to stop on the hard shoulder, an exit road or a slip road, except in an emergency.

Your vehicle

You must only drive a vehicle that's allowed on a motorway.

The following types of vehicle **MUST NOT** be used on motorways

- motorcycles under 50 cc
- certain slow-moving vehicles with oversized loads – except with special permission
- invalid carriages (powered vehicles used by disabled people) less than 254 kg unladen weight
- agricultural vehicles.

Also, motorways **MUST NOT** be used by pedestrians, cyclists, horse riders or holders of provisional car or motorcycle licences. (In 2018 it's proposed that learner car drivers will be allowed to have driving lessons on a motorway, provided that they're accompanied by an approved driving instructor (ADI) and are in a vehicle fitted with dual controls. Please check **www.gov.uk** for the latest information.)

Check your vehicle

Make sure your vehicle is safe and in good working order
High speeds and long distances increase the risk of mechanical failure.

You should carry out the following checks on your vehicle before using a motorway.

- **Tyres** They must be in good condition and inflated to the correct pressure. Follow the guidance given in the vehicle handbook, which may give different pressures to be used when the vehicle is loaded.

- **Brakes** Check they can stop you safely.
- **Steering** Check it's in good order.
- **Instruments and warning lights** Make sure they're all working correctly.
- **Mirrors** Make sure they're clean and correctly positioned.
- **Windscreen and windows** Make sure they're clean. Top up the reservoir for the windscreen washers, and the rear window washer if your vehicle has one.

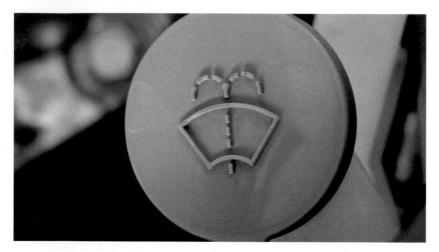

- **Lights and indicators** Make sure they're all working correctly.

For safety, convenience and good vehicle care, you should also check the following items.

- **Fuel** Make sure you have enough fuel to avoid running out between service areas.
- **Oil** High speeds may mean your engine uses oil faster. Running out can be dangerous and costly.
- **Water** Higher speeds can mean a warmer engine, especially in traffic tailbacks in hot weather.

Make sure your load is secure
Check that everything carried on your vehicle or trailer is safe and secure. If anything should fall from your vehicle or from another, stop on the hard shoulder and use the emergency telephone to inform the authorities. **Never** try to retrieve it yourself.

⊕ Motorway signs and signals

Motorway signs

Leading to the motorway

Direction signs from ordinary roads to the motorway have white lettering and figures on a blue panel, often bordered in white.

These signs may stand alone or be included in other, larger signs of various colours.

On the motorway

You may find the following types of sign on the motorway

- advance direction signs
- countdown markers
- signs giving information about service areas
- signs with a brown background. These indicate tourist attractions that can be reached by leaving at the next exit.

All these signs are very much larger than those on ordinary roads because you need to be able to see them from a distance. This is a good reminder that you must leave more room for all manoeuvres on motorways.

Each junction has an identifying number that corresponds with current road maps. This is to help you plan your route and know where you need to leave the motorway.

Speed-limit signs

- Signs that display a speed limit within a red ring indicate mandatory speed limits. You **MUST** obey these signs. If you don't, you risk prosecution.
- Black and white rectangular signs show recommended maximum speeds.

Motorway signals

Signals warn of dangers ahead, such as

- incidents
- fog
- icy roads
- delays
- standing traffic.

Flashing amber lights

Look out for flashing amber lights and signs, either on the central reservation or overhead. These warn you of

- lane closures
- roadworks
- other hazards.

They might also show a temporary speed limit. You should

- slow down to the speed limit
- be ready to slow down even further to pass the obstacle or danger
- look out for signs giving further advice
- don't speed up until you see the sign ending the temporary restriction (or there are no more flashing amber lights).

Red lights

Some signs have flashing red lights as well.

A red light (it may be a red 'X') warns you that you **MUST NOT** go beyond the red light in that lane. You should

- start to slow down in good time
- be ready to change lanes.

If the red light flashes on a slip road, you **MUST NOT** enter that slip road.

If a red light flashes on the central reservation or at the side of the road, you **MUST NOT** go beyond the signal in any lane.

⊕ Joining a motorway

You can join a motorway

- where a main road becomes a motorway. This is indicated by a specially worded sign
- by joining at any entry point. A slip road leads onto the motorway.

At an entry point where a slip road leads to the motorway, adjust your speed to that of the traffic already on the motorway before joining it. Give priority to traffic already on the motorway.

Join where there's a suitable gap in the left-hand lane. Use the Mirrors – Signal – Manoeuvre/Position – Speed – Look (MSM/PSL) routine.

A quick sideways glance might be necessary to verify the position of other vehicles. Try to avoid stopping at the end of the slip road unless queuing to join other slow-moving traffic.

At some slip roads there's no need to join by merging because the joining lane may continue as a dedicated lane. Signs and road markings normally indicate this arrangement.

Do
- indicate your intention to join the motorway
- make sure you can be seen
- assess the speed of the traffic on the motorway before you try to join.

Don't

- force your way into the traffic stream

- drive along the hard shoulder.

Once you've joined the motorway, keep in the left-hand lane until you've had time to judge and adjust to the speed of the traffic already on the motorway.

In some cases, the lane merges from the right. Take extra care when joining or meeting traffic at these locations.

⊕ On the motorway

Seeing

Make sure you start out with clean mirrors, windscreen, windows and lights. Use your washers, wipers and demisters whenever necessary to ensure you can see clearly.

You need to use your mirrors frequently and much earlier than on normal roads. Because of the higher speeds on motorways, they're even more important.

Effective observation

Keep your eyes moving between the road ahead and your mirrors, so that you always know what's happening all around you.

Continually reassess the movement of the vehicles

- directly ahead (in the near and far distance)

- alongside you

- behind you.

At high speeds, situations change rapidly. Effective observation helps you prepare for any sudden developments.

For example, an increase in the number of vehicles ahead could mean that traffic is slowing down and 'bunching'.

If you see serious congestion ahead, you can use your hazard warning lights briefly to alert drivers behind you. This can reduce the risk of rear-end collisions, especially in bad weather.

Being seen

Because of the higher speeds, your vehicle needs to be seen much earlier on a motorway than on an ordinary road.

Always try to avoid staying where you might be in another vehicle's blind spot. This is especially important when the other vehicle is a large vehicle. A good indication is, if you can't see the driver's mirror, the driver probably won't be able to see you.

Poor daylight

In poor daylight, you should use your headlights.

Fog

In fog, where visibility drops below 100 metres (328 feet), you may find it helpful to use fog lights in addition to your headlights.

You **MUST** switch your fog lights off when visibility improves. This is the law. They're misleading and can dazzle other drivers if left on. They may also make your brake lights less conspicuous.

Headlight flashing

The level of noise is higher on a motorway, particularly in wet weather, and other road users may not be able to hear your horn.

If you think a warning is necessary, flash your headlights instead.

Watch out for any such warnings intended for you.

Driving and braking

At motorway speeds, braking should normally be

- unhurried
- progressive.

If you slow down gradually without putting your foot on the brake, it allows traffic to move more freely. If you're constantly touching the brake pedal and causing your brake lights to show, it encourages those behind to do the same, causing braking and accelerating, so hindering the smooth flow of traffic.

Following traffic at the correct distance will enable you to adjust your speed without having to constantly brake and accelerate heavily. This will aid the smooth flow of traffic.

It's when you're driving on a motorway that you may find it most useful to use cruise control if it's fitted (see section 3). This will help you to maintain a constant speed and may help you save fuel.

Defensive driving

- Anticipate problems; take avoiding action before they develop.
- Slow down in good time.
- Keep your distance from the vehicle ahead.
- Take particular care when overtaking lorries, as some have poor visibility to their right.

Avoid braking suddenly

Defensive driving will reduce the likelihood of having to do so.

Read more about defensive driving in section 10.

REMEMBER, leave plenty of space between yourself and the vehicle ahead for controlled braking. Always check in your mirrors before you brake.

Keeping your distance

The faster the traffic, the more time and space you need for every driving action.

You should always

- give yourself greater margins than on ordinary roads
- make sure there's enough space between you and the vehicle ahead.

Traffic normally travels faster on motorways because there are usually no

- ordinary junctions
- sharp bends
- roundabouts
- steep hills
- traffic lights.

Slow-moving vehicles are generally forbidden.

Note: some motorway links, where motorway regulations also apply, do have roundabouts and sharp bends.

How big a gap?

Leave a gap of at least one metre or yard for each mph of your speed.

This rule is reinforced on some motorways where there are chevrons painted on the carriageway. Keep at least two chevrons between you and the vehicle in front.

Bad weather

Leave at least double the space if the road is wet.

In icy conditions, you'll need up to 10 times the stopping distance that you need in dry conditions.

Tailgating

This is a very dangerous practice, especially on motorways, where it's often the cause of serious incidents.

⊕ Lane discipline

Lane discipline is vitally important on motorways. You should normally drive in the left-hand lane.

Two-lane motorways

On a two-lane motorway, the correct position for normal driving is in the left-hand lane.

The right-hand (offside) lane is for overtaking only. Once you've overtaken you should return to the left-hand lane as soon as it's safe to do so. It isn't the 'fast lane'.

Large goods vehicles are permitted to use either lane. They're subject to the same rules on lane use described above.

Motorways with three or more lanes

Because of the volume of traffic on three-lane motorways, many are being widened to four or more lanes in each direction.

Keep to the left-hand lane unless there are slower vehicles ahead – it's possible to stay in the centre or outer lanes while you're overtaking a number of slower-moving vehicles, but don't stay in these lanes

- longer than you have to
- if you're delaying traffic behind you.

Drivers of large goods vehicles, buses, coaches or any vehicle towing a trailer aren't allowed to use the extreme right-hand lane of a motorway with more than two lanes, unless one or more lanes are temporarily closed.

Don't stay in an overtaking lane longer than it takes you to move out, overtake and move in again safely. Make sure you don't block traffic that's not allowed to use the outer lane.

Changing lanes

Don't change lanes unnecessarily. You should

- keep your vehicle steady in the centre of the lane
- not wander into another lane.

MSM routine

Always use the MSM routine well before you intend to change lanes.

At higher speeds, you must start the routine much earlier.

Look and, if necessary, signal in good time. Remember, vehicles might come up behind you very quickly.

The sooner you indicate, the sooner other drivers are warned of your intended movement. They'll expect a change in the traffic pattern and have time to prepare for it.

Be particularly aware of motorcyclists; they can be difficult to see due to their narrow profile but they may be travelling at high speeds. In congested situations they may filter between lanes of slower-moving traffic.

Crawler and climbing lanes

A steep hill on a motorway might have a crawler or climbing lane to avoid heavy vehicles slowing down the flow of traffic.

When other vehicles join

After you pass an exit, there's usually an entrance where other vehicles can join the motorway.

- Don't try to race them while they're on the slip road.
- Look well ahead; if there are several vehicles joining the motorway, be prepared to adjust your speed.
- Show consideration for traffic joining the motorway and, if it's safe, move to another lane to make it easier for joining traffic to merge.
- Take extra care if the motorway curves, as drivers on the slip road may have difficulty seeing vehicles on the motorway.

Motorway interchanges

Where motorways merge or separate you might be required to change lanes, sometimes more than once.

Pay attention to the overhead direction signs and move into the correct lane in good time.

Where the hatch markings indicate splitter islands, stay in your lane.

Assess conditions well ahead and watch for other drivers changing lane.

Changes in traffic conditions

Traffic conditions can vary as much on a motorway as on an ordinary road.

There can be rush-hour traffic near cities, heavy traffic near roadworks and constantly busy sections in other places.

⊕ Smart motorways

On some sections of motorway, technology is in place to reduce congestion and improve your journey times. These roads are known as 'smart motorways'. The technology is also referred to as active traffic management (ATM). Smart motorways use traffic management technology to vary speed limits as traffic volume increases. Drivers may also be allowed to use the hard shoulder as an extra lane during busy periods.

Types of smart motorway

Controlled motorway

Controlled motorways have three or more lanes, with variable speed limits shown on overhead signs. These speed limits are shown inside a red circle and are legally enforceable. The hard shoulder on controlled motorways should only be used in an emergency.

All-lane running

On a smart motorway converted to all-lane running, the hard shoulder is permanently used as an extra lane. Refuge areas with emergency telephones are provided at least every 2500 metres, in case of an emergency or breakdown, and drivers receive regular information updates via overhead signs. The signs display information on the current mandatory variable speed limits, as well as indicating whether lanes are closed.

Dynamic hard shoulder

Sections of smart motorway with a dynamic hard shoulder use the hard shoulder to provide extra capacity during busy periods. The hard shoulder is marked with a solid white line and drivers are only allowed to use it as a running lane when the overhead signs say it's available. If the sign above the hard shoulder displays a red X or is blank, you must only enter it in an emergency.

Driving on a smart motorway

- Overhead signs display speed limits to manage traffic and give information about incidents or driving conditions. They also tell you which lanes are available for you to use. Obey the signs; they're there to keep the traffic moving.

- Red crosses are used to show when lanes, including the hard shoulder, shouldn't be used. When you see a red X above a lane, don't drive in that lane.

- If a speed limit is displayed directly above the hard shoulder, you can drive on it. If you see a red X or no speed limit displayed above the hard shoulder, you should only use it in an emergency or breakdown.

What to do in a breakdown

If you have a problem with your vehicle when you're driving on a smart motorway, you should try to leave at the next exit or pull into a motorway service area. If you can't leave the motorway, then you should stop in one of the emergency refuge areas, where you'll be able to call for help using the roadside telephone. If it's not possible to do any of these things, try to get your vehicle off the carriageway and onto the verge or hard shoulder – if one is available.

You should

- switch on your hazard warning lights so that you can be seen more easily by other drivers and anyone coming out to help
- exit the vehicle by the left-hand door and wait behind the barrier if you're able to do so.

If, for any reason, you can't get to where it's safe to exit the vehicle, or you don't feel it's safe to do so, stay in the vehicle with your seat belt on. If you have a mobile phone, dial 999.

By making a few simple checks, like making sure you have enough fuel, checking and replacing worn or damaged tyres, and servicing your vehicle regularly, you can greatly reduce the chances of breaking down during your journey.

> For more information on smart motorways, visit
>
> **www.gov.uk/guidance/how-to-drive-on-a-smart-motorway**

⊙ Overtaking

Leave a safe distance between you and the vehicle you intend to overtake.

Use the appropriate parts of the MSM/PSL routine. For example

Mirrors Check behind to verify the speed, course and position of traffic behind you.

Position You should be able to move out smoothly to the right without making any sudden movements.

Speed Make sure you're going fast enough or can accelerate quickly enough to overtake without blocking any vehicle coming up behind.

Look Look ahead and use your mirrors to check whether there's anything preventing you from overtaking safely; for example, a lane closure ahead or traffic coming up much faster from behind in the right-hand lane.

Try to anticipate whether the vehicle ahead will move out to overtake.

A quick sideways glance into the blind area might sometimes be necessary before you change lanes.

Remember LADA

- **L**ook
- **A**ssess well ahead
- **D**ecide – don't rush
- **A**ct – only when you're sure it's safe.

Mirrors

You must use your mirrors regularly and be aware of drivers around you.

Remember that vehicles coming up in the right-hand lane are likely to be moving faster than you are. Watch out particularly for motorcyclists, as they're more difficult to see. Watch for vehicles returning to the lane you intend to use.

Signal

You should signal well before you start to move out. This gives drivers behind you plenty of time to anticipate what you intend to do and could influence any manoeuvres they're planning.

Pulling out

Check your mirrors again, and take a quick sideways glance into the blind spot, before pulling out smoothly into an overtaking lane. Overtake as quickly and safely as possible. Be aware that, for a period, you'll be in the blind spot of the vehicle you're overtaking.

Moving back to the left

Pass the vehicle and signal, if necessary, before moving back to the left as soon as you're sure it's safe to do so. Don't cut in too soon in front of the vehicle you've just passed.

Look well ahead for any vehicles about to move into the lane that you intend to join. Allow plenty of room. Finally, make sure your indicator signal cancels properly.

Overtaking on the left

Never overtake on the left, unless the traffic is moving in queues and the queue on your right is moving more slowly than the queue you're in.

Overtaking on busy motorways

If you come up behind traffic moving more slowly than you are when you're overtaking, be patient and

- don't intimidate the driver ahead by flashing your headlights and driving dangerously close behind
- wait until the vehicle ahead can move safely to the left, then proceed.

Defensive driving

Let faster traffic pass you. If other drivers are breaking the speed limit, don't add to the danger by trying to enforce the legal speed limit.

Don't move to a lane on the left to overtake.

Never use the hard shoulder to overtake – unless directed to do so by traffic signs at roadworks, by police officers or by traffic officers in uniform.

⊙ Leaving a motorway

Unless you're going to the end of the motorway, you'll leave by moving left from the left-hand lane into a slip road. Position yourself in the left-hand lane in plenty of time.

Plan well ahead, particularly on motorways with three or four lanes.

Road signs

Use the road signs and markers to help you time your exit and use your mirrors and indicators appropriately.

You'll have plenty of time to observe the signs and markers, so there's no need to rush.

One mile before the exit

There'll be a junction sign with road numbers, unless there are exits very close together.

Half a mile before the exit

You'll see a sign with the names of places you can reach from that exit.

Countdown markers

These are positioned at 270 metres (300 yards), 180 metres (200 yards) and 90 metres (100 yards) before the start of the slip road.

Where a lane splits off from the motorway as a dedicated lane, countdown markers aren't provided.

To leave the motorway

Use your mirrors and signal in good time. Remember to use the MSM/PSL routine.

Get into the left-hand lane early. On a motorway with three or four lanes, this could mean changing lanes more than once. You must follow the MSM/PSL routine for each change of lane.

> **REMEMBER,** use your mirrors and signal left in good time to move into the left-hand lane.

Don't

- move to the left more than one lane at a time

- cut straight across into the slip road at the last moment.

The hard shoulder is **not** an exit road, and you must avoid queuing on it.

Occasionally, where motorways merge, there may be an exit just before the one you intend to take. In these cases, or where there are service areas near to exits, look well ahead for the direction signs to ensure you take the right exit.

If you miss your exit, carry on to the next one.

Speed when leaving a motorway

After driving at motorway speeds for some time, your judgement of speed will almost certainly be affected: 40 or 45 mph (64 or 72 km/h) will seem more like 20 mph (32 km/h). Stay aware of your speed.

- Adjust your driving to suit the new conditions.

- Check your speedometer. It will give you the accurate speed.

Remember, even if you don't have to reduce your speed because the road you're joining is a dual carriageway, drivers of some other vehicles have to obey a lower speed limit. Be aware that they may reduce their speed.

Reduce speed at first

For the sake of safety, reduce your speed until you're used to the change of conditions. It could take you time to adjust.

Motorway slip roads and link roads often have sharp curves, which should be taken at much lower speeds.

Look ahead for traffic queuing at a roundabout or traffic signals.

End of motorway

There will be an 'end of motorway' sign wherever you leave the motorway network. This means that the road you're joining has different rules.

Remember to watch for any signs telling you what these are, particularly

- speed limits
- a dual carriageway
- two-way traffic
- a clearway
- a motorway link road
- part-time traffic lights.

⊙ Weather conditions

The advice given in section 12 is even more important on a motorway.

Wet weather

Visibility can be made worse because, at higher speeds, vehicles (especially large ones) throw up more spray. So

- use your headlights to help other drivers see you. Don't use rear fog lights unless visibility is less than 100 metres (328 feet)

- always reduce your speed when conditions are poor. Driving is safer at lower speeds

- adjust your speed to suit the conditions and leave larger separation distances, at least double the normal gap.

Ice or frost

Ice or frost on the road can seriously affect your handling of the vehicle.

Try to anticipate the road surface conditions. If your steering feels light, it's an indication that there may be frost or ice. Be very gentle with your use of the controls.

Allow up to 10 times the normal distance for braking.

Side winds

Wind is another motorway hazard.

Wind can affect your steering. If it's coming from the left on an exposed stretch of motorway, be especially careful. A sudden gust as you pass a large vehicle, or come out from under the shelter of a bridge or embankment, can send you swerving to the right.

In strong wind, drivers of high-sided vehicles or those towing caravans may experience difficulties. Motorcyclists can also be affected by strong side winds. Allow for this when overtaking these vehicles.

Fog

Driving on the motorway when the weather is foggy can be particularly hazardous.

If there's fog on the motorway, you must be able to stop well within the distance you can see to be clear.

- Use dipped headlights.
- Check your mirrors and slow down; fog affects both visibility and judgement of speed and distance.
- Check your speedometer and leave plenty of space between your vehicle and the vehicle ahead.

Fog can drift quickly and is often patchy.

If a motorway warning sign shows 'FOG'

- be prepared
- reduce your speed in good time.

Multiple pile-ups can happen in foggy conditions. They're usually caused by drivers who are

- travelling too fast
- driving too close to the vehicle in front
- assuming there's nothing in the fog ahead.

If there's fog

- switch on your fog lights if visibility drops below 100 metres (328 feet)
- be prepared to leave the motorway
- be on the alert for incidents ahead
- watch out for emergency vehicles coming up behind, possibly on the hard shoulder.

REMEMBER, don't 'hang on' to the lights of the vehicle ahead. You'll be too close to brake if it stops suddenly.

⊙ Stopping on motorways

You must only stop on a motorway if

- red lights or other signs or signals tell you to do so
- you're asked to stop by the police, traffic officers or Driver and Vehicle Standards Agency officers
- it's an emergency
- it will prevent an incident.

You mustn't stop to pick up or set down anyone on any part of a motorway, including a slip road.

The hard shoulder

When travelling on a smart motorway, use the hard shoulder as directed by the signs. On all other stretches of motorway, use the hard shoulder only in an emergency.

Slowing down and stopping

If you have to slow down or stop on the carriageway as a result of traffic congestion, switch on your hazard warning lights to warn traffic behind you of the obstruction ahead. Once you're sure they've been seen, switch them off.

Breakdowns and incidents

Information about how to deal with breakdowns and incidents on a motorway can be found in sections 15 and 16, respectively.

Parking at service areas

Service areas are the only parking places provided on motorway routes. To reach the services, follow the same procedure as for a motorway exit.

Once you're off the motorway, slow down and be aware that a low speed will feel very different after motorway driving. Watch out for sharp turns into car parking areas. Other drivers could fail to reduce their speed sufficiently. Once you've stopped in the car park, keep children and animals under control.

When you leave your vehicle, remember to lock it. Don't leave valuables (cameras, etc) on view. Be a careful pedestrian.

To rejoin the motorway, follow the same procedure as when joining the motorway at any entrance.

➡ Motorways at night

> If you've just left a well-lit service area, give your eyes time to adjust to the darkness.

Use your headlights

Always use your headlights, even on motorways that are lit. Use dipped beam if you're likely to dazzle drivers ahead or oncoming drivers, particularly on a left-hand curve.

If you're dazzled

You may have to slow down, but don't brake too hard; there might be a vehicle behind you.

Judging speed

It's harder to judge speed and distance both on a motorway and at night.

If you change lanes to overtake, or to leave the motorway, use your indicators earlier and give yourself even more time.

Reflective road studs

These can help you determine the road layout. Their positions are as follows.

- **Red** Between hard shoulder and carriageway.
- **White** Between lanes.
- **Amber** Between edge of carriageway and central reservation.
- **Green** Between carriageway and slip-road exits and entrances.
- **Fluorescent green/yellow** At contraflow systems and roadworks.

⊙ Roadworks

Incidents can happen at roadworks. Obey all signs, including speed-limit signs.

Approaching roadworks

- Reduce speed in good time when warned by advance warning signs, gantry signs or flashing signals – don't leave everything to the last minute, as this can greatly increase the chance of mistakes and incidents.
- Get into the lane indicated for use by your vehicle in good time.

- Where lanes are restricted, merge in turn.

- When you drop your speed it may seem as if you're travelling more slowly than you really are – it's important to keep to the speed limit and not just slow down to the speed that feels safe to you.

- Look out for road workers who are placing or removing signs. They might need to cross the carriageway, especially when temporary barriers and cones are being set up or taken down.

Travelling through roadworks

- Obey all speed limits – they're there for a reason. Roadworks are complicated areas and you'll need more time to spot hazards, for your own safety and the safety of road workers.

- If all drivers observe the speed limits, it helps to keep traffic moving and not 'bunching up' – this is good for journey times and the environment.

- Keep the correct separation distance from the vehicle ahead; you'll need time to brake if the vehicle in front stops suddenly.

- Avoid sharp braking and sudden steering movements.

- Don't change lanes when signs tell you to stay in your lane.

- Don't let your attention wander; there may be road workers in unexpected places, and they can be difficult to spot in cluttered areas.

Exiting roadworks

Stay within the speed limit even when you're leaving the coned area. There may be road workers' vehicles leaving the roadworks at this point. Even if you see the road worker, remember that they may not have seen you. Don't speed up until you're clear of the roadworks.

> **REMEMBER,** people may be working at roadworks sites and their safety is at risk if you don't follow the advice above.

Mobile roadworks

Minor maintenance work may sometimes be carried out without the need for major lane closures. Slow-moving or stationary works vehicles, with a large arrow on the back of the vehicle, are used to divert traffic to the right or left as appropriate.

There are no cones when these vehicles are being used.

Contraflow systems

These are temporary systems where traffic travelling in opposite directions shares the same carriageway. They allow traffic to keep moving during repairs or alterations on the other carriageway.

The lanes are often narrower than normal lanes. Red and white marker posts separate traffic travelling in opposite directions, and fluorescent or reflective bright green/yellow road studs often replace normal ones.

Contraflow systems may also be found on other roads carrying fast-moving traffic.

Watch out for
• lane-change signs
• vehicles broken down ahead – there's often no hard shoulder
• vehicles braking ahead – keep your distance.

⊛ Traffic officers

Working in partnership with the police, traffic officers are extra eyes and ears on most motorways and some 'A' class roads in England only. They're a highly trained and highly visible service patrolling the motorway to help keep traffic moving and to make your journey as safe and reliable as possible.

Traffic officers wear a full uniform, including a high-visibility orange and yellow jacket, and drive a high-visibility vehicle with yellow and black chequered markings.

Every traffic officer has a unique identification number and photographic identity card. They normally patrol in pairs. The vehicles contain a variety of equipment for use on the motorway, including temporary road signs, lights, cones, debris removal tools and a first-aid kit.

Role of traffic officers
They

- help broken-down motorists to arrange recovery
- offer safety advice to motorists
- clear debris from the carriageway
- undertake high-visibility patrols
- support the police and emergency services during incidents
- provide mobile or temporary road closures
- manage diversion routes caused by an incident.

If you have an emergency or break down on the motorway, the best action to take is to use an emergency roadside telephone.

Emergency roadside telephones are answered by operators located in a regional control centre. Control-centre operators are able to monitor any stranded motorists on closed-circuit television (CCTV) screens and despatch the nearest available traffic officer patrol to assist.

Powers of traffic officers

Unlike the police, traffic officers don't have any enforcement powers. However, they're able to stop and direct anyone travelling on the motorway. It's an offence not to comply with the directions given by a traffic officer (refer to The Highway Code, rules 107 and 108).

Extent of scheme

Seven regional control centres, managed by Highways England, are able to despatch traffic officers to any motorway in England.

⊕ The novice driver

Motorways are safer than normal roads but they're also faster. After passing your driving test, you should consider taking further professional instruction before you use a motorway. In 2018 it's proposed that learner car drivers will be allowed to have driving lessons on a motorway, provided that they're accompanied by an approved driving instructor (ADI) and are in a vehicle fitted with dual controls. Please check **www.gov.uk** for the latest information.

The Pass Plus training scheme aims to improve your driving skills and make you a safer driver, and it includes a section on motorway driving. You can get details of the Pass Plus scheme by visiting **www.gov.uk** or calling **0115 936 6504**.

If you've recently passed your test, haven't driven for a while, or your driving hasn't included heavy, fast-moving traffic, your decision-making skills might not be up to the standard needed.

You should

- ask for advice from a professional instructor who can give you valid, safe instruction
- use every chance to observe and learn as a passenger
- select fairly quiet sections of motorway to practise on
- get used to driving at 60–70 mph (96–112 km/h) and keeping up with the flow of traffic.

Section twelve

⊕ All-weather driving

This section covers

- Your vehicle
- Ensuring a clear view
- Wet roads
- Side winds
- Fog
- Snow and ice
- Bright sunshine and hot weather

⊙ Your vehicle

Tyres and brakes

Whatever the weather, make sure your vehicle and equipment are in good condition and regularly checked and serviced.

In bad weather the condition of your vehicle – especially your tyres and brakes – is even more important.

Different weather conditions can lead to a variety of different hazards, both from season to season and from region to region.

Tyres

Check tyre condition and pressures frequently. Make sure that the tyres have a good tread, that the walls are undamaged and that they're inflated to the correct pressure.

Also check your tyres for uneven wear of the tread, either across or around the tyre, which could be due to a mechanical defect. Have your vehicle checked, any fault put right and a new tyre fitted if necessary.

Good tyres are especially important in snow, on icy roads and in heavy rain. Be prepared; don't wait until the bad weather shows up the deficiency – it might be too late, and your life could depend on a few millimetres of rubber that should have been there.

Different types of tyres are available that are specially adapted for particular weather conditions (such as winter tyres or all-season tyres).

Brakes

Keep your brakes well maintained. Stopping takes much longer on wet, slippery roads, even with perfect brakes.

⊙ Ensuring a clear view

Can you see properly?

The biggest single danger to any driver is being unable to see properly. You won't be able to make the right decisions if you can't see the road clearly.

Always keep your windscreen, mirrors and windows clean and clear.

Wipers and washers

Make sure your wiper blades are effective.

Make sure washers are working and keep the reservoir filled. Use an additive, as it helps

- to prevent freezing in winter
- to clear dead insects and smears off the windscreen in summer.

Misting up

Misting up of the mirror and glass inside the car affects your ability to see. Even on a summer's day a sudden shower can make the glass mist up inside.

- Keep a dry cloth handy to clean all inside glass.
- Wipe the windows dry before you set out.
- Use your demisters. If your car has a heated windscreen, use it early. Also, use your heated rear window to maintain your rear vision.
- Open your windows to clear mist, if necessary.
- If your car is fitted with air conditioning, this can assist with clearing windows.

Read your vehicle handbook and follow the manufacturer's suggestions for effective heating and ventilation.

Many anti-mist and anti-frost accessories are available, including

- liquid for keeping glass clear
- de-icers
- prepared cloths
- electrically heated glass.

Warm, dry air works best, is by far the cheapest and is usually in plentiful supply once the engine has warmed up.

However, when you start from cold you won't be able to create warm air, so use a dry cloth or a chamois leather. If you have a passenger, ask them to help keep side windows clear – this is essential when manoeuvring.

Wait until the windscreen has cleared completely before pulling away.

In icy weather

If the weather is particularly icy, your windows and windscreen can freeze over.

You could cover your windscreen overnight to prevent ice forming on it. If ice has formed, you can use de-icer or a scraper to remove most of it. Before setting out, give yourself plenty of time to clear the windscreen. Wait until your demister and heater are working well enough to keep the whole of the windscreen and rear window clear.

Take care not to damage wiper blades, which may have frozen onto the windscreen or rear window. Never use boiling water to clear the windscreen; you could break the glass. Use water that's barely lukewarm or even cold – this is still warmer than ice and will start the defrosting process.

In rain

Use dipped headlights in poor visibility (such as rain, drizzle, mist, or very poor light) so that other drivers can see you.

Rain can drastically reduce your view through the windscreen and windows and in the outside driving mirrors.

Keeping your windscreen clean prevents smears and streaks that can reduce your vision. Always keep the washer bottle topped up and use a screen-wash additive.

Keep your speed down in very wet weather. Some windscreen wipers struggle to cope with very heavy rain.

In bad weather, clean your windscreen, windows, indicators and lights as often as necessary.

REMEMBER, whatever the weather, don't drive unless you can see properly all around.

➡ Wet roads

Wet roads reduce tyre grip, so slow down. Give yourself plenty of time and room for slowing down and stopping. Keep well back from other vehicles. On a wet road, you should allow at least double the braking distance for a dry road.

After a spell of dry weather, rain on the road can make the surface even more slippery. Take extra care, especially when cornering. Be aware that different road surfaces might affect the grip of your tyres.

> **FACTS** The less tread on your tyres, the greater the increase in braking distance.

Consider others

Pedestrians and cyclists can easily get drenched by passing vehicles. Look well ahead and show consideration by slowing down or giving them more room when it's safe to do so. Also give cyclists room to pull out to avoid large puddles.

Aquaplaning

A great danger when driving at speed in very wet weather is the build-up of water between the tyre and the road surface. As a result, your vehicle actually slides forwards on a thin film of water as your tyres lose contact with the road surface. This is called aquaplaning. Even good tyres can't grip in this situation.

A clear indication that you're aquaplaning can be that the steering suddenly feels very light. When this happens, slow down by easing off the accelerator. Never brake or try to change direction, because when you're aquaplaning, you've no control at all over steering or braking.

The higher your speed on a wet road, the more likely you are to aquaplane. You must keep your speed down and watch for water pooling on the road surface.

Even at lower speeds, if the front and rear tyres on one side of the vehicle hit a patch of deeper water, the vehicle may swerve because of the additional resistance on that side.

> Learn more about aquaplaning and the importance of tyre tread depth in this Tyresafe video.
>
> **youtube.com/watch?v=pxuYOI_uruU**

Spray

Another reason for keeping your speed down on wet roads is the amount of water thrown up by other vehicles.

Overtaking or being overtaken by heavy vehicles on a motorway can be an unnerving experience.

If necessary, slow down to increase the distance between you and the large vehicle, remembering to look in your mirrors before you do so.

Sometimes wipers can't keep the windscreen clear even when working at full speed. This results in the driver being temporarily blinded to conditions ahead; you may need to slow down.

If water sprays up under the bonnet, it can stop the engine or affect the electronic controls.

Dealing with floods

When you have to pass through a flood, take your time. Stop and assess how deep the water is. Don't just drive into it. Some roads that are likely to flood have depth gauges. Check the depth on these.

Deep water

If the water seems too deep for your vehicle, turn back and go around the flood by another road. It might take a little longer, but that's better than finding yourself stranded.

If the water is too deep it could

- flood the exhaust, causing the engine to stop
- find its way into the air intake on some vehicles, causing serious engine damage.

Shallow water

If the water isn't too deep, drive on slowly but be sure to keep to the shallowest part. Remember, because of the camber of the road, the water is probably deepest near the kerb and shallowest at the crown. By keeping to the shallowest part of the road, you'll be more likely to see lifted manhole covers or other debris.

Driving through floodwater

Drive in first gear as slowly as possible but keep the engine speed high and steady by slipping the clutch.

- If the engine speed is too low, you might stall.

- If you go too fast, you could create a bow wave. Water will flood the engine and it could cut out.

Try to strike a balance.

Engines and water

Some types of diesel engine will tolerate a certain amount of water, but many modern fuel systems are electronically controlled and are, therefore, affected by water.

All petrol engines can be seriously affected by even small amounts of water being splashed onto the electrical components; these can include engine management systems, ignition systems and so on.

Crossing a ford

The depth of water at a ford varies with the weather and is usually greater in winter. There may be a depth gauge in the area. If the water isn't too deep for your vehicle, cross using the same technique as you would for a flood.

Remember to test your brakes after you cross. There might be a notice reminding you to do so.

Don't try to displace the water by 'charging' at the flood or ford.

- You could lose control.
- Your vehicle will probably stall.
- You could end up blocking the road.

Test your brakes

Water can reduce the effectiveness of your brakes, so test your brakes whenever you've passed through water on the road. When you've driven safely through, check your mirrors first and then test your brakes.

If they don't work properly, it will help to dry them out if you apply light pressure to the brake pedal while driving along slowly. Don't drive at normal speed until you're sure they're working properly.

⊕ Side winds

Some vehicles can become unstable in strong side winds (or crosswinds), because of their large surface area and comparatively low weight.

This can happen particularly on exposed stretches of road such as motorways, viaducts and bridges.

The effect can vary from a slight pull on the steering wheel to a distinct wander, possibly into the path of another vehicle.

In very bad cases, the vehicle can be blown off the road or onto its side, with very serious results.

Cyclists and motorcyclists

In gusty conditions, watch for cyclists or motorcyclists being blown sideways and veering into your path. Allow extra room when overtaking.

High-sided vehicles and trailers

Drivers of high-sided vehicles, or those towing caravans, trailers or horseboxes (particularly empty ones), should

- pay special attention to forecasts of strong winds
- avoid well-known trouble spots and high bridges.

Drivers of these vehicles should be constantly alert for the effects of wind near bridges and embankments, even on normal journeys in reasonable conditions. If there's a severe weather warning, consider whether your journey is really necessary.

Other drivers should bear this in mind when about to overtake, or when being overtaken by, these particular types of vehicle.

⊕ Fog

Fog is one of the most dangerous weather conditions. An incident involving one vehicle can quickly involve many others, especially if they're driving too close to one another.

Motorway pile-ups in fog have sometimes involved dozens of vehicles. All too often there's a loss of life or serious injury that could easily have been prevented.

Observe the obvious

If it's foggy and you can only see a short distance ahead, you should start thinking about how the conditions will affect your driving.

Do you need to drive?

Take alternative transport or postpone your journey, if at all possible. If you must drive, give yourself time to prepare.

Check all the lights on your vehicle, clean your windscreen, and ensure you have made every effort to remain as visible to other road users as you possibly can. This should also include wiping your number plates. Remember that foggy conditions mean that your journey will take longer, so try to allow yourself more time and plan rest stops where appropriate.

REMEMBER, if the fog is thick and you can see the rear lights of the vehicle ahead, then you may be too close to stop in an emergency.

Use of lights

Correctly adjusted fog lights can be a valuable aid when driving in fog.

In daylight

You **MUST** use your dipped headlights when visibility is seriously reduced.

- They'll be seen from a much greater distance than sidelights.
- They won't dazzle other drivers or pedestrians in the daytime.

You should also use dipped headlights, or at least sidelights, in relatively light fog. Remember that, even if you think **you** can see far enough ahead, your own vehicle might not be clearly visible to others until you're too close. If in any doubt, always try to maximise your visibility in the interests of safety.

Use fog lights if your vehicle is fitted with them.

At dusk

Use dipped headlights at dusk and other times when visibility is poor.

At night

Slow down and use dipped headlights, not main beams. If you can't see for more than 100 metres, switch on your front and rear fog lights, if fitted.

High-intensity rear fog lights

If your vehicle has high-intensity rear fog lights, use them in fog only when visibility is seriously reduced. Normally this means when you can't see for more than 100 metres (328 feet).

> **REMEMBER,** you **MUST** switch fog lights off when visibility improves – it's the law. Using them at other times, such as in the rain, can dazzle drivers behind you.

Adjust your lights

Change your lighting with the conditions. For example, when you're queuing in traffic and the driver behind has already seen you, it can be helpful to switch off your rear fog lights temporarily to avoid dazzling them.

Driving in fog

Poor visibility is frustrating and a strain on the eyes. Your ability to anticipate is dangerously restricted. It's also much more difficult to judge distances and speed in fog when outlines become confusing. You can easily become disoriented – especially on an unfamiliar road.

In the interests of safety, you **MUST**

- slow down – check the speedometer from time to time
- be able to stop well within the distance you can see to be clear
- use your windscreen wipers to keep the outside of the screen clear
- use your demister to keep the inside of the screen clear. Use your heated windscreen if your vehicle has one.

Do

- give yourself plenty of time and space to deal with whatever is ahead. Decide what's a safe speed for the conditions and stick to it. Don't let other drivers push you into driving faster
- watch out for emergency vehicles. There could well be an incident ahead.

Don't

- follow the vehicle in front too closely
- try to keep up with the vehicle ahead. You'll get a false impression that the fog isn't too bad if you 'hang on' to the lights of the vehicle ahead because it will displace some of the fog
- use main beam when you're in fog as the fog reflects the light and can dazzle you, reducing your visibility even further. It can also dazzle other drivers.

Fog patches

The density of fog varies. Sometimes the fog is patchy. One moment it can be fairly clear, the next extremely dense. Avoid the temptation to speed up between the patches.

Following another vehicle

Slow down and leave plenty of room for stopping. There may be something ahead which you can't possibly see until you're too close to it.

You must leave enough space to react and brake in case the vehicle in front has to stop suddenly.

You may not see or recognise that the vehicle ahead is braking or has stopped as soon as you would in clear weather.

Remember the road surface is often wet and slippery in fog; you need to be able to brake safely.

Overtaking

Overtaking in fog can be particularly dangerous. You could well find that visibility ahead is much worse than you thought, and you won't be able to see oncoming traffic soon enough.

Dealing with junctions

Dealing with junctions in fog needs particular care, especially when turning right. You should

- open your window(s) and switch off your radio/CD player so you can hear any approaching traffic

- start indicating as early as you can

- make full use of your lights. Keep your foot on the brake pedal while you're at a standstill – your brake lights will give drivers behind an extra warning. However, when another vehicle stops immediately behind you, take your foot off the brake pedal so you don't dazzle the driver

- use the horn if you feel it will help, and listen for other vehicles.

Don't turn or emerge until you're absolutely sure it's safe.

REMEMBER, motorcyclists can be much more difficult to see in fog as they have only one headlight and tail light.

Road markings

Dipped headlights will pick out reflective road studs, but it's not so easy to recognise other road markings when driving in fog. Explanations of the different coloured road studs are given in section 6.

Try to keep a central position between lane lines or road studs. Don't mix up lane lines and centre lines. Driving too close to the centre could mean you're dangerously near someone coming the other way who might be doing the same thing. Driving on the centre line as a means of finding your way is extremely dangerous.

On rural roads, there are black-and-white marker posts, with red reflectors on the left-hand side of the road and white reflectors on the right-hand side of the road. These mark the edge of the road and are especially useful at night or at other times when visibility is reduced.

Stopping

Parking

Never park on a road in the fog if you can avoid it. Find an off-street parking place. However, if it's unavoidable, always leave your parking lights or sidelights on.

Don't leave dipped headlights or the main beam on. In foggy conditions, these can lead other road users to wrongly think they've drifted over to the extreme right-hand side of the road. If they quickly try to correct this positioning in order to keep to what they think is the left-hand side, they'll mount the pavement. This would be very dangerous for any pedestrians and other road users nearby. There might also be damage to walls, properties, street furniture and other vehicles. In rural areas there might be a ditch instead of a path, or even an embankment leading down to water.

Breaking down

If you break down, get your vehicle off the road if you possibly can. Inform the police, and make arrangements to remove it as soon as possible if it creates an obstruction. Never leave it without warning lights of some kind, or on the wrong side of the road.

⊙ Snow and ice

Is your journey really necessary?

In winter, especially if the weather doesn't look good, check the local weather forecast before setting out. If snow or ice is forecast, don't drive unless your journey is essential.

Before setting off

If you consider it necessary to travel, it's useful to carry the following in case you get stuck or your vehicle breaks down

- warm drink and emergency food
- warm clothing and boots
- de-icer/ice scraper
- torch
- first-aid kit
- spade or shovel
- jump leads
- blanket
- old sacks.

You should also

- clear all snow and ice from all of your windows so that you can see clearly all round
- ensure all lights are clean and free from snow so they can be seen by other road users
- make sure the mirrors are clear and the windows are demisted thoroughly so that you have the best visibility possible
- clear snow from the bonnet and roof so that it doesn't fly off and cause a danger to other road users such as motorcyclists or cyclists.

Starting off on snow

If you experience wheelspin when you're starting off in deep snow, don't race the engine, because the wheels will dig in further.

Try to move the car slightly backwards and then forwards out of the rut. Use the highest gear you can.

In these conditions, it's worthwhile carrying a spade and some old sacks to put under the wheels. These can be useful to help get you going when you've become stuck in snow.

Moving off in snow and ice can sometimes be improved if your vehicle is equipped with traction control. Traction control works by using sensors that 'brake' the wheels that have wheelspin while supplying more power to the wheels with the most traction. Some vehicles also have features that limit the amount of power coming from the engine. Remember that traction control doesn't mean you'll never get stuck in snow – it's designed to stop the wheels of your vehicle spinning out of control on slippery surfaces.

Snow chains are also available. These can be fitted over existing wheels and tyres to help avoid getting stuck and to reduce the danger of skidding.

Snow socks are a popular alternative to snow chains. They can be fitted on to the wheel quickly and are relatively lightweight.

Driving in snow

When falling snow reduces visibility, use your dipped headlights as you would in heavy rain or fog. Falling or freshly fallen snow need not cause too much difficulty, providing you remember to

* increase the gap between you and the vehicle in front, remembering to look in your mirror before slowing down

- test your brakes, very gently, from time to time, but be sure to look in your mirrors before braking. Snow can pack behind the front wheels or around brake linkages under the car and so affect steering and braking

- be prepared to clear the windscreen by hand. Your wipers, even with the aid of the heater, may not be able to sweep the snow clear. Snow might collect and pack around your lights and indicators

- drive with care, even if the roads have been treated. Conditions can change over very short distances

- try to find out about weather and traffic conditions ahead by listening to travel bulletins on the radio and noting any information on the variable message signs.

In areas that are subject to prolonged periods of snow, it may be an advantage to fit

- snow chains or socks

- mud and snow (M and S) tyres with a tread pattern designed for these conditions.

Snow will cover up road markings – take care when you can't see which road has priority.

Driving in icy conditions

Overnight freezing can result in an icy surface, especially on less frequently used roads. Look for signs of frost on verges, etc.

It's even more dangerous when the roads are just beginning to freeze or thaw. The combination of water and ice adds up to an extremely slippery surface.

Rain freezing on roads as it falls (black ice) is an invisible danger. If you skid on black ice it will be similar to aquaplaning and your steering will feel especially light.

When driving on ice

• you need to keep your speed down

• treat every control – brakes, accelerator, steering, clutch and gears – very delicately.

If it's very cold, treat all wet-looking surfaces as though they're frozen, because they probably are. If the road looks wet but there's no sound from the tyres, expect ice.

Braking on snow and ice

All but the most gentle braking will lock your wheels on packed snow and ice.

If your front wheels lock, you can't steer. If you can't steer, you can't keep out of trouble.

For vehicles without anti-lock brakes (ABS), in slippery conditions, repeatedly applying and releasing the brakes will slow the vehicle down and enable you to keep control.

Using this method will allow some degree of steering control.

Get into a lower gear earlier than normal. Allow your speed to fall and use the brake pedal gently and early to keep your speed well under control.

Braking distances

Braking distances on ice can easily be 10 times normal distances.

Downhill braking

Downhill braking calls for careful speed control well before reaching the actual hill, as well as while you're on it.

By selecting a low gear, the engine compression will help to hold the vehicle back and reduce the overall speed.

Anti-lock brakes

ABS may reduce the risk of vehicle instability when braking on snow and ice. However, it can't compensate for poor judgement or excessive speed, and it won't give the vehicle's tyres any more grip.

Cornering on snow and ice

Time your driving and adjust your speed so that you don't have to use your brakes at all on a bend.

Approach a corner at a steady speed, using the highest gear possible.

- Be gentle with the accelerator.
- Don't use the clutch unless you absolutely have to.
- Steer smoothly – sudden movements must be avoided.
- Take just as much care coming out of a turn.

Braking on an icy or snow-covered bend can be dangerous. The cornering force will continue to pull you outwards and the wheels won't grip very well. This could cause your vehicle to spin.

Climbing hills on snow and ice

Speed must be kept down on icy and slippery roads. But this can bring with it other problems.

For example, when going uphill you might lose momentum. Trying to regain speed and keep going could cause wheelspin and loss of control.

If you have to stop, it could be difficult to start again.

Leave a good gap between you and the vehicle in front. If it stops you'll at least have a chance to keep going while it restarts, or even pass it altogether.

To reduce the chances of wheelspin, use the highest gear you reasonably can.

Don't rush a hill thinking you'll change into a lower gear on the way up. Before reaching the hill, change into a gear that will take you all the way up.

Changing gear isn't easy on an icy slope. It takes very delicate footwork to avoid wheelspin and loss of speed.

Winter service vehicles

In winter, look out for large vehicles with flashing amber beacons, such as salt spreaders (also known as 'gritters') or snow ploughs. These vehicles travel at slow speeds – around 40 mph – even on the motorway.

Salt spreaders

Salt spreaders are used to treat roads when freezing temperatures are forecast. Salt lowers the freezing point of the road surface and prevents ice from forming.

FACTS The salt spreaders used by Highways England can carry 8–12 tonnes of salt and typically will treat 40–60 miles before returning to their depot.

If you see a salt spreader ahead

• slow down

• stay well back because salt or spray can be thrown across the road

• only overtake when it's safe to do so.

In freezing conditions, always drive with great care even if the roads have been treated.

Snow ploughs

Snow ploughs are sent out to clear the roads when snow falls.

If you see a snow plough ahead

• keep well back as often snow can be thrown up on either side

• don't overtake unless it's safe to do so – there may be uncleared snow on the road ahead.

Other vehicles causing a hazard

If a vehicle heading towards you is obviously out of control, try to make maximum use of engine braking if there's time. If you must use the brake pedal, be as gentle as possible.

Avoid braking and steering at the same time to get out of the way. Both can lead to loss of control in icy conditions.

Constantly assess what's ahead. Be prepared, and look for escape routes.

⊕ Bright sunshine and hot weather

Be prepared

Before you begin a long journey, make sure you're prepared for the weather.

Tyres

Tyre pressures should be checked and adjusted when they're cold.

Don't check the pressure when you've been driving for a while because the tyres will be warm and you won't be able to tell whether the tyre pressure is correct.

Coolant

Before you start your journey, check the level of coolant in the system.

Clear windscreen

There are generally more flies and insects about in hot weather, and your windscreen needs to be kept clean.

Keep the windscreen as clear as possible of water and grease marks. This helps to cut down glare.

Check the level in the washer reservoir and top up if necessary. Using an additive may help to keep the windscreen free of smears and streaks.

It's also important to stay hydrated when driving in hot weather. The Food Standards Agency suggests that adults should drink at least 1.2 litres (6 to 8 glasses) of water a day. In warm weather you may find you need even more than this, so make sure you've had something to drink before you start out and carry additional bottles of water in the car. It's also essential to schedule proper breaks to eat, drink and rest if you're driving long distances.

Dealing with glare

Glare

One of the main problems when driving in sunny conditions is glare. This can seriously reduce your ability to see.

Reduce your speed and take extra care. If the roads are wet, reflected glare can increase the problem.

Drive slowly and carefully if you're being dazzled by bright sunshine. Watch out particularly for pedestrians and cyclists, and make sure you can stop quickly if necessary.

Constant sun in your eyes can be exhausting on a long journey and may well affect your concentration.

Even if you don't feel the need for them, the correct sunglasses can reduce the glare and keep your eyesight effective for longer. This is especially important if you're driving abroad, where conditions are hotter and the sunlight brighter than you may be used to.

Low-angle sun

Glare can be worse in the winter when the sun is low in the sky. Wear sunglasses and/or use your visor to cut out as much glare as possible. Avoid looking directly into the sun.

Coping with heat

Make sure you have adequate ventilation inside the car. Air conditioning helps, if you have it. Take plenty of breaks and refreshment on a long trip.

If you feel sleepy, stop and rest where it's safe. Never stop on the hard shoulder of a motorway when you feel tired. Use the service areas or get off the motorway.

Listen to travel information and try to avoid known traffic hold-ups.

Overheated engines in long traffic queues are the most frequent causes of breakdowns in these conditions.

If you're travelling with pets, make sure that your vehicle is sufficiently ventilated to keep them cool. Dogs are particularly vulnerable in hot weather, so it's advisable to take some water that's specifically for them and make scheduled stops to ensure their comfort. Never leave your pet in a hot, unventilated car.

Road surfaces

Soft tarmac
During long periods of hot weather, many tarmac road surfaces become extremely soft. Take care when braking and cornering.

Oil
Oil, water and rubber dust from tyres can make the hot surface of the road slippery and dangerous, particularly if there's a sudden rain shower after a long dry spell.

Take extra care; watch your speed and keep your distance.

Loose chippings
Many highway authorities replace the granite-chipping road surfaces during the summer. Always observe the special warning speed limits and keep well back from the vehicle in front.

Flying stone chips can cause not only expensive damage to your vehicle, but also serious injury to pedestrians and other road users.

Section thirteen
➡ Driving at night

This section covers

- Your vehicle lights
- Driving in the dark
- Built-up areas
- Overtaking at night
- Following at night
- Parking at night
- Meeting other vehicles

⊙ Your vehicle lights

In the dark, your vehicle lights are the most important source of information both for you and for other road users. Use them with care and consideration.

Always

- keep your headlights clean
- use your headlights at night, dipped or full beam, as appropriate
- use dipped headlights at any time when the light is poor, even during the day, as this will make you more visible to others.

You should

- check all your lights before and during a long journey

- fix any lighting fault immediately, for your own safety and the safety of others. Carry spare bulbs where applicable

- remember that extra weight at the rear of your vehicle could cause your headlights to 'aim high' and dazzle other road users. Some models have headlight adjusters to deal with this.

Auxiliary driving lights

Auxiliary driving lights may be used to improve the view of the road ahead. However, they must only be used in conjunction with the obligatory main-beam headlights and they must switch off at the same time as the main beams.

Only one pair of dipped-beam headlights may be fitted to a vehicle. Front fog lights **MUST NOT** be used to improve the view of the road ahead, except in seriously reduced visibility such as thick fog.

Junctions at night

Brake lights can dazzle. Unless it's foggy, don't keep your foot on the brake pedal while you're waiting at a junction or queuing in traffic. Use your parking brake instead.

⊕ Driving in the dark

You can't see as far ahead when driving at night. With less information available to you, hazards can be more difficult to make out, and vulnerable road users – such as cyclists, pedestrians and motorcyclists – may not be as easy to spot as they are in daylight. The potential problems can vary with the type of road and the amount of traffic.

Speed at night

You need to be aware that driving quickly at night (and at dawn and dusk) will limit your ability to drive safely. It's more difficult to judge distance and hazards can appear to be further away than they actually are. The faster you drive, the more difficult it becomes.

Never drive so fast that you can't stop well within the distance you can see to be clear. That is, within the range of your lights.

To enable you to see the greatest distance, you should normally use main-beam headlights on unlit roads unless

• you're following another vehicle
• you're meeting oncoming traffic.

On lit roads you should normally use dipped headlights.

If you can't stop safely within the range of your lights, you're going too fast.

Note
Fluorescent material shows up well in daylight or at dusk, but is of little use in the dark. Only reflective material shows up well in headlights.

Avoid dazzling others

If you meet any other road user, including cyclists and pedestrians, dip your headlights in good time to avoid dazzling them.

At dusk

You may find it best to put your headlights on at dusk, just before lighting-up time. At this time in the evening many shades of vehicle paintwork, such as black, blues and greys, and surprisingly white and silver as well, seem to blend in with the failing light.

Colours, particularly the more neutral ones, become less easy to distinguish than you would expect in the half-light of dusk. The situation is often made worse by the fact that some vehicles will already be using lights and some won't.

Ultimately, it can mean that some unlit vehicles can be almost invisible until you're very close to them. Don't be afraid to be the first driver to switch on – it's better to see and be seen.

At dawn

The opposite applies. Don't switch off your headlights until you're sure it's safe. Make sure you can see and be seen.

When you drive with your headlights on, other drivers can

- see you earlier
- tell which way you're heading. This is often difficult in the half-light without lights.

Your eyes in the dark

If you find that you can't see so well in the dark, it might be that you need to book an appointment with an optician for an eye test.

How far can you see?

Test yourself in a suitable place.

Pick an object within the range of your lights and see if you can stop by the time you reach it. You'll be surprised how difficult this is with dipped lights on an unlit road. It shows that you should take a good look before you dip your lights.

Lighter-coloured objects are easier to see at night.

Adjusting to darkness

Give your eyes a minute or two to adjust to the darkness, particularly when you're coming out of a brightly lit area or building.

You can always use the time to clean your lights, mirrors, windscreen, etc. Remember this when you leave a motorway service area after a rest or refuelling stop.

A dirty windscreen increases glare and dazzle, so keep it clean.

Don't

• wear tinted glasses or sunglasses while driving at night

• spray the windscreen or windows with tints.

⊕ Built-up areas

The phrase 'built-up area' refers to areas such as town centres and residential streets. These areas also have regularly spaced street lighting. Unless signs show otherwise, this would normally mean that there's a 30 mph (48 km/h) speed limit (see rules 113 and 124, as well as the speed limits table in the 'General rules, techniques and advice for all drivers and riders' section of The Highway Code).

Always use dipped headlights, or dim–dip if fitted, in built-up areas at night. It helps others to see you. In areas where street lights cause patches of shadow, watch out for pedestrians, especially those in dark clothes, who can be difficult to see.

Remember to

- be on the alert for pedestrians
- approach pedestrian crossings at a speed at which you can stop safely if necessary
- watch out for cyclists and joggers.

Noise at night

Keep all noise to a minimum.

- Don't rev your engine.
- Close your car doors quietly.

Remember that neighbours and children may be asleep. Take extra care setting and disarming the anti-theft alarm on your vehicle.

Using the horn at night

You **MUST NOT** use your horn between 11.30 pm and 7.00 am in a built-up area (except to avoid danger from a moving vehicle).

If you need to warn other road users of your presence at night, flash your headlights.

⊕ Overtaking at night

You'll need to take extra care before attempting to overtake at night. It's more difficult because you can see less. Only overtake if you can see that the road ahead will remain clear until after you've finished the manoeuvre. Don't overtake if there's a chance you're approaching

- a road junction
- a bend or hidden dip in the road
- the brow of a bridge or hill, except on a dual carriageway
- a pedestrian crossing
- road markings indicating double white lines ahead

or if there's likely to be

- a vehicle overtaking or turning right
- any other potential hazard.

If you're being overtaken

Dip your lights as soon as the vehicle starts to pass you, to avoid causing glare in the mirrors of the overtaking vehicle.

⊕ Following at night

Stay clear and dip

Make sure you don't get too close to the vehicle ahead, and always dip your lights so you don't dazzle the driver. Your light beam should fall short of the rear of the vehicle in front. Remember your separation distance.

On a dual carriageway or motorway where it's possible to overtake, don't use full beam in the face of oncoming drivers.

⊕ Parking at night

FACTS Cars and light goods vehicles (up to 2500 kg laden weight), invalid carriages and motorcycles can park without lights on roads with a speed limit of 30 mph (48 km/h) or less. They must comply with any parking restrictions, and not park within 10 metres (32 feet) of a junction.

They must also be parked parallel to, and close to, the side of the road or in a designated parking place and facing in the direction of the traffic flow.

If you have to park on any other road, you should never

- leave your vehicle without side or parking lights unless a sign indicates that lights aren't required. It would be better to get it off the road altogether

- leave your vehicle standing on the right-hand side of the road, except in a one-way street.

Always switch your headlights off when you stop, even for a short while. It's an offence to leave them on when the vehicle is parked. The fixed glare can be very dazzling – especially if, for any reason, the vehicle is on the offside of the road facing oncoming traffic. Leaving lights on can also drain the battery.

⊕ Meeting other vehicles

Another vehicle's lights can tell you in which direction they're heading and can give you an idea of their speed. Oncoming lights should raise a number of questions in your mind, such as

- How far away is the vehicle and how fast is it moving?
- Should I slow down while we pass each other?
- How soon should I dip my lights?
- How far ahead can I see before I dip?

- Before I dip, is there anything on my side of the road

  - that I might endanger?

  - that might endanger me?

Examples include a stationary vehicle, a cyclist, a pedestrian, or an unlit skip.

When your headlights are on full beam

- dip early enough to avoid dazzling oncoming drivers, but not too early

- check the left-hand verge before you dip.

If you're dazzled

If the headlights of oncoming vehicles dazzle you, slow down and, if necessary, stop. Don't look directly at oncoming headlights.

Don't retaliate by leaving your lights on full beam and dazzling the oncoming driver.

On a left-hand bend

Dip earlier. Your headlights will cut straight across the eyes of anyone coming towards you. On a right-hand bend this might not happen, or it won't happen so soon.

Section fourteen
➡ Basic maintenance

This section covers

- Vehicle checks
- Fuel
- Oils and coolant
- Steering and suspension
- Brakes
- Tyres
- Electrical systems
- Basic fault-finding

⊕ Vehicle checks

Everyday vehicle checks

Before driving, you should check your vehicle to make sure it's safe and ready for the road.

Make a habit of checking daily that

- the windscreen, windows and mirrors are clean
- all lights (including brake lights and indicators) are working; replace any dead bulbs immediately (it's a good idea to carry spare fuses and bulbs)
- the brakes are working; **don't drive with faulty brakes.**

Periodic checks

These checks are necessary both for safety and for good vehicle maintenance.

Check and top up if necessary

- engine oil
- water level in the radiator or expansion tank
- brake-fluid level
- battery; top up with distilled water if necessary (some batteries are maintenance-free and don't need topping up)
- windscreen and rear window washer bottles.

You should also check tyres and make sure they're

- legal; they must have the correct tread depth and be free of dangerous cuts and defects
- at the right pressure.

How often you make the checks depends on how much you drive. Consult your vehicle handbook. If you drive a lot, you may need to do these every day.

Regular servicing

Have your vehicle serviced regularly. The vehicle handbook will tell you when servicing is recommended.

Having your vehicle serviced according to its maintenance schedule helps prevent the engine from becoming inefficient. This avoids wasted fuel and increased exhaust emissions.

 Fuel

Make sure you have enough fuel

Don't let the fuel in your tank run too low. This can cause running problems and even damage the engine. Fill up before you reach that stage. Some vehicles have a warning light which shows when the fuel is getting low.

Fuel cans

If you carry reserve fuel in a can, make sure the can is of an approved type for carrying fuel. It's illegal and dangerous to carry fuel in a container not intended for that purpose.

Motorway driving

Before driving onto a motorway, make sure you have at least enough fuel to reach the next service area. It's better if you have much more than this, in case you encounter unexpected delays or there are problems at the service area you planned to use.

Driving at higher speeds tends to use more fuel and there can sometimes be quite a distance between service areas.

Petrol engines

All modern petrol-engined vehicles are fitted with a catalytic converter to help reduce exhaust emissions. These vehicles must use unleaded fuel for the system to operate correctly.

LPG and natural gas engines

Liquefied petroleum gas (LPG) and natural gas can both be used in spark ignition engines. Unlike petrol and diesel, the fuel is gaseous at room temperature and is stored in steel tanks. These tanks can add extra weight to the vehicle, particularly if it has two tanks and is able to operate on gas or conventional fuels.

Refuelling differs from petrol and diesel vehicles in that the refuelling hose is locked in place to create a pressurised, sealed system.

If you're planning a long trip, it's worth remembering that not all garage forecourts have LPG refuelling points. Satellite navigation (sat-nav) systems can usually direct you to the nearest LPG refuelling point; if you don't have that facility, make a note of gas-ready service stations before you leave home. Always make sure that you have enough fuel to reach your first refuelling stop.

Electric cars

Electric cars use an on-board battery and convert energy stored in the cells to provide power. They require recharging from the mains – either at home or at on-street charging points.

Remember that current electric cars have a limited range before they require a recharge. Make sure that your vehicle is fully charged before you start your journey and factor in any additional time that charging the battery will require if you need to power up.

Diesel engines

With the development of clean diesel technology and good fuel economy, diesel vehicles are environmentally friendly, provided the engine is tuned correctly.

Diesel particulate matter can be harmful, but most diesel cars are now fitted with a diesel particulate filter (DPF), a device that filters particulates from exhaust gases. These filters reduce diesel particulate emissions, helping vehicles to meet European emission standards and improving air quality and public

health. It's therefore important to maintain the vehicle's DPF in accordance with the manufacturer's recommendations.

Take care to avoid spilling diesel fuel when refuelling, since it will create an extremely slippery surface.

Take care never to put petrol into a diesel vehicle, or diesel fuel into a petrol-engined vehicle. Look carefully at the pump you're going to use.

⊕ Oils and coolant

Engine oil

Oil is necessary to lubricate your engine. You need to keep the oil at the level recommended by the vehicle manufacturer. Check regularly and top up the oil when necessary, especially before a long journey.

Ideally you should check the oil level every time you fill up with fuel.

How to check the oil level

The dipstick will tell you the amount of oil in the engine.

Some manufacturers recommend that you check the oil while the engine is cold, whereas others suggest you check it while it's warm. Your vehicle handbook will give you this information.

You'll need a clean, dry cloth to wipe the dipstick.

- Ensure the vehicle is on a level area and not on a slope.
- Look for the dipstick on the engine block of your vehicle.
- Take particular care if your vehicle is fitted with automatic transmission. There may be an additional dipstick for checks on the level of transmission oil. Consult the vehicle handbook.

Oil changes

Follow the manufacturer's recommendations. Remember to have the oil filter changed at the same time as the oil.

Oil is toxic and, if it comes into contact with skin, can cause skin problems. Use protective gloves or a barrier cream and always wash oil off your hands immediately.

Keep containers storing oil out of reach of children.

Oil use

The amount of oil an engine will use depends on

- the type of engine
- the amount of wear
- how you drive.

Don't

- run the engine when the oil level is below the minimum mark
- add so much oil that the level rises above the maximum mark. You'll create excess pressure that could damage the engine seals and gaskets, and cause oil leaks. Moving internal parts can hit the oil surface in an overfull engine and may do serious or even terminal damage.

Warning light

If the oil pressure warning light on your instrument panel comes on when you're driving, stop as soon as you can and check the oil level.

The oil in your engine has to perform several tasks at high pressures and temperatures up to 300°C. It helps to

- resist wear on the moving surfaces

- counteract the corrosive acids formed as the hydrocarbons in the fuel are burnt in the engine

- keep the engine cool.

Over time the oil will become contaminated with combustion products, metal particles and moisture. Regular oil and filter changes are necessary to ensure the engine is protected by clean oil.

Make sure you always use the lubricants recommended in the vehicle handbook.

Coolant

Most vehicles today use a mixture of water and anti-freeze to make up the coolant. This stays in the radiator all year round and helps to keep the engine comparatively cool while it's running. The anti-freeze stops the coolant from freezing in cold conditions.

The anti-freeze also contains a corrosion inhibitor, which reduces rust and oxidation and prolongs the life of the system. In cold weather, keep the recommended strength of anti-freeze. Have it checked at least annually – late summer or early autumn is best.

You should check the coolant level frequently, particularly before a long trip, topping it up as necessary. Look for the high/low level markings on the header tank, where one is fitted. The need to top up often might indicate a leak or other fault in the cooling system. Have it checked by your garage or dealer.

It's a good idea to carry a spare supply of coolant in your vehicle.

Warning

- Never remove a radiator or header tank cap when the engine is hot.

- Never add cold water to an overheated engine; let it cool for a while first.

- Don't overfill or the system will blow the excess out as soon as it warms up.

→ Steering and suspension

Issues to look out for

If you feel or hear any knocking or rattling noises from the steering or suspension, you should seek advice.

Excessive movement or play in the steering wheel may indicate wear in the steering mechanism. You should seek qualified advice without delay.

Power-assisted steering

When the ignition is on and/or the engine is running, movement of the steering wheel will cause hydraulic pressure or electrical energy to assist the driver and make the steering easier. If the steering needs a lot of effort (becomes heavy) the power-assistance system may not be working properly.

Before starting a journey, two simple checks can be made.

- Gentle pressure on the steering wheel, maintained while the ignition switch is moved to 'on' or the engine is started, should result in a slight but noticeable movement as the system begins to operate.

- Alternatively, turning the steering wheel just after moving off will tell you immediately whether the power assistance is functioning.

Check the level of fluid in the pump reservoir regularly when the engine is switched off. The level should be between the 'min' and 'max' marks.

Never run the engine without oil in the pump reservoir. You could severely damage the pump or cause it to seize up completely.

Suspension

Check the condition of shock absorbers by examining them for signs of fluid leaks and by bouncing the vehicle. It shouldn't continue to bounce unduly when tested. If in doubt, seek qualified help.

Worn shock absorbers make a vehicle difficult to control and can increase your stopping distance.

 Brakes

Regular servicing

Regular servicing will help to ensure your brakes work properly. Follow the manufacturer's recommendation on service intervals. Unless you're a skilled mechanic, leave brake checking, adjustment and replacement of brake pads and shoes to your garage.

If you're in any doubt about your vehicle's brakes, don't use the vehicle. Have it checked immediately.

Warning lights

Most vehicles are equipped with a warning signal to indicate certain faults within the braking system. If the red warning signal shows, consult your vehicle handbook or obtain guidance from a mechanic. Driving the vehicle with faulty brakes could be dangerous and may be illegal.

Anti-lock braking systems

If your vehicle has anti-lock brakes (ABS), there will also be a warning light for that system to indicate a fault. If this light comes on, have the system checked immediately. Consult your vehicle handbook or your garage before driving the vehicle. Only if it's safe, drive carefully to the nearest garage.

Footbrake

Note any variations in braking efficiency. If the brakes feel spongy or slack, have them checked by a qualified mechanic. They're too important to be ignored.

Testing your brakes

Test the brakes every day as you set out. Choose a safe spot on the road.

If you hear any strange noises, or if the vehicle pulls to one side, consult your garage immediately.

Check the brake-fluid level regularly, but don't overfill. Look for the high/low markings on the reservoir. Make sure the brake-fluid reservoir is kept topped up. If the brake-fluid level is allowed to get too low, air will enter the system, causing reduced brake efficiency. If the cause of the low fluid level is a leak, it could lead to complete brake failure.

Parking brake

Check for excessive wear on the parking brake in the following way.

When applying the brake, ensure that there's no excessive travel of the brake lever and that the lever locks securely. The parking brake must prevent the vehicle from moving.

Have the parking brake checked if

- the amount of travel is above the limit specified in the vehicle handbook
- the vehicle can roll on a gradient when the parking brake is fully set.

 Tyres

Your tyres are your only contact with the road. The area of contact is as small as the sole of a shoe for each tyre. Tyres won't grip properly and safely unless they're in good condition and correctly inflated. They can easily become damaged, so check for wear and tear and replace them when necessary.

The penalties for using faulty tyres or tyres worn beyond the minimum legal tread depth are very severe. They may include a fixed fine, driving licence endorsement for every faulty tyre and discretionary disqualification.

Checking the condition of your tyres

- Check that the walls of the tyres are free from cuts and bulges.
- Check that all your tyres have a good depth of tread right across and all around them. The legal requirement for cars, vans, trailers and caravans is no less than 1.6 mm tread depth across the central three-quarters of the breadth of the tyre and around the entire outer circumference. However, it's recommended that you replace your tyres before this legal limit is reached.
- Have the wheel alignment and wheel balance, suspension and braking system checked regularly. If there's a fault, have it put right as soon as you can, otherwise the wear on the tyres will be excessive or uneven.
- If you see that parts of the tread are wearing before others, seek advice. This can indicate a tyre, brake, steering or suspension fault.

Remove anything (stones, glass, etc) caught in the treads. These can work their way in and cause damage.

How to save wear and tear on tyres

- Check tyre pressures frequently.

- Avoid driving over potholes and broken road surfaces. If you can't avoid them, slow down.

- Don't drive over kerbs or scrape the wheels along them when manoeuvring. You'll damage the wall of the tyre and this could cause a blow-out later.

- Hitting the kerb can also affect the tracking of the front wheels. If there are any signs of uneven front tyre wear, have the tracking checked.

- Think and plan ahead. High speeds, fast cornering and heavy braking all increase tyre wear.

Tyre pressure

You can't guess pressures just by looking at a tyre, except when it's obviously flat.

Check your tyres' pressures regularly – at least once a week. The vehicle handbook will show the correct pressure.

Check your tyres and adjust the pressure when they're cold. Don't forget the spare tyre and remember to refit the valve caps.

The handbook will also tell you if you need different pressures for different conditions.

Generally, the pressure should be higher for a heavily loaded vehicle or if you're intending to drive at high speed for a long distance – for example, a long motorway journey.

Find out more about tyre safety on this YouTube channel.

youtube.com/user/TyreSafe

⊙ Electrical systems

Battery

Most modern batteries are maintenance-free and sealed for life. The terminals should be secure, clean and greased.

If the battery is fitted with a filler cap or caps, check the level of the fluid. The plates in each cell should be covered. Top up with distilled water if necessary, but avoid overfilling.

Lights

Check the operation of the front and rear lights, brake lights and indicators, including hazard lights, each time you use the vehicle.

Make use of reflections in windows and garage doors, or ask someone to help you.

Carry a selection of spare bulbs and replace any faulty ones immediately. Your vehicle handbook should give the bulb replacement procedure.

Headlights **MUST** be properly adjusted to

- avoid dazzling other road users
- enable the driver to see the road ahead.

All lights **MUST**

- be clean and in good working order
- show a steady light.

Indicators **MUST**

- be clearly visible
- be in good working order
- show the correct colour
- flash between once and twice per second.

Windscreen washers and wipers

Check the windscreen washer mechanism and the washer reservoirs. Make sure there's enough liquid.

The washer can be very important in wet, muddy conditions. If you carry a supply of water, you can use a sponge to wash away dirt wherever you happen to be.

Check the wipers. Replace worn or damaged blades. If your vehicle is fitted with headlight washers, the same attention should be paid to these.

The horn

Check the horn is working properly and sounding clearly. Take care not to alarm or annoy others when doing so.

⊕ Basic fault-finding

For detailed advice, consult the vehicle handbook, a workshop maintenance manual or a qualified mechanic.

The table that follows gives only a brief guide to simple fault-finding and remedies.

If you have any doubts about the roadworthiness of the vehicle, seek specialist help without delay. Don't ignore any warning signs.

Some minor faults can be easily identified and corrected, but problems with more complex engine management and electronic systems are better left to qualified mechanics – especially when the vehicle's warranty might be affected.

> **REMEMBER,** prevention is better (and cheaper) than cure. Having your vehicle serviced according to the maintenance schedule helps the engine work more efficiently. This will save fuel and reduce the effect on the environment by cutting emissions. If you notice any fault, consult your garage.

Recognising basic faults

Symptom	Probable cause	Remedy
Brakes		
Vehicle pulls to one side when braking	Incorrect adjustment	Seek qualified help
Warning light shows	Undue wear in pads/ shoes	Seek qualified help
	System fault	Seek qualified help
	Low brake-fluid level	Check level. If low, seek qualified help
	Brake light failed	Replace bulb
Brakes not working well on good road surfaces	Possible component failure	Seek qualified help
	Brakes need adjusting	Seek qualified help
Parking brake won't hold vehicle	Cable adjustment or replacement needed	Seek qualified help
Lights		
Light doesn't come on	Bulb failure	Check and replace
	Fuse failure	Check and replace
Indicator flashing irregularly	Possible bulb failure	Check and replace
	Relay failure	Check and replace
Main/dip beam not lit	Part failure of unit	Check and replace
Tyres/steering		
Steering 'heavy' or erratic	Puncture	Change wheel and repair or replace tyre
	Fault in power-assisted steering unit	Seek qualified help
Vibration in steering at specific speeds	Front wheel out of balance or tyre defect	Have the wheel balanced or tyre changed
Engine		
Misfiring or won't run	Fuel or electrical fault	Examine connections and seek help
	Defective spark plugs	Examine and replace if necessary

Symptom	Probable cause	Remedy
Engine, continued		
Fails to start	Out of fuel	Check gauge
	Damp in electrical circuits	Use anti-damp spray
Starter doesn't operate	Battery discharged (flat)	Charge or change battery
		Jump start
		Push start
Starter or solenoid clicks	Starter motor jammed	Rock vehicle backwards and forwards in gear with ignition off
		Turn 'square' end on starter with a spanner
Overheating	Fan belt snapped or hose leaking	Replace belt or hose
		Tape hose for temporary repair
	Fuse blown on electric cooling fan	Replace fuse

Maintenance

Check all levels and systems as recommended.

Changing filters and spark plugs at the recommended intervals will help keep your vehicle reliable and prolong its life.

Air filter

Replace the air filter at the intervals recommended by the manufacturer, or sooner if the vehicle is used in exceptionally dusty conditions.

Overhead camshaft engines

On this design of engine it's vital to have the camshaft drive belt (if fitted) replaced at the recommended intervals. Serious damage can be caused to the engine if the belt breaks.

Section fifteen
⊙ Breakdowns

This section covers

- Be prepared
- If you break down
- Breakdowns on motorways
- Breakdowns on dual carriageways
- Punctures and blow-outs

⊕ Be prepared

Reducing the chances of breaking down

You can reduce the chances of breaking down with preventive maintenance and regular vehicle checks. However, no matter how careful you are, your vehicle can still break down; for example, a puncture or engine problem is always possible.

Knowing how to deal with such a situation efficiently and safely is essential for every driver.

Many breakdowns are the result of

- failing to make the recommended vehicle checks
- poor vehicle maintenance
- harsh use of the vehicle.

Don't drive on, ignoring unusual noises or symptoms. If left uncorrected, a minor problem could develop into a serious fault, making the vehicle dangerous to drive.

Useful equipment

Carry a tool kit in your vehicle. The following items are useful to keep for emergency use or to make essential repairs during your journey.

- a warning triangle (or other permitted warning device)
- spare bulbs and fuses
- a torch
- vinyl tape
- wire
- jump leads
- a tow rope
- pliers
- a plastic container of water.

If you do break down, it's a good idea to wear high-visibility clothing so that you can be seen by other road users. Consider carrying a fluorescent and reflective waistcoat (fluorescent so it can be seen in daylight and reflective so it can be seen at night).

Warning devices

Permitted warning devices

There are various warning devices that you can buy to place on the road to warn other drivers when you've broken down. Don't use any of these warning devices

• on a motorway

• as an excuse to leave your car in a dangerous position.

Advance warning triangles

Advance warning triangles fold flat and don't take up much space in the car. You should carry one and use it to warn other road users if your car is obstructing the highway or is in a dangerous position as a result of a breakdown or a road traffic incident.

Where to position the triangle

You should place the triangle on the road, well back from the car.

• On a straight, level road, put the triangle 45 metres (147 feet) from your vehicle.

• On a winding or hilly road, put the triangle where drivers will see it before they have to deal with any bend or hump in the road.

- On a very narrow road, put the triangle on the nearside verge or footpath.

Always use your hazard warning lights as well as a warning triangle.

Other warning devices

These include traffic cones, collapsible traffic cones and traffic delineators (posts). At least four of any of these should be placed in a line behind your vehicle to guide traffic past. A flashing amber light may be used with any of these warning devices, but may not be used on its own.

Alternatively, a flexible yellow sheet displaying a red triangle can be placed on the vehicle as long as it doesn't obscure the number plate, lights or reflectors.

National breakdown/motoring organisations

By joining a national organisation or taking out breakdown insurance, you'll save a great deal of time and money if you break down.

Most services include an option to take your vehicle and passengers either to your destination or to your home.

The annual fee is usually less than the cost of a single motorway breakdown call-out.

⊕ If you break down

As a general rule, brake as gently as possible and pull over as far to the left as possible to keep your vehicle away from approaching traffic.

If the breakdown affects your control of the car

- try to keep in a straight line by holding the steering wheel firmly
- avoid braking severely
- steer gently on to the side of the road as you lose speed.

If possible, get your car off the road and

- use your hazard warning lights to warn others

- keep your sidelights on if it's dark or visibility is poor
- wear high-visibility clothing to help other road users see you if you need to get out of your car
- don't stand behind your vehicle where you might obscure the lights
- use a warning device, particularly if you've broken down near a bend or over the brow of a hill. Don't use one if you've broken down on a motorway.

Keep children and animals under control, and away from the road.

Always take great care when you're placing or retrieving a warning device.

Contact the police if your vehicle is causing an obstruction, and a breakdown service if you're unable to rectify the fault yourself.

Don't

- accept a lift from a stranger, however helpful they may be in the situation
- leave your vehicle for any longer than you really have to.

Drivers travelling alone

You might feel vulnerable if you're travelling alone and you break down – especially on an isolated stretch of road, a dual carriageway or a motorway.

When you telephone for assistance, make it clear to the operator that you're travelling alone. Priority will often be given in these cases.

Being recovered

If your vehicle can't be repaired where it has broken down, it will need to be moved.

There are three options

- being recovered by your breakdown organisation (the best option)
- calling out a local garage (probably the most costly)

- being towed by a friend (the most dangerous – in no circumstances should an inexperienced driver consider this).

If you're being towed, remember that the braking won't be as effective and the steering will feel heavier if the engine isn't running.

Free recovery at roadworks

If you break down on a stretch of road with roadworks, and the road is managed by Highways England, you'll be able to get free recovery if

- there's no access to hard shoulders and lay-bys
- the standard lane widths have been reduced
- the use of emergency telephones has been suspended.

See **www.gov.uk/highways** for more information.

⊕ Breakdowns on motorways

According to a survey by the Highways Agency (now Highways England), 11 200 people ran out of petrol on the English motorway network between April 2010 and September 2011. Before you join a motorway, make sure that you have enough fuel to reach your destination. If you find that you're running low, pull in to the nearest service station rather than risk running your vehicle on an empty tank, as this can lead to dirt and sediment clogging your fuel filter or injectors.

If you know that you're going to need to fill up more than once on your journey, plan ahead by looking at the intervals between service stations on your route. You should be able to find this information online by using station locator and route planner tools. Most satellite navigation (sat-nav) systems will also have service stations marked on their maps.

If you do break down on the motorway, try and reach the next exit or service area. If you can't do this, steer your vehicle onto the hard shoulder as safely as possible, and as far to the left as you can, away from traffic.

When you stop, it's a good idea to have your wheels turned to the left so that, if you're hit from behind, your vehicle isn't pushed onto the main carriageway.

When you stop

Once you've stopped

- switch on your hazard lights to warn other drivers that you've broken down
- make sure your sidelights are on in poor visibility or at night
- don't open the offside doors
- warn your passengers of the dangers of passing vehicles
- keep animals inside
- with your passengers, leave the vehicle by the nearside door away from the traffic. Lock all doors, except the front passenger door
- ask your passengers to wait near the vehicle, but on the embankment away from the hard shoulder

- telephone the emergency services. (Let them know if you're a vulnerable motorist such as a disabled or older person, or are travelling alone or with young children.) If possible, use a roadside emergency telephone, which will pinpoint your position, rather than a mobile phone.

Never

- attempt even simple repairs on the motorway
- place any kind of warning device on the carriageway or hard shoulder.

Disabled drivers
If you have any kind of mobility difficulty, you should stay in your vehicle and

- keep your seat belt fastened
- switch on your hazard warning lights
- display a 'help' pennant or use a mobile phone, if you have one in your vehicle, and be prepared to advise the emergency services of your location.

If you pass a broken-down vehicle displaying a 'help' pennant, you may feel you should do something to help. However, you mustn't stop and approach the vehicle. If you think the incident needs to be reported, you should leave the motorway or dual carriageway at the next exit or service area and report what you've seen, making sure you know the location of the vehicle before you call.

Calling for help

Emergency telephones
These telephones are connected to control centres and are on most stretches of motorway at one-mile intervals.

Look for a telephone symbol and arrow on marker posts 100 metres (328 feet) apart along the hard shoulder.

The arrow directs you to the nearest phone on your side of the carriageway. Walk to the telephone, keeping on the inside of the hard shoulder.

Never cross the carriageway or an exit or entry slip road to reach a telephone or for any other purpose.

Using the emergency telephone

The telephone connects you to a control centre, which will put you through to a breakdown service. Always face the traffic when you speak on the telephone.

You'll be asked for

- the number on the telephone, which gives your precise location
- details of your vehicle and your membership details, if you belong to one of the motoring organisations
- details of the fault.

If you're a vulnerable motorist, such as a woman travelling alone, make this clear to the operator. You'll be told approximately how long you'll have to wait.

Mobile phones

If you're unable to use an emergency telephone, use a mobile phone if you have one in your vehicle.

However, before you call, make sure that you can provide precise details of your location. Marker posts on the side of the hard shoulder identify your location and you should provide these details when you call.

Find out more about what to do if you break down on a motorway at this link.

surivegroup.org/pages/safety-information/stopping-on-the-hard-shoulder

Waiting for the emergency services

Wait on the bank near your vehicle, so you can see the emergency services arriving.

Don't wait in your vehicle unless another vehicle pulls up near you and you feel at risk.

Motorway deaths have been caused by vehicles being driven into people on the hard shoulder. When you're on the hard shoulder you're much more likely to be injured by motorway traffic than suffer a personal attack.

If you're approached by anyone you don't recognise as a member of the emergency services, think carefully before you speak to them.

If they try to speak to you, ask for some identification and tell them that the police or control centre have been told and the emergency services are coming.

A traffic officer or a person claiming to be from the emergency services should have

• an identity card

• your details: your name and information about the breakdown.

Leave your vehicle again as soon as you feel the danger has passed.

If you can't get your vehicle onto the hard shoulder, switch on your hazard warning lights and leave your vehicle only when you can safely get clear of the carriageway.

Rejoining the motorway

Use the hard shoulder to build up speed before joining the other traffic when it's safe to do so. Don't try to move out from behind another vehicle or force your way into the stream of traffic.

Remember to switch off your hazard warning lights before moving off.

⊕ Breakdowns on dual carriageways

Some dual carriageways are similar to motorways; they have

- a hard shoulder
- emergency telephones at regular intervals.

Most dual carriageways don't have a hard shoulder. If you break down here, get your car safely away from the road if you can – onto the grass verge or lay-by if there is one.

Don't stop on unprotected lay-bys on dual carriageways if at all possible. Unprotected lay-bys are those where there's no kerbed island between the main carriageway and the lay-by.

Fatal incidents involving stopped vehicles on dual carriageways have happened at unprotected lay-bys. Try to find a protected lay-by if at all possible; you'll be much safer there.

If you have to stop on a grass verge, take care as long grass could be set on fire by the heat of a catalytic converter.

You should also

- use your hazard warning lights
- use your warning triangle or other device – but only if it's safe to do so
- move your passengers to a safe position off the carriageway, well away from the vehicle
- go to the nearest telephone and arrange assistance
- keep animals safely in the car.

⊕ Punctures and blow-outs

If your car suddenly becomes unstable or you begin to notice steering problems, you might have a puncture or a blow-out (burst tyre).

Try not to panic.

- Take your foot off the accelerator.
- Don't brake suddenly.
- Try to keep a straight course by holding the steering wheel firmly.
- Stop gradually at the side of the road.
- Get the vehicle away from the traffic (onto the hard shoulder if you're on a motorway).

If you have to move the vehicle, do so very slowly to avoid further damage to the tyre or wheel rim.

On a motorway, never attempt to change a wheel yourself. Always use the emergency telephones to call for assistance.

On all other roads, get the vehicle to a place of safety before attempting repairs or changing the wheel.

Changing a wheel

If you do have to change a wheel and can do so safely, follow this procedure.

- Pull in at the nearest available lay-by or designated parking place. If neither of these options is available to you, then try and stop somewhere that's far enough from the highway to avoid causing a safety hazard. Don't try and change your wheel at the side of the road. If you can't get off the road altogether, use your warning triangle, or any other permitted warning device, to warn other drivers, particularly if you're near a bend. If necessary, wait for assistance.
- Some new cars have puncture repair kits rather than spare wheels. If your car doesn't have a spare wheel as standard, follow the manufacturer's directions to use the kit to provide a temporary fix.

- Don't try and change the wheel on soft or loose ground as jacking up the car on this kind of surface could cause an accident.

- Turn off the engine and make sure that you switch on your hazard warning lights.

- Make sure the handbrake is applied and the car is in first gear.

- Take out the jack and the spare wheel from the car. These are usually stored under the lining in the boot of your vehicle. The spare wheel may be screwed in – if this is the case, then carefully undo the screw bolt and lift the wheel out of the boot.

- Remove the wheel cap.

- Use the wheel nut wrench to slightly loosen the wheel nuts. Most nuts turn anti-clockwise.

- Place the jack underneath a lifting point that's near the wheel that you're removing.

- Turn the jack's handle until the head of the jack is flush against the lifting point. Keep turning until the car is slightly raised. If you need more information about lifting your car with a jack, your manufacturer's handbook should be able to help you.

- Jack up your vehicle until the wheel is raised off the ground. Fully remove the wheel nuts and carefully lift the wheel off the hub.

- Place the spare wheel on the hub, replace the wheel nuts, then tighten each nut by hand. The nuts will normally tighten in a clockwise direction.

- Tighten the top nut first, then tighten the others in a diagonal pattern.

- Lower the jack until your vehicle's wheel is touching the ground. Use the wrench to tighten the nuts until the wheel is fully secured.

Section sixteen

⊙ **Incidents, accidents and emergencies**

This section covers

- The scene of an incident
- First aid on the road
- Fire and electric shock
- Tunnels

⊙ The scene of an incident

Arriving at the scene of an incident

You can reduce the chances of being involved in an incident by driving defensively. Unfortunately, road traffic incidents are always possible, even with the greatest care.

You might also come upon the scene of an incident. It could be that you're the first to arrive and the safety of existing casualties and other road users might be in your hands.

Knowledge and preparation can save lives. If you're involved in an incident, you **MUST** stop.

If you're the first or among the first to arrive at the scene of an incident, avoid becoming a casualty yourself. Remember that

- further collisions can, and do, happen
- fire is a major hazard.

Take extra care when visibility is very poor.

What to do at the scene of an incident

Warn other traffic
Do this by

- switching on hazard warning lights or other lights
- displaying an advance warning triangle (unless you're on a motorway)
- using any other means to warn other drivers.

Put out cigarettes or other fire hazards. Switch off your engine and warn others to do the same.

Call the emergency services if necessary.

Calling emergency services
Give full details of the location and casualties. On a motorway, this could mean going to the nearest emergency telephone.

Mobile phones

It can be very tempting to reach immediately for your mobile phone to call the emergency services.

Before you do, make sure you'll be able to tell them exactly where you are. This is particularly important on a motorway, where imprecise details can cause great problems for the emergency services. Location details are given on marker posts located on the hard shoulder. Always check these before you make your call.

Additionally, you will find driver location signs on motorways and primary routes. These identify the precise location and help the emergency services to get to the scene quickly.

M42 A 194.7

Dealing with those involved

Move uninjured people away from the vehicles involved to a place of safety. On a motorway this should be away from the carriageway, hard shoulder or central reservation.

Don't move casualties trapped in vehicles unless they're in danger. Be prepared to give first aid as described later in this section.

Don't remove a motorcyclist's helmet unless it's essential to do so; for example, if they're having breathing difficulties.

When an ambulance arrives, give the crew as many facts as you can (but not assumptions, diagnoses, etc).

Incidents involving dangerous goods

If the incident involves a vehicle containing dangerous goods

- switch off your engine and don't smoke
- keep well away from the vehicle
- call the emergency services and give the police or fire brigade as much information as possible about the labels and other markings. Don't use a mobile phone close to a vehicle carrying flammable loads

- beware of dangerous liquids, dust or vapours, no matter how small a concentration, or however minor the effects on you may seem.

Full details of hazard warning plates, such as the one shown above, are given in The Highway Code.

Passing the scene of an incident

If you're not one of the first to arrive at the scene of an incident and enough people have already stopped to give assistance, you should drive past carefully and not be distracted by the incident.

If the incident is on the other side of a dual carriageway or motorway, don't slow down to look. You may cause another collision on your side of the road or, at the very least, additional and unnecessary traffic congestion.

Always give way to emergency and incident support vehicles. Watch out for their flashing lights and listen for their warning sirens. Depending on the type of vehicle, the flashing lights used could be red, blue, amber or green (see rules 106, 107, 219 and 281 in The Highway Code).

Police cones or vehicles
If these are obstructing the road, don't drive round them; you should stop. They mean that the road ahead is closed or blocked for an unspecified time.

If you're involved in a road traffic incident

You **MUST** stop. If there are injuries, either call an ambulance and the police yourself or ask someone else to do it. Ask them to return to you when they've made the call to confirm that they've made it. You should

- give whatever help you can. People who seem to be unhurt may be suffering from shock and may, in fact, be unaware of their injuries
- ask yourself whether you're hurt too. If in doubt, get a check-up at the hospital.

If you hit a domestic or farm animal, try to find the owner to report any injuries.

For any incident involving

- injury to another person or animal
- damage to another vehicle or property

give your name and address, the name and address of the vehicle's owner and the registration number of the vehicle to anyone having reasonable grounds for requiring them. If this isn't possible at the time of the incident, you **MUST** report the incident to the police as soon as possible and in any case within 24 hours. In Northern Ireland you must do this immediately.

If there has been an injury, you must also give insurance details to the police. If you can't produce the insurance documents when you report the incident, you have up to seven days to produce them at a police station of your choice.

Witnesses

Note any witnesses and try to make sure they don't leave before you get their names and addresses.

Make a note of the numbers of any vehicles whose occupants might have witnessed the incident.

You'll need to exchange details and obtain

- the other driver's name, address and phone number
- the make and registration number(s) of the other vehicle(s) involved
- insurance details.

Find out the vehicle owner's details too, if different.

Information

Gather as much information as you can, such as

- vehicle damage and/or injuries you're aware of
- the number of people present in the vehicle(s)
- weather conditions
- road conditions
- details of other vehicles. Record all information: the colour, condition, whether the lights were on, and whether they were showing any indicator signals
- what was said by you and other people
- identification numbers of police involved
- any other possible factor in the incident.

Take photographs

If you have a camera or a mobile phone with a camera

- take pictures at the scene, including the registration plates of the vehicles involved
- try to record the conditions, vehicle damage and number of passengers present.

Some smartphone apps have a checklist feature designed to help you gather all the information you need in the event that you witness – or are involved in – a road traffic incident.

In gathering information, don't place yourself in any danger.

Draw a map

Show the situation before and after the incident, and give approximate distances

- between vehicles
- from road signs or junctions
- away from the kerb.

Note skid marks, where any witnesses were situated, street names, car speeds and directions.

Statements

If the police ask you for a statement, you don't have to make one straight away. It could be better to wait a while, even if you don't appear to be suffering from shock. Write your statement later. Take care with the wording, and keep a copy.

Fraud

The Insurance Fraud Enforcement Department (IFED) is a dedicated police investigation unit based at the City of London Police. They're investigating insurance fraud and arresting suspected Insurance fraudsters across the UK. IFED targets all kinds of insurance fraud, from organised gangs operating 'crash for cash' rings, through to individuals making fraudulent claims on personal injury and motor vehicle policies.

Therefore, it's important to record as many details about the incident as you can, in order to prevent fraudulent insurance and personal injury claims.

⊕ First aid on the road

The following information was compiled with the assistance of St John Ambulance, the British Heart Foundation and the British Red Cross. It's intended as a general guide for those without first-aid training but shouldn't be considered a substitute for proper training. Any first aid given at the scene of an incident should be looked on only as a temporary measure until the emergency services arrive.

1. Deal with danger

Further collisions and fire are the main dangers following a crash. Approach any vehicle involved with care, watching out for spilt oil or broken glass. Switch off all engines and, if possible, warn other traffic. If you have a vehicle, switch on your hazard warning lights. Stop anyone from smoking, and put on the gloves from your first-aid kit if you have one.

2. Get help

If you can do so safely, try to get the assistance of bystanders. Ask someone to call the appropriate emergency services on 999 or 112 as soon as possible. The operator will need to know the exact location of the incident (including the direction of traffic, eg northbound) and the number of vehicles involved. Try to give information about the condition of any casualties; for example, if anyone is having difficulty breathing, is bleeding heavily, is trapped in a vehicle or doesn't respond when spoken to.

3. Help those involved

Don't move casualties from their vehicles unless there's the threat of further danger.

Don't remove a motorcyclist's helmet unless it's essential.

Try to keep casualties warm, dry and as comfortable as you can.

Give reassurance confidently and try not to leave a casualty alone or let them wander into the path of other traffic.

Don't give a casualty anything to eat or drink.

4. Provide emergency care

If you need to provide emergency care, follow the DR ABC code.		
Danger		Check that it's safe to approach.
Response		Try to get a response by gently shaking the casualty's shoulders and asking loudly 'Are you all right?' If they respond, check for injuries.
Airway		If there's no response, open the casualty's airway by placing your fingers under their chin and lifting it forward.
Breathing		Check that the casualty is breathing normally. Look for chest movements, look and listen for breathing, and feel for breath on your cheek. If there are no signs of breathing, start CPR. Interlock your fingers, place them in the centre of the casualty's chest and press down hard and fast – around 5–6 centimetres and about twice a second. You may only need one hand for a child and shouldn't press down as far. For infants, use two fingers in the middle of the chest and press down about a third of the chest depth. Don't stop until the casualty starts breathing again or a medical professional takes over.

Circulation		If the casualty is responsive and breathing, check for signs of bleeding. Protect yourself from exposure to blood and check for anything that may be in the wound, such as glass. Don't remove anything that's stuck in the wound. Taking care not to press on the object, build up padding on either side of the object. If nothing is embedded, apply firm pressure over the wound to stem the flow of blood. As soon as practical, fasten a pad to the wound with a bandage or length of cloth. Use the cleanest material available.

Unconscious and breathing

Don't move a casualty unless there's further danger. Moving a casualty unnecessarily could worsen any injury they may have sustained. If breathing stops, treat as recommended under 'DR ABC'.

Don't attempt to remove a motorcyclist's helmet unless it's essential; for example, if the casualty isn't breathing normally. Otherwise, serious injury could result.

If an adult or child is unconscious and breathing, but otherwise uninjured, place them on their side in the recovery position (as shown below).

- Start with the casualty on their back and sit or crouch to one side of them.
- Place the arm nearest you straight out, at a right angle to their body.
- Roll them onto their side towards you.
- Turn the casualty's other arm palm upwards, and place this hand between the ground and the casualty's cheek.
- With your other hand, grasp the casualty's top leg just above the knee and pull it up at a right angle, keeping the foot on the ground. This will prevent them from rolling over any further.
- Make sure that the casualty's airway remains open and that you monitor their condition until a medical professional takes over..

Dealing with shock

The effects of shock may not be immediately obvious. Warning signs to look for include

- paleness of the face (pallor)
- cold, clammy skin
- fast, shallow breathing
- fast, weak pulse
- yawning or sighing
- confusion
- loss of consciousness (in extreme cases).

Prompt treatment can help to deal with shock.

- Don't give the person anything to eat or drink. Their condition may be severe enough to require surgery, in which case it's better if the stomach is empty.
- Lay them down, with their head low and legs raised and supported, to increase the flow of blood to their head.
- Call 999 or 112 for medical help. Say that you think the person is in shock, and explain what you think caused it (such as bleeding or a heart attack).
- Loosen any tight clothing around the person's neck, chest and waist to make sure it doesn't constrict their blood flow.

- Fear and pain can make shock worse, by increasing the body's demand for oxygen, so, while you wait for help to arrive, it's important to keep the person comfortable, warm and calm. Do this by covering them with a coat or blanket and comforting and reassuring them.
- Keep checking their breathing, pulse and level of response.
- If they lose consciousness at any point, open their airway, check their breathing, and prepare to treat someone who has become unconscious.

Burns

Put out any flames, taking care for your own safety. Cool the burn for at least 10 minutes with plenty of clean, cool water. Cover the burn with cling film if available. Don't try to remove anything that's sticking to the burn.

Be prepared

Always carry a first-aid kit – you might never need it, but it could save a life.

Learn first aid – you can get first-aid training from a qualified organisation such as St John Ambulance, St Andrew's First Aid, British Red Cross Society or any suitable qualified body.

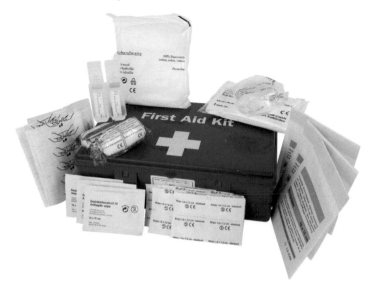

⊕ Fire and electric shock

Fire

Carrying a suitable fire extinguisher in your vehicle may help you to put out a small fire.

If you suspect a fire in the engine compartment

- pull up as safely and as quickly as possible
- get all passengers out safely
- summon assistance or get someone to dial 999 or 112
- **don't** open the bonnet
- you may be able to direct any available fire extinguisher through the small gap available when the release catch is operated.
- if the fire appears to be large, **don't** try to tackle it; get well clear of the vehicle and leave it to the fire service
- **don't** take any risks.

Remember, fire can spread through a vehicle with alarming speed.

If you notice a strong smell of petrol, don't ignore it – alert the emergency services to it when they arrive.

Electric shock

Some incidents involve a vehicle hitting overhead cables or electrical supplies to traffic bollards, traffic lights or street lights. Check before trying to get someone out of a vehicle in such cases.

Don't touch any person who's obviously in contact with live electricity unless you can use some non-conducting item, such as a piece of dry wood, plastic or similar – anything wet shouldn't be used. You mustn't try to give first aid until electrical contact has been broken.

A person can also be electrocuted simply by being too close to a high-voltage overhead cable. Contact the provider (their telephone number may be shown on a nearby pole), then follow their advice.

⊕ Tunnels

If you break down or are involved in a road traffic incident in a tunnel

- switch on your hazard warning lights
- switch off the engine
- leave your vehicle
- give first aid to any injured people, if you're able
- call for help from an emergency point.

If your vehicle is on fire and you can drive it out of the tunnel, do so. If not

- pull over to the side and switch off the engine
- leave the vehicle immediately
- put out the fire using the vehicle's extinguisher or the one available in the tunnel
- move without delay to an emergency exit if you can't put out the fire
- call for help from the nearest emergency point.

If the vehicle in front is on fire, switch on your hazard warning lights, then follow the above procedure, giving first aid to the injured if possible.

Some tunnels have signs with specific advice about what to do if you break down or are involved in an incident inside them. Make sure you follow these instructions and inform the tunnel controller of your location as soon as you can.

Section seventeen

→ Ecosafe driving and the environment

This section covers

- What you can do
- Ecosafe driving
- Choosing a vehicle
- Vehicle maintenance
- Alternatives to driving

⊕ What you can do

Transport is an essential part of modern life, but we can't ignore its environmental consequences – local, regional and global. There's increasing public concern for the protection of our environment, with the result that many motor manufacturers are devoting more time, effort and resources to the development of environmentally friendly vehicles.

But you, as a driver, can also help. If you follow the principles of ecosafe driving set out in the following pages, you'll become a more environmentally friendly driver and

- your journeys will be more comfortable
- you could considerably reduce your fuel bills
- you could reduce those emissions that cause damage to the atmosphere.

In addition, you'll become a safer driver as you develop your planning, perception and anticipation skills to a high level.

Try to drive in an ecosafe manner at all times, whether you're driving for business or for pleasure. Fuel, like all forms of power, costs money as well as having an impact on the environment. Minimising the fuel or power you use is always important, both for the planet and for your pocket.

However, although it's good to save fuel, you mustn't compromise your own safety or that of other road users when attempting to do so. Road safety is more important than saving fuel. At all times you should be prepared to adapt to changing conditions and it may be that you have to sacrifice fuel-saving for safety.

The effects of pollution

Air pollution contributes to health problems for many people. In densely populated areas, traffic is the biggest source of air pollution. Road transport accounts for a significant proportion of all emissions and how we drive can make a surprising difference to local air quality.

The particular problem with emissions from vehicles is that they're at ground level. People with conditions such as respiratory problems, heart disease or vascular disease are particularly exposed.

In addition, pollution from motor vehicles causes changes to communities and the landscape, including

- damage to vegetation
- deterioration and weakening of buildings and bridges
- the depletion of natural resources
- disruption of wildlife.

Fuel combustion produces

- carbon dioxide, a major greenhouse gas; transport accounts for about one-fifth of the carbon dioxide we produce in this country
- nitric oxides; these add nitrogen to the atmosphere, causing damage and disturbance to the ecosystem.

Catalytic converters in good working order reduce these emissions.

Information about air pollution is available online at **https://uk-air.defra.gov.uk and www.gov.uk/defra**. You can also phone the free air pollution recorded information helpline on **0800 556 677**.

What you can do to help

The car has become a central feature in our lives, but it's still possible to drive in a manner that's less harmful to the environment by taking care and giving some thought to how, and when, we drive.

We give some suggestions on the following pages about what you can do to help.

⊖ Ecosafe driving

Ecosafe driving is a recognised and proven style of driving that contributes to road safety while also reducing fuel consumption and emissions.

One of the main factors in increasing road safety is the emphasis on planning ahead so that you're prepared for potential hazards. By increasing your hazard perception and planning skills you can make maximum use of your vehicle's momentum and engine braking. By doing this, you can reduce damage to the environment.

Hazard awareness and planning

You should be constantly scanning all around as you drive. Look into the far distance, middle distance and foreground, and also check behind and to the sides with frequent use of your mirrors.

Early recognition of potential hazards is important, but just looking isn't enough; you need to act correctly on what you've seen.

If you anticipate problems and take appropriate action to deal with hazards in plenty of time, you'll avoid

• late braking

• harsh acceleration.

Both of these actions lead to higher fuel consumption.

Keep a safe distance from the vehicle in front, as this will help you to plan your driving. Don't always use the brake when the vehicle in front of you slows down. By just taking your foot off the accelerator, your vehicle will slow down and fuel consumption will then be reduced.

If you plan early for hazards

- you'll avoid the need for sudden, harsh braking
- traffic will flow more smoothly (see section 18)
- you'll use less fuel.

Starting up and driving away

Avoid over-revving your engine when you start your vehicle and pull away.

Don't leave your engine running unnecessarily. If you're stationary and are likely to be so for more than a few minutes, you should switch off your engine to reduce emissions and noise pollution.

If your vehicle is fitted with a stop–start system, make sure it's active. This will save you the effort of switching off and restarting your engine when waiting in traffic queues.

Choosing your speed

Keep within the speed limit
Exceeding a speed limit by only a few miles per hour will mean that you use more fuel but, more importantly, you're breaking the law and increasing the risk of a collision.

Slow down
Vehicles travelling at 70 mph (112 km/h) use up to 30% more fuel to cover the same distance as those travelling at 50 mph (80 km/h). However, don't travel so slowly that you inconvenience other road users.

Cruise control

When appropriate, use cruise control if it's fitted. Cruise control keeps the vehicle travelling at a constant speed. It uses sophisticated control systems and is very fuel-efficient. It can also help to maintain your speed within the speed limit.

Cruise control shouldn't be used in heavy traffic or when driving on wet or slippery roads. Remember, when cruise control is activated, your feet may not be in their usual position in relation to the foot controls.

The accelerator

Try to use the accelerator smoothly and progressively. When appropriate, take your foot off the accelerator and allow the momentum of the car to take you forward.

Taking your foot off the accelerator when going downhill can save a considerable amount of fuel without any loss of control over the vehicle.

Wherever possible, avoid rapid acceleration or heavy braking, as this leads to greater fuel consumption and more pollution.

Driving smoothly can reduce fuel consumption by about 15%, as well as reducing wear and tear on your vehicle.

Selecting gears

It's not always necessary to change up or down through each gear; it's possible to miss out intermediate gears. This is known as 'block' gear changing. It helps to reduce the amount of time you're accelerating and, as this is when fuel consumption is at its highest, it will help you to save fuel (see section 5).

As soon as conditions allow, use the highest gear possible without making the engine struggle.

Some modern cars have a display that suggests when to change gear and which gear to use. Following these suggestions can help you save fuel.

Check fuel consumption

Check your fuel consumption regularly. To make sure you're getting the most from your car, simply record the amount of fuel you put in your car against miles travelled. This will help you to check whether you're using fuel efficiently.

If you haven't changed your method of driving, or the conditions in which you're driving, an increase in average fuel consumption can mean you need to have your car serviced. Ecosafe car drivers are constantly aware of how much fuel their vehicles use.

If your car is fitted with a trip computer, it can help you check your fuel consumption.

Engine braking

With your foot fully off the accelerator, there will only be enough fuel reaching the engine for it to tick over. The momentum of the moving car will turn the engine but, without fuel, the engine's compression creates a resistance. It's this resistance that slows the car and is termed 'engine braking'.

Engine power

Modern cars are designed to deliver power even when engine revs are quite low. You'll find that you can make use of the higher gears at low speeds.

Route planning

Plan your route and avoid known hold-ups and roadworks. Always know where you're going – you'll use a lot of fuel by getting lost.

Plan your journey beforehand.

* Use a map.
* Check a route planner on the internet.
* Program your satellite navigation (sat-nav) system, if you have one.
* Consider using an alternative route suggested by the sat-nav. This may add a few extra miles to a journey but can work out more fuel-efficient and less stressful.

If you're driving to a busy town or city, remember to plan where you're going to park. This can

* reduce journey times, emissions and costs
* allow you to arrive at your destination without the stress of having to start looking for a car park
* provide better opportunities to park in secure locations.

Try to use uncongested routes. Researchers have discovered new methods of helping the environment by easing traffic flow and congestion on certain routes. One example is the introduction of active traffic management (ATM) or 'smart motorways'. You can read about smart motorways in section 11, and more information about avoiding congestion can be found in section 18.

Minimise weight and drag

Save fuel by not carrying unnecessary weight in your car. Remove items from your boot if they're not required and avoid topping up your tank with fuel if it's not needed.

Remove cycle carriers and roof racks when they're not in use to reduce wind resistance.

FACTS The drag on a roof box can increase a vehicle's fuel consumption by more than 15%.

Opening windows or a sun roof will increase drag and, consequently, fuel consumption when you're driving at higher speeds.

Air conditioning and climate control

If air conditioning is fitted, use it only when you really need to – running air conditioning continuously may increase fuel consumption by about 15%.

Climate control is now an option on many cars. This monitors humidity, temperature (external and internal) and the quality of the air entering the vehicle. It adjusts the use of the air conditioning as required and reduces fuel waste. In hot, humid conditions, it can also help to reduce the driver stress that can contribute to 'road rage' situations.

Turn it off

Modern cars come with a variety of electrical devices, but using them will increase your fuel consumption, so make sure you switch them off when you don't need them. These devices include

- heated windscreens
- heated seats
- audio systems
- demisters.

If you have to make a prolonged stop at a level crossing or roadworks (say, two minutes), it may be better to stop the engine. Modern cars use very little extra fuel when they're restarted without pressing the accelerator, so you won't waste lots of fuel by turning the engine back on.

Stop–start technology
This technology automatically shuts down the engine when the vehicle is stationary and restarts it when required, thus reducing fuel consumption and emissions. Use it if it's fitted in your vehicle.

Parking

Always try to reverse into a parking space, so that you can drive out of it.

Manoeuvring while the engine is cold uses a lot of fuel. When you park in a garage or car park and intend to stay for a long time, reverse the car into the space or garage while the engine is warm, and drive out forwards when it's cold.

⊛ Choosing a vehicle

When choosing a vehicle, try to bear in mind economy and emissions.

Try to choose a vehicle with low fuel consumption and low emissions. The Vehicle Certification Agency produces a guide to the fuel consumption of new vehicles.

Search for fuel consumption, carbon-dioxide emissions, and tax bands for new and used cars on the Vehicle Certification Agency (VCA) website.

dft.gov.uk/vca

Manual versus automatic

In the past, vehicles with automatic transmission were generally less fuel-efficient than those with manual transmission. However, recent improvements in technology have resulted in much more fuel-efficient automatic vehicles. Now, some automatic vehicles are more economical and have better emission statistics than their manual counterparts. As with manual vehicles, check the carbon-dioxide and fuel-economy statistics when choosing an automatic.

Petrol engines

There are advantages and disadvantages to all types of fuel. To help you make an informed choice and understand the effect each has on the environment, some of the differences are explained below.

The modern petrol engine has been designed to operate more efficiently to meet increasingly stringent emissions standards.

Key factors in this improvement in reducing exhaust pollution are

- fuel injection
- electronic engine management systems
- redesigned exhaust systems.

Ever stricter controls on exhaust emissions require catalytic converters to be fitted to the exhaust systems of all new petrol-engined vehicles.

Catalytic converters

These are exhaust-treatment systems that remove up to 75% of carbon monoxide, nitrogen oxide and hydrocarbons.

The converter is a honeycomb-shaped filter with a total surface area about equal to a football pitch. This surface is coated with precious metals such as platinum, palladium and rhodium. These speed up a chemical reaction in the exhaust gases as the engine heats up.

The oxygen content of the exhaust is monitored and a sensor triggers controls to adjust the air–fuel mixture.

The converter only deals with toxic and polluting gases. Carbon dioxide is still produced.

Leaded petrol can't be used in vehicles fitted with a catalytic converter. Even one tankful can permanently damage the system.

If you over-accelerate or exceed 3000 rpm, the catalytic converter can't clean up emissions completely and will release some that are contaminated. Make sure, therefore, that you don't drive in such a way that this will occur.

Diesel engines

These engines are very fuel-efficient and produce less carbon dioxide than any other road transport fuel.

Compared with petrol-engined cars, they also emit less carbon monoxide and fewer hydrocarbons. They do, however, produce more emissions of nitric oxides and particulates that are bad for local air quality.

Newer vehicles have to meet strict new emissions standards aimed at reducing these pollutants.

New fuels

All road fuels sold in the EU now have a very low sulphur content. They've been specially formulated to meet EU laws concerning the use of this chemical.

Sulphur is the main component of particulates in exhaust emissions, and it also produces acidic gases. The lower sulphur content in these fuels helps to reduce this source of pollution.

More advanced fuels are still becoming available, and motorists should always consider using the most up-to-date type of fuel for their vehicle.

Liquefied petroleum gas

Vehicles powered by liquefied petroleum gas (LPG) are now commercially available and the number of fuel stations supplying LPG is increasing steadily.

This fuel is cheaper to use than petrol or diesel and the emissions cause less air pollution. However, LPG does produce more carbon dioxide per mile travelled than diesel.

Electric and hybrid vehicles

Manufacturers are offering an increased choice of electric and hybrid vehicles, which offer reduced local pollution and lower running costs. Hybrid vehicles can also help overcome the worry about running out of power that's associated with driving an electric car for a long distance.

⊕ Vehicle maintenance

Keeping your vehicle well maintained is important to ensure maximum economy and the least damage to the environment.

You should make sure that your vehicle is serviced and maintained regularly.

Servicing

Have your vehicle serviced as recommended by the manufacturer.

The cost of a service may well be less than the cost of running a badly maintained vehicle. For example, even slight brake drag can increase a vehicle's fuel consumption.

Make sure your garage includes an emissions check in the service.

Tyres

Make sure that your tyres are properly inflated. Incorrect tyre pressure

- results in shorter tyre life
- may create a danger, as it can affect stability and stopping distance
- can increase fuel consumption and emissions.

When replacing tyres, consider buying energy-saving types that have reduced rolling resistance. These increase fuel efficiency while maintaining a good grip on the road.

Engines

Make sure the engine is tuned correctly. Badly tuned engines

- use more fuel
- emit more exhaust fumes.

MOT tests include a strict exhaust emission test to ensure that engines are properly tuned. This means they operate more efficiently and cause less air pollution.

Recycling

If you do your own maintenance, make sure that you send oil, old batteries and used tyres to a garage or local authority site for recycling or safe disposal.

Don't pour oil down the drain; it's

- illegal and could lead to prosecution
- harmful to the environment.

⊕ Alternatives to driving

Try to help lessen pollution by using your car only when it's really necessary. You should

- avoid using your car for very short journeys, especially when the engine is cold
- walk or cycle for short journeys
- use public transport when you can. Light rapid transit (LRT) systems ('metros') and trams are being introduced in many cities and large towns to provide more efficient public transport. These vehicles are more environmentally friendly because they use electricity, rather than fossil fuels
- consider car sharing if there's no suitable public transport. There may be a colleague or friend who's making the same journey (for example, to work or on the 'school run')
- if at all possible, avoid using your car when air pollution is high.

As well as the environmental effects of driving, consider also the relative costs, safety and travelling times of various forms of transport.

Costs

When considering the costs of driving, remember that it isn't just the cost of fuel that you need to take into account; you also need to consider insurance, depreciation, maintenance and vehicle tax.

Safety

Statistics have proven that travelling by bus or coach is about as safe as travelling by air, rail or on water. All of these transport methods are less risky than driving a car or riding a motorcycle.

Travelling times

Remember that it's sometimes difficult to estimate the time for a journey by car because of delays that can be caused by congestion, incidents and roadworks. These factors should always be taken into account, especially if it's necessary to travel at busy times.

Section eighteen

→ Avoiding and dealing with congestion

This section covers

- Journey planning
- While driving
- Urban congestion

⊕ Journey planning

The information available to the modern driver means that journey planning to avoid congestion can often be just a matter of checking online or using a satellite navigation (sat-nav) device. Using this information can help you work out what time of day to travel, as well as whether there are any major route disruptions. It can also help you to schedule refuelling stops if you're travelling long distances.

Time of day

Much congestion is caused by work- and school-related travel. This causes delays in the early morning and late afternoon/early evening. If you don't have to travel at these times, try to avoid them. This will

- allow you to have an easier and more pleasant journey, and one that's less likely to be delayed
- ease traffic congestion.

Try to arrange appointments so that you avoid these times.

⊕ While driving

Delays and diversions

Carry a map with you so that you can stop and check your position or identify an alternative route if you get held up or diverted.

If you're using a sat-nav system

• Your sat-nav won't always be correct, so take a hard-copy map with you in case of errors.

• You should always be aware that your sat-nav can be a distraction. Don't spend time looking at it when your attention should be focused on the road. If you're confused by any of its instructions, find a safe place to stop and review the route.

• Don't be distracted from making your own judgement about the safety of any manoeuvres.

• Before you turn, make sure you're allowed to do so by looking at any road signs.

Mobile phones

A mobile phone can be useful in the event of delays or breakdowns. However, remember that it's illegal to use one while driving. This includes while you're waiting in a queue of traffic.

If you have a passenger, get them to make the call. When you're travelling alone and you need to call, find a safe place to stop first. If you're on a motorway, you must leave the motorway before using your phone.

Hazard perception

Looking well ahead to see what the traffic in front of you is doing will help you to plan your driving.

If you see the traffic ahead slowing down, ease off the accelerator and slow down gradually, rather than leaving it late and having to brake harshly.

Plan your driving and slow down early – if you do this, the traffic situation ahead may have cleared by the time you get there.

Constant speed

When you can see well ahead and the road conditions are good, you should drive at a steady cruising speed. This is the time to use cruise control if it's fitted to your vehicle.

Whether or not you have cruise control, choose a speed that's within the speed limit and one which you and your vehicle can handle safely.

Make sure you also keep a safe distance from the vehicle in front. Remember to increase the gap on wet or icy roads. In foggy conditions you'll have to slow down to a speed that allows you to stop within the distance you can see to be clear.

At busy times, some stretches of motorway have variable speed limits shown above the lanes. The speed limits shown on these signs are mandatory and appear on the gantries above the lanes to which they apply.

These speed limits are in place to allow traffic to travel at a constant speed. This has been shown to reduce 'bunching'.

Keeping traffic at a constant speed over a longer distance has been shown to ease congestion.

Your overall journey time normally improves by keeping to a constant speed, even though at times it may appear that you could have travelled faster for shorter periods.

Lane discipline

You should drive in the left-hand lane of a dual carriageway or motorway if the road ahead is clear. If you're overtaking a number of slower-moving vehicles, it may be safer to remain in the centre or outer lane until the manoeuvre is completed, rather than continually changing lanes. Return to the left-hand lane once you've overtaken all the vehicles, or if you're delaying traffic behind you.

Don't stay in the middle lane. Remember that some vehicles are prohibited from using the right-hand lane, so if you remain in the middle lane they won't be able to get past you. If you stay in the middle lane an unnecessarily long time, you effectively turn a three-lane motorway into a two-lane motorway.

You mustn't normally drive on the hard shoulder but, at roadworks and certain places where signs direct, the hard shoulder may become the left-hand lane.

Using sign information

Look well ahead for signals or signs, especially on a motorway. Signals situated on the central reservation apply to all lanes.

On very busy stretches, there may be overhead gantries with messages about congestion ahead and a separate sign for each lane. The messages may also give an alternative route, which you should use if at all possible.

If you're not sure whether to use the alternative route (for example, whether you can reach your destination if you use the route suggested), take the next exit, pull over at the first available safe area (lay-by or service area) and look at a map.

On a motorway, once you've passed an exit and meet congestion, there may not be another chance to leave and you could be stuck in slow-moving or stationary traffic for some time. Take the opportunity to leave the motorway as soon as possible; you can always rejoin the motorway if you feel that's the best course of action once you've had time to consider the options.

If you need to change lanes to leave the motorway, do so in good time. At some junctions a lane may lead directly off the motorway. Only get in that lane if you wish to go in the direction indicated on the overhead signs.

Motorway signals can be used to warn you of a danger ahead. For example, there may be an incident, fog, or a spillage, that you're unable to see.

Amber flashing lights warn of a hazard ahead. The signal may show

- a temporary maximum speed limit
- lanes that are closed
- a message such as 'Fog' or 'Queue'.

Adjust your speed and look out for the danger.

Don't increase your speed until you pass a signal that isn't flashing or one that gives the 'all clear' sign and you're sure it's safe to increase your speed.

⊕ Urban congestion

Congestion in urban areas leads to

- longer journey times
- frustration
- pollution through standing and slow-moving traffic.

London suffers the worst traffic congestion in the UK and amongst the worst in Europe. Various measures have been introduced to try to reduce the congestion and make traffic flow more freely. Red Routes and congestion charging are two of the schemes initiated in the London area. These are also being introduced into other congested towns and cities.

Transport strategy

A wide range of other measures have been designed to make public transport easier, cheaper, faster and more reliable.

If it isn't necessary to make your journey by car, you might want to consider alternative forms of transport.

For London, the Transport for London (TfL) journey planner (**tfl.gov.uk**) can help you discover the quickest and easiest routes for your journey using public transport. Alternatively, you can call TfL's Travel Information Call Centre on **0343 222 1234**.

Red Routes

Red Routes keep traffic moving and reduce the pollution that comes from vehicle emissions. Stopping and parking are allowed only within marked boxes.

Overnight and on Sundays most controls are relaxed to allow unrestricted stopping.

There's a fixed penalty for an offence and illegally parked vehicles may be towed away.

There are five main types of Red Route markings.

Double red lines
Stopping isn't allowed at any time, for any reason. These lines are normally placed at road junctions or where parking or loading would be dangerous or cause serious congestion.

Single red lines
Parking, loading or picking up passengers isn't allowed during the day (generally 7 am to 7 pm). Stopping is allowed outside these hours and on Sundays.

Red boxes
These indicate that parking or loading is permitted during the day at off-peak times, normally 10 am to 4 pm. Some boxes allow loading and some allow parking; the rules in each case are clearly shown on the sign.

White boxes
Parking or loading is allowed throughout the day, subject to restrictions shown on the sign.

Red Route clearway
There are no road markings but clearway signs indicate that stopping isn't allowed at any time, apart from in marked lay-bys.

Congestion charging

Congestion charging is a way of ensuring that those using valuable and congested road space make a financial contribution. It encourages the use of other modes of transport and is also intended to ensure that journey times are quicker and more reliable for those who have to use the roads.

The London scheme requires drivers to pay if they wish to drive in central London during the scheme's hours of operation.

Extent of zone

Traffic signs make it very clear when you're approaching, entering and leaving the charging zone. Advance information is provided on the main approach roads. These signs advise how far ahead the zone starts and the hours of operation, and some give the amount of the charge.

As you approach the charging zone, directional signs indicate which routes take you into the charging zone and which you can take if you wish to avoid it.

As you enter and exit the zone, signs indicate the boundary of the zone. The sign on entry also gives hours of operation.

Paying and exemptions

You can pay the congestion charge

- in advance or on the day of travel before, during or after your journey
- daily, weekly, monthly or even for the whole year.

To find out more about how to pay and where you can pay, visit **tfl.gov.uk** or call **0343 222 2222**.

At midnight, images of all the vehicles that have been in the charging zone are checked against the registration numbers of vehicles that have paid their congestion charge for that day. The computer keeps the registration numbers of vehicles that should have paid but haven't done so. A penalty charge notice is issued to the registered keeper of the vehicle.

Not all drivers have to pay the charge. Those who are exempt include

- disabled people who hold a Blue Badge
- riders of two-wheelers.

There are also exemptions for low- or no-emission vehicles. To check whether your vehicle qualifies, visit **tfl.gov.uk**

Residents living within the zone obtain a reduced rate but aren't exempt unless their vehicle meets the minimum exemption requirement.

Some people may be able to claim reimbursement; for example, staff, firefighters and patients too ill to travel to an appointment on public transport.

Emission Zone London also operates an emissions zone for diesel vehicles with high carbon-dioxide outputs. The zone covers most of Greater London and operates for 24 hours a day, all year round. Charging days run from midnight to midnight, so if you entered the zone before midnight and were still driving through it at 1.30 am you'd need to pay the charge for both days. To see if your vehicle is affected by Low Emission Zone charges, visit **tfl.gov.uk**

Section nineteen

→ Towing a trailer

This section covers

- Towing regulations
- Towing a caravan
- Towing a horse trailer
- Caravan and trailer safety
- Driving techniques

⊕ Towing regulations

Throughout this section, reference is made to the maximum authorised mass (MAM) of vehicles and trailers. This should, in all cases, be taken to mean the maximum permissible weight – also known as the gross vehicle weight. You may not be planning to drive a vehicle, or a vehicle towing a trailer, at these maximum weights, but they're key factors that determine driver licensing requirements.

If you passed your test before 1 January 1997

You're generally allowed to drive a vehicle and trailer combination up to 8.25 tonnes.

If you passed your test on or after 1 January 1997

You may tow a trailer behind a category B* vehicle without taking a further test as long as the trailer doesn't exceed 750 kg.

If the trailer you wish to tow exceeds 750 kg, you may tow it behind a category B vehicle provided that the vehicle and trailer combination doesn't exceed 3.5 tonnes. If you wish to drive a category B vehicle towing a trailer that exceeds the limits given above, you'll have to pass a practical category B+E test.

If you wish to drive a vehicle with a MAM exceeding 3.5 tonnes (for example, a motorhome or recreational vehicle), you'll need to pass a category C or C1 test.

* A category B vehicle is a four-wheeled vehicle with a MAM not exceeding 3.5 tonnes which has no more than eight passenger seats (in addition to the driver's seat).

Category B+E test

Details of the test and the minimum test vehicle and trailer requirements may be found in **The Official DVSA Guide to Learning to Drive**.

More detailed information about towing trailers can be found in DVLA factsheet INF30 'Requirements for towing trailers in Great Britain'. This also includes information about towing while driving a larger vehicle. DVLA factsheets are available free of charge at **www.gov.uk** or by telephoning **0300 790 6801**.

Further useful information on towing can be found on the National Trailer and Towing Association website.

ntta.co.uk

In 2013, new European requirements came into force that change towing regulations. New car and light van drivers wanting to tow trailers will be able to tow a slightly larger trailer on a normal car driving licence.

Since 19 January 2013, drivers passing a category B (car and small vehicle) test have been allowed to tow

- small trailers weighing no more than 750 kg
- a trailer over 750 kg as long as the combined weight of the trailer and the towing vehicle is no more than 3500 kg MAM.

If you want to tow a trailer weighing more than 750 kg, when the combined weight of the towing vehicle and the trailer is more than 3500 kg, you'll have to pass a further test to obtain B+E entitlement on your licence. You'll then be able to tow trailers up to 3500 kg.

The combination

The vehicle handbook or the manufacturer's agent will normally have information on

- the maximum permissible trailer mass that can be towed by your vehicle
- the maximum noseweight that should be applied to the tow ball.

You shouldn't exceed either limit.

There are separate and also legal limits on the laden weight of unbraked trailers. Make sure that you know what the limits are for your vehicle.

As a general rule, even if the vehicle manufacturer's limits are higher, it may be safer if the weight of the loaded trailer or caravan doesn't exceed 85 per cent of the kerbside (empty) weight of the towing vehicle. This applies particularly if you're not experienced at towing.

Remember that the overall length of the combination is generally double that of the normal family car.

Mirrors

You'll need to fit exterior towing mirrors so that you have a clear view along both sides of the caravan or trailer.

Stabiliser

A good stabiliser fitted to the tow bar can make the combination safer to handle, but you'll still be responsible for loading the combination correctly. A stabiliser won't cure instability caused by a poor towing vehicle/trailer combination.

The stabiliser will give you added security in side winds, especially when large goods vehicles overtake you on the motorway.

⊙ Towing a caravan

Basic requirements

Most of the skills and precautions involved in towing a caravan are the same as those needed for towing a trailer. You must have a full category B (car) driving licence before towing a trailer or caravan of any size.

Weight distribution

The overall stability of both the caravan and the towing vehicle depends on correct weight distribution.

For example, heavy items should be loaded as low as possible in the caravan so that the weight is mainly over the axle(s).

Bulkier, lighter items, such as bedding or clothing, should be distributed to give a suitable 'noseweight' at the towing coupling. The noseweight should never exceed the vehicle manufacturer's recommendations.

If in doubt, the noseweight may be measured by using an inexpensive gauge available from caravan accessory stockists.

> **REMEMBER,** the more weight you carry, the more fuel you use.

⊙ Towing a horse trailer

Before setting out on any journey with a horse trailer, you should perform the following checks.

Tow-ball height

Trailer manufacturers will usually specify the height at which the trailer should be attached to the towing vehicle. If the tow bar is too low for your horse trailer, it's likely to result in too much stress being placed on the rear axle of the towing vehicle. It can also affect the front axle of the trailer by overloading it, leading to poor control, excessive tyre wear and reduced braking action.

Setting the tow bar too high transfers the load to the rear of the trailer and can lead to the towing vehicle becoming detached from the trailer. Before you hitch the trailer to the towing vehicle, make sure that the tow bar is set up to provide equal distribution of weight between the towing vehicle, the coupling and the trailer. Grease the tow ball and check it for signs of wear. You should be able to check tow-ball wear by looking at the wear indicators in the trailer's hitch. If you have any doubts at all about the condition of your tow ball, get professional advice.

⊕ Caravan and trailer safety

Any load must be carried so that it doesn't endanger other road users. It must be securely stowed within the size and weight limits for the vehicle.

The load needs to be secure so that it can't move or fall from the vehicle when cornering or braking.

Before starting a journey, check that the caravan or trailer

- is loaded correctly, with the right noseweight on the tow bar
- is correctly hitched up, with the breakaway cable or secondary coupling properly connected and the coupling head fully engaged and locked
- lights and indicators are connected and working correctly
- jockey wheel and assembly is fully retracted and in the stowed position
- braking system is working correctly
- windows, roof light and door are closed
- tyre pressures are correct.

In addition

- check the caravan or trailer tyres for tread depth, damage and cracking of the sidewalls. Even if the tread shows little wear or is above the legal minimum depth, the tyre may be suffering from the effects of ageing
- remember that tyre regulations also cover the tyres on your caravan or trailer
- a caravan that has to be left standing for long periods should be raised on supports that take the weight off the tyres. This will help prolong tyre life

- check that your caravan or trailer is fitted with tyres of the specified rating (see the vehicle handbook)
- check that you've secured and turned off all fuel supplies, such as liquid gas cylinders.

Riding in the caravan

Don't allow anyone to ride in the caravan when it's being towed.

If you stop for a break, always lower the jockey wheel and corner steadies of the caravan before entering or letting anyone in. Don't forget to raise them fully before you move off.

⊕ Driving techniques

If you haven't towed a caravan before, seek advice from one of the large caravanning organisations.

You should also consider attending one of their courses, which cover safety aspects such as loading, manoeuvring and driving techniques.

You can find detailed guidance on all aspects of towing in the booklet **The Caravan Towing Guide**, which is available from

National Caravan Council Ltd
Catherine House, Victoria Road
Aldershot, Hants GU11 1SS
Tel 01252 318251
Fax 01252 322596
Email info@thencc.org.uk
thencc.org.uk

Manoeuvring

Drivers without experience of towing need to take great care, particularly when manoeuvring.

Don't be afraid to practise reversing in a quiet car park until you've mastered the technique.

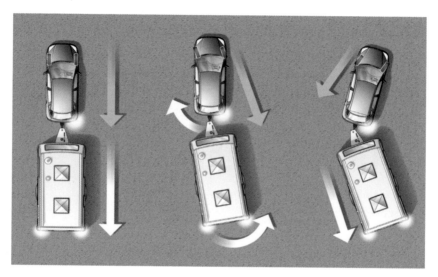

On the road

Always be aware of the increased weight, length and width of the combined vehicles.

You'll soon adjust to the different techniques involved in towing, so long as you remember not to hurry any manoeuvres and to plan well ahead. You should

- allow more time and brake earlier when slowing down or stopping
- give yourself three times the normal distance and time to overtake safely
- take account of the extra length, particularly when turning or emerging at junctions.

Snaking

Never attempt to correct swerving or 'snaking' by increasing speed, steering sharply (zigzagging), or braking hard.

The safe technique is to

- ease off the accelerator slowly
- allow a certain amount of 'twitch' in the steering
- reduce speed until the snaking has stopped.

High-sided vehicles

You need to take extra care when passing or being passed by high-sided vehicles.

Allow as much space as possible to avoid the effects of turbulence or buffeting.

Speed limits

Some speed limits are lower than normal when you're towing. Unless road signs tell you otherwise, you mustn't exceed

- 30 mph (48 km/h) in built-up areas
- 50 mph (80 km/h) on single carriageways
- 60 mph (96 km/h) on dual carriageways or motorways.

Reduce your speed

- in high winds or side winds
- when going downhill
- in poor visibility.

REMEMBER, check your mirrors frequently. If you're holding up a queue of traffic, you should be prepared to pull in where it's safe to let other, faster traffic pass.

Motorway driving

Caravans or trailers mustn't be towed in the outside lane of a motorway that has more than two lanes, unless other lanes are closed.

Side winds

You should be aware of the dangers of side winds when towing a caravan or high-sided trailer. See pages 321–2 for more information.

Section twenty

➡ Vehicle security

This section covers

- Security measures
- Parking

⊙ Security measures

Car thieves vary from opportunists to professionals who work in gangs, so it's important that you take sensible precautions and perform some basic checks before you leave your vehicle.

Having your vehicle stolen or broken into is at best an inconvenience and at worst very distressing. While determined thieves would probably be able to steal or get into any vehicle, they're usually too busy with the poorly secured ones. If your vehicle is secured, alarmed and immobilised, they may well leave it alone.

This section deals with the precautions you can take to secure your vehicle.

Modern cars come with engine immobilisers and many also have alarms fitted as standard, but there are extra precautions you can take to make it more difficult for the would-be thief.

- Use a physical immobiliser, such as a steering-wheel lock or parking-brake lock, or some other visible security device.

- Have the vehicle registration number etched on all windows.

- Install a GPS device so you can track your vehicle's location in the event of it being stolen.

- Use a Thatcham-approved vehicle marking scheme.

Vehicle Watch

Join a Vehicle Watch scheme, if there's one in your area. The scheme's high-visibility stickers, displayed on the front and rear windscreens of your vehicle, act as a deterrent to would-be thieves. There are two types of sticker

- **Vehicle Watch** By displaying this sticker you're inviting the police to stop your vehicle if they see it in use between midnight and 5.00 am

- **25-plus** By displaying this sticker you're also inviting the police to stop your vehicle at any time of day if it's being driven by anyone who appears to be under the age of 25.

Stickers and additional information about the scheme can be obtained from the crime prevention officer at your local police station.

Property registers

The police have a national record of stolen property called the National Mobile Property Register. They use this searchable record of registered owners in order to return their property in the event that it's stolen.

You can register your property through this website.

immobilise.com

 Parking

Avoid leaving your vehicle unattended in poorly lit areas. The risk of vehicle crime is known to be higher in these locations.

Whenever possible

- use attended and secure car parks
- at night, park in an area that will be well lit
- if you have a garage, use it.

When you leave your vehicle

- stop the engine
- close all windows completely (but don't leave pets in a vehicle with the windows completely closed)
- remove the key

- engage the steering lock
- set the alarm or anti-theft device, if you have one
- either remove all valuables or lock them out of sight
- lock the doors.

Never leave the vehicle documents inside your vehicle.

Car parks

Using parking facilities that have won the Park Mark® Safer Parking award means that you're parking in an area that has been approved by the police. They make sure that the site has measures in place to create a safe environment.

These facilities are run by responsible operators who are concerned about your safety and the safety of your vehicle. The police will be assured that these operators have done the best they can to reduce crime and the fear of crime on their site.

To find your nearest Park Mark® awarded site, visit **parkmark.co.uk** and enter your postcode into the search box.

Soft-top vehicles

Never leave a cabriolet or soft-top vehicle where it will obviously be vulnerable.

REMEMBER, lock it or lose it!

Valuables

Car audio systems

Many modern cars have tuners installed as part of the dashboard, which makes them difficult for thieves to remove. Despite this, there's a large market for people who want to upgrade their car audio systems. For this reason, tuners/CD players and Bluetooth media receivers remain prime targets for thieves, so it's important to take some simple precautions every time you leave your vehicle.

- If the faceplate (the control panel with the buttons and the frequency display) is removable, take it with you. Removing it will mean that a would-be thief won't be able to power on or operate the device. You may also be able to install a removable radio. It looks exactly like any other radio, but it slides out of its housing. You can lock it away in the boot or take it with you.

- If your car audio system can't be operated without a code, don't leave the code card in the car. Memorise the code and store the card safely at home in case you forget the number.

- Prime any security devices that are installed before you leave your vehicle.

- Remove all accessories, such as adapters, audio cables and MP3 devices, from the glovebox and take them with you.

Satellite navigation systems

- If you have a portable system, take it with you when you leave the car; also take the support cradle and suction pad.

- Wipe away any marks on the windscreen or dashboard that have been left by the suction pads. These marks are a clue to would-be thieves that a device may be stored in the vehicle and they may break in to look for it.

Catalytic converters

Catalytic converters contain valuable metals and have become targets for thieves. Vehicles with high ground clearance are most vulnerable to this crime, because the catalytic converter can be removed without having to jack up the vehicle.

Protect yourself from this crime by

- parking in a locked garage if possible
- parking in a well-lit area overlooked by residents
- having the catalytic converter marked with a Thatcham-approved security marking scheme.

If you see anyone acting suspiciously around or under a vehicle, report it to the police.

Section twenty-one
➡ Driving abroad

This section covers

- Planning your journey
- Driving your own vehicle
- Hiring a vehicle
- Driving in Europe
- Other things to consider

⊕ Planning your journey

Before you drive abroad, it's vital that you know the rules and practices related to driving in the country you're visiting. You'll need to consider

- driving rules and regulations, such as speed limits and which side of the road to drive on
- what documentation is needed for the country you're visiting
- whether you have the right insurance and breakdown cover
- equipment that you must carry by law, such as warning triangles.

You'll also need to decide whether to take your own vehicle or hire one when you get there.

The major motoring organisations, the AA and RAC, can help you to organise and plan the details of your trip.

They can

- save you time and money
- set up medical, travel and vehicle insurance
- provide equipment for minor repairs and breakdowns
- help you organise the correct documents for your car, trailer or caravan.

You can often make your trip much easier by using their facilities and experience.

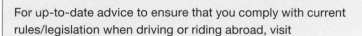

For up-to-date advice to ensure that you comply with current rules/legislation when driving or riding abroad, visit

www.gov.uk

Regulations

Speed limits

There are speed limits in all countries, but they vary from country to country. The motoring organisations provide a list of these various speed limits on their websites. Make sure you know the limits for those countries you'll be travelling through. Many countries have severe on-the-spot fines for offenders, while others prosecute through the courts.

Alcohol and driving

Don't drink alcohol and drive. The laws and penalties abroad are often more severe than those in the UK.

Passengers

Never take more passengers than your vehicle is built to carry. Make sure you use your seat belts and that everyone is secure before setting out on any journey.

Tunnels

Be aware that some tunnels in Europe can be several miles in length. Make sure you comply with any regulations that apply to them.

Plates

You need to display

- a registration plate on your caravan or trailer, if you're towing one
- a nationality plate of the approved size and design at the rear of your vehicle and caravan or trailer.

Documents

Insurance

Third-party motor vehicle insurance is compulsory in most countries. Contact your insurer to make sure you're adequately covered.

Most insurance policies issued in the UK automatically provide third-party cover in EC countries as well as in some others. They don't provide comprehensive cover unless you arrange this with your insurer, which may charge an extra premium.

Make sure you have the appropriate insurance certificate with you.

Your driving licence

You must carry your national driving licence when driving abroad. Even if you need an International Driving Permit (IDP), take your national licence too.

If you want to drive a hired or borrowed vehicle in the country you're visiting, ask about minimum age requirements in case they apply to you.

The hire company may also ask for a 'check code' so they can view your driving licence. You can find out how to get this code at
www.gov.uk/view-driving-licence

International Driving Permit

Many non-EC countries still require an IDP. To qualify for one, you must be 18 or over.

To apply you'll need

- your driving licence
- a passport-sized photograph
- a fee.

Major motoring organisations and the Post Office can issue your IDP.

Note 17 year-olds aren't allowed to drive in most European countries.

Vehicle registration certificate

You must carry the original vehicle registration certificate with you.

If you don't have your vehicle registration certificate, apply to a vehicle registration office for a temporary certificate of registration (V379). Apply through your local post office well in advance of your journey.

If you plan to hire, borrow or lease a vehicle, you must ensure you have all the relevant documents before you drive.

Blue Badges

If you hold a Blue Badge you should take it with you. Many European countries recognise this badge and allow special parking for any vehicle displaying it.

Passport/visa

All persons travelling must hold an up-to-date passport, valid for all countries through which they intend to travel. **Carry your passport(s) at all times.**

Keep a separate note of the number, date and place of issue of each passport, in case they're stolen or lost.

Travellers need a visa for some European countries. Check well in advance with the embassies or consulates concerned. This is particularly important if you hold a UK passport not issued in this country, or the passport of any other country.

Medical expenses insurance

You're strongly advised to take out comprehensive medical insurance cover for any trip abroad.

Most medical treatment can be obtained free of charge or at reduced cost from the healthcare schemes of countries with which the UK has reciprocal healthcare arrangements. However, you shouldn't rely on these arrangements alone.

European Health Insurance Card (EHIC)

This is issued free of charge and can be used to cover medical treatment for either an incident or illness within the European Economic Area (EEA).

The quickest and easiest way to get an EHIC is to apply online.

For more information, visit **nhs.uk/nhsengland/healthcareabroad**

You can also apply by phone on **0300 330 1350** or pick up an EHIC form from a post office.

Carnet de Passage

If you're planning to take your own vehicle outside Europe you may need a Carnet de Passage. This is a customs document required in some countries to temporarily import a vehicle duty-free.

To download an application form for a Carnet de Passage, visit

rac.co.uk

Equipment

In many countries, emergency equipment must be carried. Check with the motoring organisations to find out what's required in the countries you'll be visiting. This equipment may include the following.

Advance warning triangle

The use of a warning triangle is compulsory in most countries for all vehicles with more than two wheels. Hazard warning lights shouldn't be used instead of a triangle, but in addition to it. Some countries require two advance warning triangles.

Fluorescent vests

In some countries, such as France, the law requires motorists to carry a fluorescent vest in their vehicle and to put it on before leaving the vehicle if they're involved in a breakdown or incident.

Spare bulbs

Some countries require you to carry a spare set of bulbs in your vehicle.

Fire extinguisher

A fire extinguisher is compulsory in some countries and strongly recommended.

First-aid kit

Make sure your vehicle carries a first-aid kit. It's compulsory in some countries and strongly recommended in many others.

Breathalyser

In France it's now compulsory for all motorists (except moped riders) to carry a breathalyser in their vehicle.

As part of your planning, make a checklist of equipment, documents and other items you'll need. If you're travelling through several countries, check whether each item is compulsory or strongly recommended.

Winter equipment

Winter tyres are a legal requirement in many countries during certain periods of the year. Winter tyres provide a better grip on the road than normal tyres and are suitable for use in icy, snowy and wet conditions.

Snow chains are compulsory in some parts of Europe (depending on local conditions), although different countries have different snow-chain laws, so it's important to check these before travelling abroad. When fitting them, always follow the manufacturer's guidelines and, if in any doubt, seek help from a qualified professional.

Only use snow chains when the road surface is covered in snow or ice. If you try to use chains on a road that has been cleared of snow and gritted, you risk damaging the road surface and your vehicle.

In some countries you may be required to carry skis, or anything else you carry on your roof, in a purpose-made box, securely fitted to your roof rack.

⊙ Driving your own vehicle

If you intend to drive your own vehicle abroad, have it thoroughly checked and serviced. Checks include the spare tyre (make sure it's in good condition), your tool kit and jack (make sure all items are complete and in working order). Also make sure you have your spare car keys.

Lights
Your lights may need to be altered for driving on the right. Deflectors are required in some countries. These prevent your dipped beam from dazzling drivers approaching on the left. Yellow-tinted headlights are no longer required in most countries. Always carry a set of replacement bulbs and fuses.

Your mirrors

Check your mirrors. You must have clear all-round vision. You'll need to have exterior rear-view mirrors, especially on the left, for driving on the right-hand side of the road.

If you're towing a caravan or trailer, make sure you can see clearly behind you, down both sides of the combination.

Seat belts

Check seat belts and child restraints, including booster seats. Make sure that the fittings are secure and that the belts and restraints are functioning correctly.

Precautions against breakdown

Dealing with breakdowns abroad can be especially time-consuming and worrying without the help of one of the motoring organisations or breakdown services.

The best prevention is to have your car thoroughly serviced before you leave and to make regular checks along the way. Make sure you're prepared for minor breakdowns.

You must have all the necessary documents before leaving. Again, the motoring organisations will be able to tell you what's required for each country.

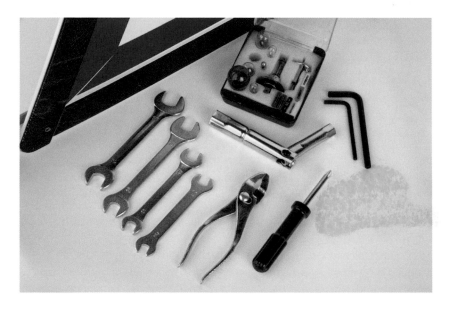

⊙ Hiring a vehicle

If you choose to hire a vehicle abroad, book in advance with a reputable firm. Booking in advance will allow you the time to fully understand the terms and conditions of the agreement, the level of insurance cover, and any additional charges that might be incurred.

The hire company abroad may ask for a 'check code' so they can view your driving licence. You can find out how to get this code at **www.gov.uk/view-driving-licence**

As when driving your own vehicle, it's vital that you understand the rules of the road and have all the necessary documentation for the areas you're visiting.

When you receive your vehicle, make sure that

- you're familiar with the controls, and that the vehicle has any essential equipment for the country you're in
- any existing damage on the vehicle is noted
- you understand what the fuel requirements are (normally you'll be required to return the vehicle with either a full or empty tank – failure to comply with the specific requirements can be costly)
- you have the rental agreements in writing
- you're provided with information on what you need to do in the event of a breakdown or an incident.

For more information on hiring a car abroad, visit

theaa.com

⊙ Driving in Europe

It can take you time to adjust to driving on the right, especially if you're in a right-hand-drive car.

> **REMEMBER,** hire vehicles will normally be left-hand drive. These may feel unfamiliar at first. Make sure you understand the controls before you drive.

Get into the habit of using all your mirrors before making any manoeuvre. This is particularly important before deciding to overtake. Remember to check the left exterior mirror. Don't attempt to overtake until you're used to driving on the right.

Don't let your attention wander. It can be dangerous to forget where you are, even for a moment.

- Each time you set out, remember that you're in a foreign country where you must drive on the right.
- Take special care when you have to drive on the road again after a rest.

Avoid driving for long periods and don't drive when you're tired.

Take extra care at roundabouts. Be aware of the possibility of changed priority.

Each time you move away, remember on which side of the road traffic will be approaching.

Make sure that you know the rules of the road; for example, in some countries you can turn right, with caution, at an amber filter light.

Motorway tolls

Find out about these. Include them in your budget and make sure that you carry an accepted method of payment. Frequent travellers may want to find out about the automated payment systems that are available in some countries.

⊕ Other things to consider

Planning your route

You can make your journey much easier by planning your route effectively. It's especially worth doing so when travelling abroad, where

- the roads are likely to be unfamiliar
- you may wish to avoid certain routes or roads
- you'd like to know the locations of tolls.

Most satellite navigation (sat-nav) systems can be used abroad, and motoring organisations can provide

- route guides
- summaries of motoring regulations
- details of tolls.

They'll also recommend alternative routes from continental ports or airports to specific destinations; for example, using motorways for speed and convenience or scenic routes for pleasure.

Security

Don't leave handbags, wallets or other valuables within obvious view inside the vehicle, even when you're inside too.

Never leave valuables in an unattended parked vehicle overnight. Loss of possessions, passports, tickets, cash and credit cards can be distressing and inconvenient when you're abroad.

After your trip

Don't forget to adjust to driving on the left again as soon as you return.

Section twenty-two

→ Automatics and four-wheel drive

This section covers

- Automatics
- Four-wheel drive

⊕ Automatics

Vehicles with automatic and semi-automatic transmission have always been a great help to drivers with physical disabilities, because there's less work for the feet and hands to do.

They're also a popular choice with other drivers, not least because of the easier control and convenience they offer, particularly in congested urban conditions.

Vehicles with automatic transmission have no clutch pedal. The transmission senses and selects the best gear for the road speed and load on the engine. This not only makes the physical job of driving much easier but also allows you more time to concentrate on the road ahead.

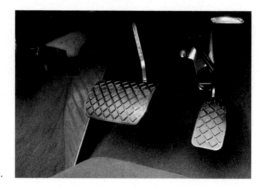

Automatic transmission usually changes to a higher gear as the road speed increases and to a lower gear as it falls. It will also change down to a lower gear going uphill as the load on the engine increases.

There are times – for example, when going down a steep hill – when you need to stay in a low gear, even if the engine load is light. The transmission often tries to change to a higher gear in these situations. However, the driver is usually able to override the transmission by using the gear selector to stay in a suitable lower gear.

Driving a vehicle with automatic transmission

Make sure you fully understand the procedure required before you attempt to drive a vehicle with automatic transmission.

Although most automatics have a cut-out switch to prevent you from starting the engine while the vehicle is in gear, always check that the selector is in the 'P' (Park) or 'N' (Neutral) position and the parking brake is fully applied before switching on the ignition.

For normal forward driving, move the selector lever to the 'D' (Drive) position. The transmission will then change gear automatically.

Alternatively, you can select one of the numbered gears. This gives you similar flexibility to a manual gearbox.

Controlled use of the accelerator is essential when driving an automatic, as it has such a direct effect when the selector is in any position other than 'P' or 'N'.

Avoid heavy acceleration; it can

- cause the vehicle to surge forward (or backwards) out of control
- delay upward gear changes
- waste fuel and increase exhaust emissions.

Controlled use of the accelerator

When carrying out manoeuvres at low speeds, use hardly any accelerator and only light braking; one foot on each pedal is often convenient and safer.

When driving, it's safer to use the right foot for both the accelerator and the brake pedal, just as you do in vehicles with a manual gearbox.

This develops anticipation by encouraging the early release of the accelerator pedal and early and progressive braking. It cuts out

- the instability and wear and tear brought about by using the brake and accelerator at the same time
- the need to learn a different method if you change from an automatic to a manual or vice versa.

The gear selector

Virtually all automatics have a gear selector. A typical gear-selector layout includes

- **P** – (Park) This mechanically locks the transmission and should only be selected when the vehicle is stationary
- **R** – (Reverse)
- **N** – (Neutral) This is the same as neutral on a manual gearbox

- **D** – (Drive) For driving forward with automatic gear selection
- **2** – (Second gear)
- **1** – (First gear).

Some automatics with four forward gears have third gear as an additional position that comes between 'D' and '2'.

The numbered gear positions enable you to prevent the transmission from automatically changing up to a higher gear. This is particularly useful

- in heavy traffic
- when manoeuvring
- when going down a steep hill.

There might be minor variations in the selector positions between different manufacturers.

With any automatic it's essential to study the vehicle handbook to understand the features of your particular model.

Kick-down

This is a feature that provides quick acceleration when you need it; for example, to overtake.

Sharply pressing the accelerator pedal fully down causes a quick change down to the next lower gear. To return to the higher gear, ease the pressure off the accelerator pedal.

The importance of the parking brake

Fully applying the parking brake whenever your vehicle is stationary is even more important on an automatic.

If the selector lever is in any position other than 'P' or 'N', the vehicle will move off under power if the accelerator is pressed (accidentally or on purpose), unless the brakes are on.

Creep

Creep happens when the tick-over, or slow running of the engine, creates enough power to move the vehicle. You'll need to use the brakes to prevent any unwanted movement.

Always check your vehicle for a tendency to creep excessively. Do this on the level (not uphill).

Never rely on creep to hold the vehicle on a hill – even though the vehicle doesn't move. The vehicle could roll back without warning if the engine stopped for any reason.

The safe rule is: apply the parking brake fully whenever you pull up.

Paddle control

Some vehicles with automatic (or semi-automatic) transmission are equipped with 'paddles' on the steering wheel. These fingertip controls allow drivers to change gear manually when they need the extra control over the engine that comes with manual switching. Being able to select the appropriate gear before a corner, for example, can have a positive impact on the vehicle's ability to negotiate the bend with maximum efficiency.

Using the paddles to generate more power from the engine can have a negative impact on fuel consumption.

Points to remember

Apart from avoiding the danger of excessive creep, you should also

* make sure the tick-over isn't set too fast. This can make your speed more difficult to control. You could, for example, find the vehicle doesn't slow down as much as you expect when you take your foot off the accelerator. This could result in you approaching a junction much too fast

- avoid overconfidence and driving too fast for the road and traffic conditions
- be aware of the reduced effect of engine braking on automatics. Use the gear selector to hold a lower gear if necessary
- control the vehicle's speed in good time, so that you approach corners, bends or other hazards safely.

Automatics sometimes change up a gear as you approach a corner, due to reduced pressure on the accelerator. To avoid this, slow down before you reach the corner, then accelerate gently as you turn.

⊛ Four-wheel drive

Four-wheel drive is where both axles of a vehicle are driven by the engine. The system may be permanently connected, or drive to the second axle may be selected by the driver to suit the conditions.

Four-wheel-drive vehicles are available in a variety of models, including off-road designs, estate cars, sports vehicles and saloons.

Vehicles that use a four-wheel-drive system by default are known as all-wheel drive (AWD). In most cases, the driver can't switch into a two-wheel-drive mode. Standard four-wheel drive differs from AWD in that four-wheel drive is selected by the driver, generally in response to situations where low traction is likely, such as on slippery surfaces.

You don't need any extra skill to drive four-wheel-drive vehicles on public roads. However, you should be aware that some large four-wheel-drive vehicles have blind spots that can easily obscure a group of pedestrians, a motorcyclist or even a small car.

Saloon cars with four-wheel drive

Some saloon cars are fitted with four-wheel drive. This can be

- an optional extra when buying a new vehicle
- part of the overall design, so that sensors in the vehicle's drive system automatically engage four-wheel drive when appropriate.

Benefits
The main benefit of four-wheel drive in a saloon car is improved traction in all weather or road conditions.

Limitations
Saloon cars with four-wheel drive can deal with some off-road conditions. However, because of their low ground clearance, they won't deal with very soft surfaces. In these conditions off-road vehicles with higher ground clearance and off-road tyres perform better.

The same applies to snow. A four-wheel-drive saloon will deal very well with snow up to a certain depth, but not with very deep snow.

Driving off-road

Off-road driving requires a very different technique from driving on asphalt. It's a good idea to have some off-road driver training to help you learn these skills. However good your technique, though, you should always keep to safe driving principles.

- Remember to take into account the nature of the terrain. This can vary a lot, from heavily rutted tracks with stones, rocks and hidden obstructions, to steep gradients with soft, slippery surfaces.
- When driving up or across a steep slope, be aware of the risk of the vehicle rolling.

- Take corners at a steady speed. The stability of the vehicle could be affected if it's driven recklessly.
- Understand both your own and the vehicle's limitations and stay within them.

Hidden obstructions, such as boulders and rocks, could damage the underside of your vehicle or suddenly deflect the steering, causing loss of control.

Whatever type of vehicle you drive, if you take part in off-road activities, remember to

- avoid damaging walls, fences, paths, grassland, crops, etc
- take care not to harm livestock or wildlife
- respect the environment
- close gates behind you
- drive in a responsible manner at all times.

Defensive driving

When travelling diagonally downhill, always look for an escape route straight down the slope in case the vehicle strikes any object or there's a danger of overturning.

Section twenty-three

⊙ Driving taxis

This section covers

- First steps to becoming a taxi driver
- Passenger care
- Professional driving
- Passengers with special needs

⊛ First steps to becoming a taxi driver

Throughout this section, 'hackney carriage drivers' and 'private hire drivers' will both be referred to as 'taxi drivers', and 'fare-paying passengers' as 'passengers'.

If you wish to become a taxi driver you should contact your local authority to enquire about licensing arrangements in your area, both for yourself as a potential taxi driver and for your vehicle. Regulations differ from one local authority to another, whether you intend to drive a hackney carriage or a private hire vehicle.

The main difference between a hackney carriage and a private hire vehicle is that a hackney carriage can be hailed on the street or wait for a fare at a taxi rank, whereas a private hire vehicle must be booked by a customer in advance.

The badging and licensing requirements for both hackney carriages and private hire vehicles are renewable and are the responsibility of the licensing authorities.

Regulations

Although regulations differ between local authorities, wherever you are, you'll definitely need

- a medical check, including an eyesight test
- a Disclosure and Barring Service check

- to hold a current driving licence – even if you have penalty points on your licence, you may still be able to apply. Check with the licensing authority
- to pay a fee for the issue of the licence.

Many authorities set a driving test of some description. Contact your local authority to find out more about their requirements.

Medical check

Consult your doctor first if you have any doubts about your fitness. You may be refused a licence if you suffer from certain conditions, including epilepsy and diabetes, or don't meet the eyesight requirements. (A full list of conditions can be found on the medical report form D4, available from **www.gov.uk**.)

You'll need to send a medical report to your taxi licensing authority. The medical examination isn't free under National Health Service rules. Your doctor may charge the current fee for this examination, and payment will be your responsibility. You'll have to send in the report form by a set date after its completion for it to be valid.

For more information on driving taxis, go to **www.gov.uk**

(→) Passenger care

Caring for your passengers is an important part of taxi driving. As the driver, you're responsible for the safety and comfort of your passengers as they get into and out of your vehicle, as well as during the journey. Your job is to carry your passengers to their destination

- safely
- comfortably
- efficiently
- courteously.

This includes the care of your passengers as you pick them up and drop them off at their destination in a safe and convenient place.

Remember that you're the representative of the licensing authority and the way you perform your role reflects on the authority.

Ask yourself the following

- Do your passengers feel safe and comfortable during the journey? Are they getting a smooth ride? If they aren't, you may need to improve your driving style to give them a more pleasant journey.
- Do they need help getting into or out of your vehicle? Be aware of passengers with special needs, particularly when they're entering or leaving the vehicle.

To help your passengers, you should

- look directly at them when you speak to them; it can help you to communicate effectively
- make sure they're comfortably seated before you move away.

In the event of a breakdown, show consideration for your passengers' safety and the completion of their journey.

Passenger seat belts

Passengers **MUST** wear seat belts where they're fitted.

- Adult passengers are responsible for their own actions.
- You're responsible for making sure that children under 14 wear their seat belts. The only exception is where there's a fixed partition separating the front and the rear of the taxi, in which case you're not responsible.

It's unreasonable to expect the right child seat or booster to be available in a taxi unless a parent or carer has brought it with them. So there's an exception to the law, which says that if child restraints aren't available in a licensed taxi or licensed private hire vehicle

- a child under three years old may travel unrestrained but in the rear only – this is the only exemption for a child under three years old
- a child aged three years and above **MUST** use an adult belt in the rear seat only.

Any child up to 135 cm (approx 4 feet 5 inches) tall and sitting in a front seat of any vehicle **MUST** use the seat belts or child restraints available.

Dealing with lost property

If you find any property in your vehicle after the passenger has left, you should normally hand it in to a police station as soon as possible.

Some licensing authorities run their own lost-property section. If this is the case in your area, you should hand in the lost property there, as soon as possible. Check with your licensing authority for the regulations in your area.

⊕ Professional driving

Professional driving means

- looking after your passengers, yourself and your vehicle
- planning well ahead – taking account of road and traffic conditions
- practising good observation
- keeping in control
- anticipating events.

It's essential that your vehicle is under control at all times. You must drive it with skill and plan ahead so that your vehicle is always travelling at the correct speed and ready for your next manoeuvre.

Consider the environment

You'll often have to wait for a fare. If you have to wait more than a few minutes, turn off your engine to reduce emissions and noise pollution.

All drivers are responsible for using their vehicles in a way that's sympathetic to the environment. This is especially the case for professional drivers, so use your skills to set an example to other road users.

Seat belts

It's always safer to wear a seat belt when driving; however, taxi drivers aren't required by law to wear a seat belt at all times. Drivers of hackney carriages don't need to wear a seat belt when they're on duty, but private hire drivers are only exempt when they're carrying a fare-paying passenger.

Communication and in-car equipment

Don't allow the use of in-car equipment to distract you from driving carefully and safely. It's illegal to use a hand-held mobile phone or other similar device when driving. Never use a hand-held microphone when driving. Find a safe place to stop before using such equipment.

If your taxi is fitted with a communications radio or telephone, you should only use it while driving if it's fitted with a hands-free microphone. However, even using hands-free equipment is likely to distract your attention from the road. It's far safer not to use this equipment, or tune the radio, while driving.

Tiredness and distractions

As a professional driver you may be driving for long hours. Even though your hours aren't restricted like those of a bus or coach driver, you should make sure that you don't drive for so long that you become exhausted. You have a duty to yourself as well as your passengers not to drive when you're tired.

You should normally take a break of at least 15 minutes after every two hours of driving.

You must make sure that you're always fit and able to concentrate for the whole of your shift.

If you know that you'll have a long journey at the end of the day, such as an airport run, plan your day and your rest periods so that you can make this journey safely.

Obviously, if you're carrying passengers, you can't stop in the middle of a journey to take a rest.

Factors causing fatigue include

- time of day – natural alertness is at a minimum between 2.00 am and 7.00 am. There's another, smaller dip in alertness between 2.00 pm and 4.00 pm
- lack of sleep
- continual glare from oncoming headlights. This is very tiring on the eyes and can lead to general tiredness
- limited lighting (street lights, pedal cycles) causing strain on the eyes when reading signs, looking for premises or seeing other vehicles.

REMEMBER, tiredness can kill.

Be aware of distractions from your passengers when you're driving.

- Your passengers may be talking among themselves, so make sure you're not distracted by what they're saying.
- Your passengers may try to chat with you, especially if they're not from your town and are trying to find out more about the area. Be polite, but make sure you're not distracted and can concentrate on your driving at all times.

All of the advice in this publication is relevant to you as a taxi driver. However, there are certain manoeuvres you'll have to carry out more frequently when driving taxis than you would when driving a private car. These are

- stopping at the side of the road
- turning in the road.

Stopping at the roadside

As a taxi driver you have to think of your passengers at all times and make sure that, when you stop, your passengers are able to get into or out of your vehicle safely and conveniently.

Make sure that

- you pull up within a reasonable distance of the kerb, in a position that's safe, legal and convenient

- you apply the parking brake and put the vehicle into neutral gear before your passenger opens the door

- your passengers can open the door fully and that their entry or exit isn't blocked by trees or street furniture – lampposts, waste bins, signs, etc

- you're there to help your passenger with loading or unloading luggage or if they're not able to get in or out without help

- all your passengers are comfortably seated before you move away.

Turning your vehicle around

As a taxi driver you're likely to have to turn your vehicle around more frequently than most other drivers – for example, if you've just dropped off a passenger and receive a call on your radio to pick up a fare in the opposite direction.

You should assess the situation and decide on the safest and most appropriate way to make the turn. You could consider

- making a U-turn within the width of the road

- using a junction on the left or right to swing around

- turning in the road using forward and reverse gears

- reversing into a side road on your left or right.

Never reverse from a side road into the main road and don't use private driveways to make your turn. Make sure that you don't mount the kerb when you're turning around, as this could endanger pedestrians and damage your vehicle.

⊕ Passengers with special needs

As a professional driver you should always be there to give help when it's needed, especially when your passenger has special needs.

Whatever vehicle you drive, be ready to help when an older passenger, or one who has limited mobility, is getting into or out of your vehicle.

Some vehicles, especially black cabs, are fitted with special equipment to allow easy access for those who may otherwise find it difficult. If you have this equipment, make full use of it to improve your passenger's comfort.

Special fittings can include

- an intermediate step
- a swivel seat
- a ramp and wheelchair fittings.

Intermediate step

It can be difficult for people with limited mobility to get into or out of some vehicles, including black cabs.

This can be because of the position of the seats and the greater distance between the floor of the vehicle and the street or pavement.

Assess your passenger's needs, and if you think it might help, offer to provide the additional step for them as they get into or out of the taxi. Follow this procedure

- Remove the step from the stowage compartment.
- Make sure the door is fully open and secured.
- Fit the step and make sure it's securely fixed before your passenger steps onto it.
- Once they're safely in, close the door and stow the step.

Swivel seat

A person with limited mobility might also find the swivel seat helpful. Often this will need to be used with the intermediate step. As the passenger gets into your vehicle, you should

- make sure the door is fully opened and secured
- pull down the seat and swing it outwards until it's locked
- help the person onto the seat if necessary
- swivel the seat back into the travelling position until it's locked
- offer to help secure the seat belt before closing the door.

Reverse the process when you reach the end of the journey.

Ramp and wheelchair fittings

If you have the facility to carry wheelchairs, you must make sure that the wheelchair is correctly loaded and secure.

To safely load a passenger in a wheelchair you should

- prepare for your passenger. Fit the wheelchair restraint and make space available for the wheelchair. Make sure the door is fully opened and secured. Pull out the ramp and add an extension if necessary
- gently push the wheelchair and its user into the vehicle and stow the ramp. If you need to let go of the wheelchair to stow the ramp, make sure you apply the wheelchair brakes
- position the wheelchair so that it can be secured using the equipment provided by the vehicle manufacturer
- make sure that all straps and belts that secure the wheelchair and its user are fastened according to the manufacturer's instructions
- close the door.

To unload the wheelchair at the end of the journey, you should

- open the door fully and secure it
- release the restraining straps and belts
- pull out the ramp and fit the extension if it's needed. If you need to move the wheelchair to do this, make sure you apply the brakes before letting go of the wheelchair
- wheel out the wheelchair. Walk backwards for the safety of your passenger and so that you can retain full control
- remove the ramp and stow any equipment in the appropriate place
- close the door.

Drivers of taxis designated by the local licensing authority as being wheelchair accessible must comply with the requirements of Section 165 of the Equality Act 2010, unless they have been issued with an exemption certificate. The Act requires the drivers of those vehicles to carry passengers in wheelchairs and provide assistance to those passengers, and it prohibits them from charging extra for doing so.

⊛ Further information

Selected sources and recommended reading are detailed below.

Government agencies and websites

GOV.UK
www.gov.uk

Driver and Vehicle Standards Agency (DVSA)
www.gov.uk/dvsa

Safe Driving for Life
safedrivingforlife.info

Highways England
www.gov.uk/highways

THINK! road safety campaign
http://think.direct.gov.uk

Travel information

AA travel
theaa.com/travel

Traffic England
trafficengland.com

Advanced motoring organisations

IAM RoadSmart
iamroadsmart.com

DIAmond Advanced Motorists
driving.org/diamond

RoSPA Advanced Drivers and Riders
roadar.org

Mobility

Driving Mobility
drivingmobility.org.uk

Motability
motability.co.uk

Miscellaneous

TyreSafe
tyresafe.org

YouTube: Driver and Vehicle Standards Agency
youtube.com/dvsagovuk

YouTube: Highways England
Visit youtube.com and search for 'Highways England'

Government statistics

Department for Transport (DfT), Reported Road Casualties, Great Britain: 2015 annual report
www.gov.uk/government/uploads/system/uploads/attachment_data/file/568484/rrcgb-2015.pdf

DfT, Reported Road Casualties in Great Britain: main results 2015
www.gov.uk/government/uploads/system/uploads/attachment_data/file/556396/rrcgb2015-01.pdf

DfT, Reported Road Casualties, Great Britain: 2013 annual report – focus on pedal cyclists
www.gov.uk/government/uploads/system/uploads/attachment_data/file/358042/rrcgb2013-02.pdf

DfT, Contributory factors for reported road accidents (RAS50) – statistical data set
www.gov.uk/government/statistical-data-sets/ras50-contributory-factors

➡ Photographic credits

⊙ Index

Or Dead Slow?
Your Choice

Horses are unpredictable. Passing horses wide and slow can prevent deaths of drivers, riders and horses.

The
British
Horse
Society

#thinkhorsethink15

Dead Slow?

Good Choice

It's not just the horse that will suffer when involved in a road accident. The average horse weighs half a tonne and on impact can cause significant damage to a vehicle and the people inside.

Protect yourself. Protect your car. Protect horses and riders.

15

When passing horses

1. Slow down to a maximum of 15mph
2. Be patient, don't sound your horn or rev your engine
3. Pass horse wide and slow (at least a car's width)
4. Drive slowly away

Thank you for driving safely around horses.

bhs.org.uk/deadslow